Open Source: The Unauthorized White Papers

Open Source: The Unauthorized White Papers

Donald K. Rosenberg

IDG Books Worldwide, Inc.
An imprint of IDG Books Worldwide, Inc.
Foster City, CA ■ Chicago, IL ■ Indianapolis, IN ■ New York, NY

Open Source: The Unauthorized White Papers

Published by
M&T Books
An imprint of IDG Books Worldwide, Inc.
919 E. Hillsdale Blvd., Suite 400
Foster City, CA 94404
www.idgbooks.com (IDG Books Worldwide
Web site)

Library of Congress Card Number: 00-105673

ISBN: 0-7645-4660-0

Printed in the United States of America

10 9 8 7 6 5 4 3 2 1

1O/SQ/QX/QQ/FC

Distributed in the United States by IDG Books
Worldwide, Inc.

Distributed by CDG Books Canada Inc. for Canada;
by Transworld Publishers Limited in the United
Kingdom; by IDG Norge Books for Norway; by IDG
Sweden Books for Sweden; by IDG Books Australia
Publishing Corporation Pty. Ltd. for Australia and
New Zealand; by TransQuest Publishers Pte Ltd. for
Singapore, Malaysia, Thailand, Indonesia, and Hong
Kong; by Gotop Information Inc. for Taiwan; by ICG
Muse, Inc. for Japan; by Intersoft for South Africa; by
Eyrolles for France; by International Thomson
Publishing for Germany, Austria, and Switzerland; by
Distribuidora Cuspide for Argentina; by LR
International for Brazil; by Galileo Libros for Chile; by
Ediciones ZETA S.C.R. Ltda. for Peru; by WS
Computer Publishing Corporation, Inc., for the
Philippines; by Contemporanea de Ediciones for
Venezuela; by Express Computer Distributors for the
Caribbean and West Indies; by Micronesia Media
Distributor, Inc. for Micronesia; by Chips
Computadoras S.A. de C.V. for Mexico; by Editorial
Norma de Panama S.A. for Panama; by American
Bookshops for Finland.

For general information on IDG Books Worldwide's
books in the U.S., please call our Consumer Customer
Service department at 800-762-2974. For reseller
information, including discounts and premium sales,
please call our Reseller Customer Service department
at 800-434-3422.

For information on where to purchase IDG Books
Worldwide's books outside the U.S., please contact our
International Sales department at 317-596-5530 or fax
317-572-4002.

For consumer information on foreign language translations, please contact our Customer Service department
at 800-434-3422, fax 317-572-4002, or e-mail
rights@idgbooks.com.

For information on licensing foreign or domestic
rights, please phone +1-650-653-7098.

For sales inquiries and special prices for bulk quanti-
ties, please contact our Order Services department at
800-434-3422 or write to the address above.

For information on using IDG Books Worldwide's
books in the classroom or for ordering examination
copies, please contact our Educational Sales department at 800-434-2086 or fax 317-572-4005.

For press review copies, author interviews, or other
publicity information, please contact our Public
Relations department at 650-653-7000 or fax
650-653-7500.

For authorization to photocopy items for corporate,
personal, or educational use, please contact Copyright
Clearance Center, 222 Rosewood Drive, Danvers, MA
01923, or fax 978-750-4470.

Library of Congress Card Number: 00-105673

is a registered trademark or trademark under
exclusive license to IDG Books Worldwide, Inc.
from International Data Group, Inc. in the
United States and/or other countries.

is a trademark of
IDG Books Worldwide, Inc.

ABOUT IDG BOOKS WORLDWIDE

Welcome to the world of IDG Books Worldwide.

IDG Books Worldwide, Inc., is a subsidiary of International Data Group, the world's largest publisher of computer-related information and the leading global provider of information services on information technology. IDG was founded more than 30 years ago by Patrick J. McGovern and now employs more than 9,000 people worldwide. IDG publishes more than 290 computer publications in over 75 countries. More than 90 million people read one or more IDG publications each month.

Launched in 1990, IDG Books Worldwide is today the #1 publisher of best-selling computer books in the United States. We are proud to have received eight awards from the Computer Press Association in recognition of editorial excellence and three from Computer Currents' First Annual Readers' Choice Awards. Our best-selling ...For Dummies® series has more than 50 million copies in print with translations in 31 languages. IDG Books Worldwide, through a joint venture with IDG's Hi-Tech Beijing, became the first U.S. publisher to publish a computer book in the People's Republic of China. In record time, IDG Books Worldwide has become the first choice for millions of readers around the world who want to learn how to better manage their businesses.

Our mission is simple: Every one of our books is designed to bring extra value and skill-building instructions to the reader. Our books are written by experts who understand and care about our readers. The knowledge base of our editorial staff comes from years of experience in publishing, education, and journalism — experience we use to produce books to carry us into the new millennium. In short, we care about books, so we attract the best people. We devote special attention to details such as audience, interior design, use of icons, and illustrations. And because we use an efficient process of authoring, editing, and desktop publishing our books electronically, we can spend more time ensuring superior content and less time on the technicalities of making books.

You can count on our commitment to deliver high-quality books at competitive prices on topics you want to read about. At IDG Books Worldwide, we continue in the IDG tradition of delivering quality for more than 30 years. You'll find no better book on a subject than one from IDG Books Worldwide.

John J. Kilcullen

John Kilcullen
Chairman and CEO
IDG Books Worldwide, Inc.

Eighth Annual Computer Press Awards ≥1992

WINNER

Ninth Annual Computer Press Awards ≥1993

WINNER

WINNER

Tenth Annual Computer Press Awards ≥1994

WINNER

Eleventh Annual Computer Press Awards ≥1995

IDG is the world's leading IT media, research and exposition company. Founded in 1964, IDG had 1997 revenues of $2.05 billion and has more than 9,000 employees worldwide. IDG offers the widest range of media options that reach IT buyers in 75 countries representing 95% of worldwide IT spending. IDG's diverse product and services portfolio spans six key areas including print publishing, online publishing, expositions and conferences, market research, education and training, and global marketing services. More than 90 million people read one or more of IDG's 290 magazines and newspapers, including IDG's leading global brands — Computerworld, PC World, Network World, Macworld and the Channel World family of publications. IDG Books Worldwide is one of the fastest-growing computer book publishers in the world, with more than 700 titles in 36 languages. The "...For Dummies®" series alone has more than 50 million copies in print. IDG offers online users the largest network of technology-specific Web sites around the world through IDG.net (http://www.idg.net), which comprises more than 225 targeted Web sites in 55 countries worldwide. International Data Corporation (IDC) is the world's largest provider of information technology data, analysis and consulting, with research centers in over 41 countries and more than 400 research analysts worldwide. IDG World Expo is a leading producer of more than 168 globally branded conferences and expositions in 35 countries including E3 (Electronic Entertainment Expo), Macworld Expo, ComNet, Windows World Expo, ICE (Internet Commerce Expo), Agenda, DEMO, and Spotlight. IDG's training subsidiary, ExecuTrain, is the world's largest computer training company, with more than 230 locations worldwide and 785 training courses. IDG Marketing Services helps industry-leading IT companies build international brand recognition by developing global integrated marketing programs via IDG's print, online and exposition products worldwide. Further information about the company can be found at www.idg.com.   1/26/00

Credits

Acquisitions Editor
Laura Lewin

Project Editors
Terry O'Donnell
Terri Varveris

Technical Editor
Joseph Traub

Copy Editors
Richard Adin
Mildred Sanchez

Proof Editor
Neil Romanosky

Project Coordinator
Marcos Vergara

Graphics and Production Specialists
Robert Bihlmayer
Jude Levinson
Michael Lewis
Victor Varela
Ramses Ramirez

Quality Control Technician
Dina F Quan

Book Designer
Kurt Krames

Illustrator
Gabriele McCann

Proofreading and Indexing
York Production Services

About the Author

Donald K. Rosenberg is president of Stromian Technologies, an international consultancy for software marketing, distribution, and licensing. He is the publisher of the OEM Software Licensing Guide, the Open Source Software Licensing Page, and other on-line marketing resources at www.stromian.com. Dr. Rosenberg has 20 years of marketing experience and has worked with companies large and small in the U.S. and Europe, both in Open Source and in more traditional software markets and channels. A speaker on Open Source licensing issues at USENIX, ALS, Linux Expo, and Comdex, he is on the Advisory Boards of the Linux Mall and other Open Source companies.

For Karla Anne, quae diutius libello proprio carebat

Foreword

Even Being a Forward Kind of Guy......

I am still flattered when asked to write a forward to a person's book...particularly when that person is Donald Rosenberg.

I met Don at the first Freenix track that was given by USENIX in January of 1997. Don was easy to spot, since he was the one person out of 500 that was wearing a suit, and was second in age only to me.

"What are you speaking on," I asked, seeing his speaker's ribbon. "I am here to talk about licensing," Don answered, with a shy smile and the twinkle in his eye that he often shows. "Thank Heaven that someone is doing it," I remember thinking at the time.

Linux licensing seems to be the most confusing thing about Linux, and it should be a very easy thing to understand. Free software! How can it get any simpler than that? Yet people kept having issues with understanding the General Public License (GPL) and other licenses associated with what most people call "Free Software" and/or "Open Source."

I have heard many questions over the years. When do I have to ship the sources to my product, and when can I keep the sources to myself if I want to do so? What benefits do my customer and I have from making my source code available? What parts of a Linux distribution are "free," and what do I have to pay for on a system by system basis? Can I really copy a whole CD-ROM of software and sell it for money as long as I acknowledge the people who worked on it? Why do Linux people keep saying there are two meanings of "free" (freedom *and* "no cost") and that they do not always just talk about "freedom," particularly when the conversation turns to beer.

There *are* a variety of licenses that have similar meanings, even if the results of applying them are vastly different over time. For example, the Berkeley Software Distribution was one of the most popular versions of Unix, but its license (which did not require changes to the OS to be freely distributed) allowed to other versions of Unix systems based on BSD to diverge in functionality. This allowed the commercial Unix systems to diverge, creating an insurmountable obstacle for independent software vendors (ISVs).

There also exists the whole concept of making money on something that is free of cost, or the perception that people are charging money on something they are supposedly giving away. One can begin to understand why there is confusion in the common marketplace, a marketplace that has existed for years on protecting and selling intellectual property.

But we are going into a new marketplace, a marketplace created by the Internet, which is so big and so diverse that you can find a large enough market to think a different way. The entire computer marketplace at the start of the New Millennium is about 400 million units. Imagine what the marketplace will be like (and the amount of money that will be made using traditional means of selling software) as the market expands to embrace the emerging nations, a marketplace of an additional 5.6 billion people?

This market may be of people who wish to modify an already existing (and free) operating system platform and who might pay a person good money to tailor it to their needs. You might also find a large enough group of people willing to donate their time and energies to create the basis of this platform and give it away for free. Then have these two groups of people come together to help support each other, all the time building on that which has been built before.

This new market may reject the concept of paying (and repaying) for software developed two, three or four years ago, which is what we do today.

For a long while, I could not explain why people created good software, then gave away both the binaries and the source code to it. Then it hit me. It was the same as an amateur painter.

Very few amateur painters put their paintings in a dark closet. They then typically hang it on the wall. Sometimes they take it to an art show to have it judged by people they feel are better then themselves in various techniques. They might be told how to mix their colors better, or how to use certain artist's tools and tricks to make their pictures better. Finally they apply these techniques to create even better paintings, but they do want their paintings seen and admired. This is why they hang them on the wall.

The equivalent for software of "hanging on the wall" is to be distributed and used by people all over the world.

And if you can do it with an operating system, could you also do it with other things too? Perhaps you could find musicians who played music because they wanted to create art. Old songs would be distributed for free, and could be modified to create new songs without royalty to the original artist as long as the modifications were also distributed for free. Perhaps in the larger audience of the Internet there would be enough people willing to pay for modifying the old songs (or having new ones written) that artists would be paid for creation of new works rather than just living off the royalties of old works.

But I digress. In this book we are talking about software, and Shawn "Napster" Fanning now knows that music is not like software. Or so the music industry lawyers have told him.

Perhaps, however, Don's book will cause these people to stop and think. Perhaps people will be brave enough to entertain new methods of generating revenue from artistic endeavors. Perhaps with the more immediate "suddenness'" of the Internet market, patents and copyrights should have a shorter lifetime, to allow the original artist to make some money, yet allow others to transform an artist's works later on. Or perhaps as John Perry Barlow, a lyricist for my own favorite band "The Grateful Dead," explains that artists should make the bulk of their money out of public displays of their art (i.e., concerts). Perhaps an artist should give away his creation, but sell his performance. This might be extended to streaming video concerts. Then concepts like Napster would help the music market, not hurt it.

I am a great fan of the Star Trek series of TV shows. In those shows people worked because they enjoyed doing their jobs, not because they were paid. It may take several decades for us to get to that stage, but perhaps the ideals of the Open Source community can help get us started, to "boldly go where no man has gone before." But we have to take that first step.

I hope that Don's book lights the fire of ideas for you, no matter what your endeavor might be.

Warmest wishes,

Jon "maddog" Hall

Preface

Do you need this book? You probably do if you are curious about Linux and Open Source. Nowadays you can open your newspaper or newsmagazine or turn on your television or radio, and find a lot of small news stories about both. You will have a harder time, however, finding a source that covers the whole Open Source world from top to bottom. You can buy Eric Raymond's book on theoretical writings about Open Source, *The Cathedral and the Bazaar;* Bob Young's story of how he got Red Hat, Inc., up and running, *Under the Radar;* or the perspectives of Open Source leaders in *Open Sources: Voices from the Open Source Revolution.* They each contribute their part of the picture.

If you want to know more, there are a couple of magazines that cover Linux. To become well informed, you must spend a lot of time on the Internet (where Open Source lives) and visit an Open Source or Linux conference or trade show or two. And you will have to try to pull it all together. That's where this book comes in. It is intended for a variety of readers — you may be one of them — to pull all the information together.

Who This Book Is For

This book is for general readers and computer users who wish the entire subjects of Open Source and Linux would sit still in one place long enough for them to get a look at it (and they do in this book). These general readers are unsatisfied by media accounts and don't know where to look for detailed information on the Internet. (There's a large collection of Web links at the end of this book, besides links scattered through the text.) This book is also for corporate IT managers who want to know more about how Open

Source will fit in with corporate computing strategies. And, finally, it is for those members of the Open Source community who would like a chance to look back at where they came from and see their movement in a larger context.

If a chapter (or group of chapters) doesn't interest you at first, go ahead and skip it for now. There's a glossary in the back. Turn to it if you don't see terms explained on the spot. Although the more specialized chapters are written in more specialized language, this is not a technical book; it is written primarily from a business point of view. The book spends little time on software development tools because technical people generally have their own ways of learning about new tools.

A Guide to the New Land

If the past looks like a foreign country, certainly the future is even more strange to us; if Open Source is that future, then it will seem even stranger to the ordinary computer users, most of whom are deeply immersed in the Windows world. You may understand about Linux that it is an operating system, that it is free, and that some people are making fabulous amounts of money from it, but the details are unclear, and it all seems to have something to do with dot-com IPO hype. As for Open Source, you may have heard that it's good, but there is a strange haze hanging over it. It seems to be associated with a closed community of arrogant juvenile geniuses with overly-dramatic or difficult personalities, with demonstrations outside Microsoft offices demanding refunds...and what does that penguin have to do with it, anyway? And will it really destroy Microsoft?

This book takes up these questions and stereotypes. For now let me assure you that the Open Source community is very interested in offering ordinary users a superior computing experience; how they hope to do this forms part of the book. There are plenty of young people in the movement, and they do attract attention. The community also includes many experienced coders and managers with gray hair who are trusted members of the corporate world.

How I Came to Write This Book

My own work is software marketing and licensing. In the mid-1990s I began hearing a low buzz around the Research Triangle area of North Carolina about a little Linux company called Red Hat. I had tried a couple of times to find them, but no one seemed to know where they were (access was through the Internet, and the company was still run out of an apartment in those days). I found them in 1996 when someone gave me the name of Michael K. Johnson, who was one of a dozen Red Hat employees now settled in their new offices. Like so many in the Open Source community (which did not even have that name in those days) he was very helpful and free with information. He had just given up editorship of the *Linux Journal*, and gave me 18 back issues to help me get started in understanding what was going on.

I had been aware of Richard Stallman and his Free Software Foundation since his early days in the 1980s; he appeared to be in the same category as the man who runs Project Gutenberg, whose goal is to put as much public domain literature on the Internet as possible. There seemed to be no commercial application for either. Red Hat, on the other hand, had a business plan and an aggressive marketer, Bob Young. Bob was quite open and voluble in explaining his branding strategy for Red Hat.

Note

During one visit in early 1998 Bob Young sketched the diagram that I titled Unified Field Theory of Licensing? and used in talks and in Chapter 7. At the time he told me I was free to use it, but without his name. Since Bob subsequently put it in his own book, I thought I would explain its appearance here, and the fact that I have been free with it for a couple of years now.

As I began to meet more Linux people (via e-mail), it was inevitable that I should run into Jon "maddog" Hall, executive director of Linux International. Through his efforts, I was invited to give a talk at the Freenix section of Usenix in January 1997. The talk covered the methods of distribution in the commercial software world; it was by now apparent that Linux was headed there (nobody dreamed how soon), and we wanted Linux developers to start thinking about commercializing their software and how it could be done.

From that time on I gave more talks to Open Source developer groups, and as I learned more and accumulated more material, it occurred to me that there was no book explaining the Open Source world to those outside it, or to those who had only a partial view of it from inside. A book is always a larger undertaking than one thinks at first, and I owe apologies to the publisher and to my family for having spent so much time on it. Part of the difficulty was the speed at which things change in the Open Source world; the trick is to keep current while putting in the book the long-term truths about Open Source. Only its readers can tell me whether I have succeeded.

This Book's Organization

The book is divided into six sections, the first looking back into the past, and the last looking ahead into the future. Within the running text there are sidebars that take up related topics in more detail and notes that supplement or update the material. There are also two appendixes and a short glossary.

Part I: Open Source Software Is Linux...and More

This part delves into the origins of Open Source software and what has already been done to commercialize it. Open Source is not so much a revolutionary idea as an earlier way of doing things that is being vindicated as everyone moves deeper into the computer world.

Part II: Open Source Software in Your Business

This part explores the idea of adopting Open Source software in your business, and the advantages and problems of such a move. This part includes a quick survey of available software that any office would expect to use and a comparison of Windows and Linux.

Part III: Open Source Licensing: Does It Have to Be This Hard?

This part gets to the heart of what is unique about Open Source software. The licensing can be complicated, but problems are simplified if you know what you want to accomplish and pick the license accordingly. In this part, you also learn to look the legendary UNIX bug-a-boo, fear of forking, in the eye.

Part IV: Linux Is Moving UP...and DOWN

This part deals with the flexibility of Linux. It describes how Linux now runs on mainframe computers, runs gangs of PC's that behave like supercomputers, and runs the software in new cell phones, Internet access devices, and industrial equipment.

Part V: Open Source Software AS Your Business

This part looks at the ways companies are making money in the growing Open Source market. You may find your own opportunity in this part.

Part VI: The Future of Open Source

This part looks at companies and community projects that are moving Open Source forward, and how Open Source is becoming a factor in the competition between companies such as IBM, Sun Microsystems, and Microsoft. You also learn of the plans the large entertainment and intellectual property companies have for your future use of books, movies, music, and software, and how Open Source software and attitudes are in the middle of controversies that can be settled only by Congress or the Supreme Court.

Appendixes

Appendix A contains the complete text of the following public software licenses: GNU General Public License, GNU Lesser General Public License, Open Source Definition, QT Free Edition License, X Window License, Apache License, Q Public License, Mozilla Public License, IBM Public License, and BitKeeper. Appendix B lists many Web resources that provide a wealth of information.

Reach Out

The publisher and I want your feedback. After you have the chance to use this book, please take a moment to register this book on the http://my2cents.idgbooks.com Web site. (Details are listed on the my2cents page in the back of the book.) Please be honest with your evaluation. Positive or negative, the information you provide can help to shape future versions and editions of this book.

Feel free to send e-mail with specific questions regarding the material in this book. I'll do my best to help you out and answer your questions by return e-mail. You can use the form on the above listed Web site, or just send an e-mail to:

donr@stromian.com

Please put "Book" in the subject line of the e-mail.

Acknowledgments

A great many people have been helpful to me during the writing of this book: Tom Adelstein, of Bynari Systems, Inc.; Mitchell Baker of mozilla.org; "The BRU Guys," Enhanced Software Technologies, Inc.; Sam Byassee, of Smith Helms Mullis & Moore; Elizabeth Coolbaugh, of *Linux Weekly News;* Frank Hecker, of Collab.Net; Chris Herrnberger, of Linux Studio; Dan Kusnetzky, of International Data Corp.; Frank LaMonica, of Precision Insight; Jacques Le Marois, of MandrakeSoft; Bruce Perens, of the Linux Capital Group; Nicholas Petreley, of Caldera Systems, Inc.; Stacey Quandt, of the Giga Information Group; Pamela Samuelson, of the University of California at Berkeley; and Marc Torres, of Atipa Linux Solutions.

The preceding list includes many individuals who gave instant response to pestering questions. I hope no one will hold these people responsible for my own shortcomings in this book, and that the many others who have been helpful to me will not feel slighted at not appearing here.

Contents at a Glance

Contents

Part IV: Linux Is Moving UP ...and DOWN 121

Part I

Open Source Software Is Linux...and More

Chapter 1

The Origins of Open Source Software

Open Source is not a new way of doing things — it is the original computer way of doing things. Linux did not suddenly appear like a mushroom — it is (as Microsoft scornfully puts it) a "30-year-old operating system technology and architecture." Linux is not the first free mimic of UNIX — that was BSD, which is still with us and growing stronger. It's not an obvious joke when Linus Torvalds and his followers talk about World Domination and laugh — they laugh because they enjoy sounding like comic-strip villains, and because they know they mean it. To follow all these threads in computer history and social history, we need to go back about 40 years.

In the Beginning...

International Data Corporation (IDC, http://idc.com/) currently rates the number of Linux users (not systems) in the world at anywhere from 7 to 21 million; the predicted growth rate is 200 percent for 2000. This large number did not spring up overnight, although it looks like that. The forces that brought on Linux go back many years, and, to set the proper context, we will have to go back and look in places besides computer companies and laboratories.

The 1960s and early 1970s – datapriests and hippies

In the early days of computing, hardware manufacturers gave away their software because their machines would not operate without it. Digital Equipment Corporation did not bother to copyright its operating system and even provided customers with a large catalog of free software that was distributed originally on punched paper tape and later on "Linc tape." Users paid five dollars to cover the cost of copying a program and could then make their own copies for free. There might be jokes that came along with the operating system, and there were third-party games, such as Spacewar, which MIT computer students wrote and freely distributed. No one thought about rights to the software, let alone business practices; the software was a give-away needed to sell the actual article of commerce—the expensive hardware. Because none of the software would run on a competitor's machine, no one gave "software piracy" a thought, let alone a name.

The machines were distant deities, dwelling in glass houses and approachable only through the intermediation of the datapriests. Students in the outer courtyard of the temple prepared forms from which keypunch "girls" prepared the actual cards for eventual offering to the computer. After this step, the hopeful carried their box(es) of cards (it was very bad luck to drop them) to the datapriests, who fed them to Moloch. Results might be days in coming, and only then were results or errors known.

Life in California in those days had not reached the frenetic pitch of today, even in the emerging Silicon Valley. There were some workaholic engineers in the aerospace and silicon chip industries, but for the most part California remained the land that had invented modern leisure (or inherited it from the original Mexican settlers). Here the hippies arose and flourished and preached and practiced their main tenets of charity and antiauthoritarianism. They believed that the quest for material possessions was corrupting the world, and that life would be better if lived more simply, particularly if everyone cooperated and shared freely what they had. At the same time they were highly resistant to authority, and burned with a self-righteous zeal to smash the state. Self-dramatization was part of the ethos.

In the California of leisure, many young people believed that their jobs were merely the means to support their real lives. Living in an alternative reality (when not at work) was popular in a land with flourishing groups like the Society for Creative Anachronism and various sci-fi fan clubs, and with nature religions mixing varying proportions of masquerade, ritual, and belief. The recession at the end of the 1960s left many creative and energetic young people without jobs, and activities like the original Renaissance Faire flourished because its promoters took full advantage of the many volunteers eager to play at living in another world. After the spread of the microcomputer industry across the Santa Clara (now Silicon) Valley, the Renaissance Faire went into a decline and eventual takeover.

Computers were not absent from this world; the first big microcomputer show in San Francisco called itself the Computer Faire. Marshall McLuhan was the chief of the prophets of a coming convergence of media, computing, and telecommunications that would enable truly public discussion and give real "Power to the People!" Ted Nelson began his Xanadu Project, which aimed to place in hyperlinked cyberspace everything that anyone had ever written or said, or written or said in comment thereon. Xanadu would be powerfully democratic because it would be electronically accessible to everyone. In Berkeley, cradle (and later, museum) of the Revolution, Lee Felsenstein toiled at the beginnings of such a network he called Community Memory as he worked to put computer terminals in public places so that anyone could read and post to an electronic bulletin board. The antiauthoritarian message of these projects was clear: no gatekeepers, no datapriests, no mediators.

If all of this seems a product of fantasy, it was. In addition to the alternative existences mentioned previously, there were elaborate role-playing games (RPGs) such as *Dungeons and Dragons* (played without computers in those days). Young technical employees and computer students found these appealing, along with the science fiction that spoke of computer realms of the future. Tolkien's fantasy work, *The Lord of the Rings*, was particularly popular; it echoes today in the computer industry with names like Gandalf and Palantir. There were even more products of these grandiose and fruitful fantasies of power. Ted Nelson's dream of universal access to the collective mind embodied itself in the World Wide Web; and Lee Felsenstein went on to design the Osborne 1 in 1980. The biggest change the hippies made in society was the personal computer, and the personal power and attitudes that still surround it.

The 1970s – The MIT AI laboratory

Although California had several important sites contributing to the progress of computer technology and education, we need to move across the country to the Massachusetts Institute of Technology (MIT) for the next part of our story.

Hacker vs. Cracker

The Open Source world is *hacker*-driven, and hackers define themselves as clever software programmers who push the limits of the doable. This attitude – "It wasn't meant to do this but I can make it do this" – is the antiauthoritarian germ that flowers freely in the *cracker*, a person who illegally breaks into others' systems and exploits their resources. Crackers believe they are the cleverest of the hackers because they are pushing the systems (computer and legal) hardest.

Law-abiding, ethical hackers (the majority) resent the popular use of the term hacker to describe the disruptive and lawless crackers, and proposed the term *cracker* to describe them. This book observes the distinction between the two terms.

For a few years, the Artificial Intelligence lab at MIT was a center of hackers — young men who lived to program and freely share their clever exploits with others. During the close of these golden hacker years, it was the home of Richard M. Stallman, known familiarly by his computer handle of RMS. Stallman began the Free Software movement, whose extension is the much newer Open Source Initiative.

Some Resources on Hackers, UNIX, and Linux

If you are looking for some background to the hacker culture at MIT and other places in the 1970s, Steven Levy's 1985 book, *Hackers*, provides a history; the Internet's Jargon File carries some of its folklore – in fact, Stallman was one of the original authors. You can find the file in many places on the Web, but you might start at http://www.tuxedo.org/~esr/jargon/ because the site belongs to Eric S. Raymond, who does the printed versions known as *The New Hacker's Dictionary*. Here you will find entries such as the Hacker Ethic.

Raymond has written a number of pieces on "hacker anthropology," including "The Cathedral and the Bazaar," which contrasts Open Source software development with centralized, proprietary development. He recently published these pieces in book form, but they have existed for years on the Internet. You can find them at http://www.tuxedo.org/~esr/writings/.

UNIX veteran and historian Peter H. Salus published *A Quarter Century of UNIX* in 1994, if you want the facts; the mythic dimensions of Linux are handled in my "Copyleft and the Religious Wars of the 21st Century" at http://www.stromian.com/copyleft. htm. Don Libes and Sandy Ressler cover the early period in *Life with UNIX: A Guide for Everyone*.

As Richard Stallman tells it, the MIT AI lab was a computer paradise in the 1970s, a democracy of learning. Everyone shared the programs they had written; there were no passwords to exclude users, either from using the computer or reading anyone's files; and people were always ready to help each other. Users were free to improve any program they felt needed improving, because with an open system the users were in full control, and free of central authority. When professors had terminals in their offices, and the students had none, they felt justified in breaking into locked offices to use them. It was self-evidently selfish or thoughtless for a professor to deny them the use of a terminal at 3 a.m. when the professor was hardly there to use it himself. When the AI lab introduced passwords to comply with government requirements, Stallman fought against them, urging people to use a single carriage return as a password, so that effectively there would be none.

New restrictions such as passwords were harbingers of coming rough winds in paradise. Previously, users had programmed the system so that the printer sent messages if the paper had jammed. The new computer, on the other hand, did not provide the source code for its printer driver, so that users could not hack it to add the summons. Even worse, Stallman was outraged to discover a person at Carnegie-Mellon University who admitted to having the driver source code, but who told him that the code could not be shared because the holder had received it under a non-disclosure agreement (NDA). This was Stallman's first encounter with the secrecy of the proprietary software world, which guards its source code as an asset and releases only binary code, readable by machines but not by humans. Stallman regarded the signer as a traitor who had betrayed the hacker culture and humanity, depriving everyone of the benefits that would otherwise flow from being able to modify the driver.

The worst finally came: stalwarts of the AI lab broke away to form two rival companies to exploit the LISP language they had developed there, and by the early 1980s, the companies had drained off the skilled personnel. As the expert programmers were hired away, the lab replaced its open system with a closed, proprietary system that was maintained by the vendor. Without source code, hacking was over. Stallman, who refused to join any proprietary venture, was left alone. Where he went, and what he did, we will take up in a moment.

The 1980s – UNIX and the great betrayal

Besides the universities, there were other great centers of software development in the United States, among them Bell Labs. This was better than a university—there didn't seem to be a lack of money. In this rarified atmosphere of abstract thought and pure research, work looked like play. A small robot might race down the halls carrying files, nudge your office door open, and demand to be put on your desk so its remote operator (your colleague) could look at you through the robot's camera, talk to you through its sound system, and discuss the files it had brought from the colleague's office. One scientist recalled a Bell Labs meeting he had attended remotely from California: as he used the camera to scan those seated around the table, he noticed two other robots perched on the table, likewise sent by remote attendees.

This was the perfect place to invent the perfect computer system. On early computer systems, software was written in machine language specific to the machine on which it was run. Development tools were also specific to a system. The result was duplication of effort; each machine had all its software written from the ground up. The idea of Bell Labs' UNIX was to write an operating system that would be cross-platform and that could be implemented on each type of machine. The software could simply be compiled as it moved from platform to platform. The theory of UNIX was simple, but the practice was complex; UNIX was not user-friendly and chose its friends carefully.

Hardware manufacturers, who had originally seen software only as something that had to be supplied to sell machines, began to realize that not only could the software that came with the machine benefit the customer, it could also tie the customer to the machine.

Programs could not be moved from one platform to another, forcing customers to be loyal. UNIX was to be a way around this problem. The resulting portability made it popular in the universities. Bell Labs made it easily available to other software researchers, and students studied its source code in their classes. From around the world, bug fixes and improvements poured into Bell Labs.

This open-source software paradise, like that of the MIT AI lab, ended because of commercial pressures. As AT&T and its Bell Labs were being broken up in the late 1970s and early 1980s, UNIX was recognized as a commercial asset, and a price tag was put on the source code. It was too rich for the universities. UNIX, however, did appeal to the new generation of hardware companies then rising: the makers of minicomputers. Licensing UNIX provided them with a dependable operating system developed by a responsible third party. It was scalable to large numbers of transactions for large companies. But rather than enjoy the benefits of portability and interoperability, the hardware vendors applied the lessons of lock-in. As each tweaked the source code they had received so that it would run faster on their particular machines, they also differentiated themselves so that their programs would run only on their own software/hardware systems. Customers were still locked in. Because the emphasis was still on hardware, software was merely the means to the end. The UNIX Wars saw as many varieties of UNIX as there were vendors.

The blighting of these twin paradises set new forces in motion. Stung that all their UNIX contributions had been taken from them, locked up, and sold to large corporations for large sums that they could not themselves afford to pay, developers in the universities quietly plotted their next move. In Amsterdam, Andrew Tannenbaum sat down and wrote a UNIX imitation called MINIX, so students would have a system to study. The University of California at Berkeley was a strong center of UNIX development, and had already begun distributing a version of its own: BSD. BSD at times surpassed Bell's UNIX, and its freely modifiable and distributable code made its way into numerous commercial versions of UNIX. It also formed the basis of Sun Microsystems' operating system. Critics who say that Open Source software must always lag behind and imitate proprietary software should study the history of BSD and see how many innovations and improvements originated there.

Over the years, and under legal pressure from AT&T, the BSD developers dropped every line of Bell Labs' code and substituted their own. Meanwhile, Richard Stallman was contemplating the ruins of his programmer's paradise. What he had experienced there, he would recreate for all mankind. He resigned from the AI lab, though he was allowed to occupy space there. He founded the Free Software Foundation (`http://www.fsf.org`) to serve as the vehicle for making real his grand vision of an operating system that would be forever free for all developers, and which would turn the whole world into a programmer's paradise.

He began by creating tools to build the new system, using (for the moment) proprietary tools because they were the only ones available. He created EMACS (an acronym for Editing MACroS), an editor and general-purpose tool still in use. Stallman supported himself by providing free copies of it, but charging $150 for actually making the copy and for support. He asked that all changes and improvements be sent back to him. In this way, he evolved the model of the GNU General Public License (GPL), which allows free use, modification, and distribution of the software and any changes to it, restricted only by the stipulation that those who received the software pass it with identical freedoms to obtain source code, modify it, and redistribute it. The products of a developer's mind must remain free for all developers to use and reuse. Free does not mean that no money changes hands, but it does mean that no authority or non-disclosure agreement will prevent developers from sharing code. Because of the freedoms conferred by the Free Software licensing method, and because the legal means of its enforcement is the copyrighting of the software itself, the use of the GNU GPL is often called "copylefting."

The 1990s – the arrival of Linux

Stallman says that he chose UNIX as his model because that way he would not have to make any design decisions. He called the system GNU (GNU's not UNIX), and the GNU tools that he built remain important and widely distributed to this day. The task of building the kernel he left to last; it was intended to be much better than the UNIX kernel and was called the HURD. By the time Stallman had reached this stage of the process, some ten years later, a Finnish computer student, disgusted with MINIX, had begun his own project to clone UNIX, using the popular GNU tools. This was the Linux kernel of Linus Torvalds, and when added to the GNU material already available, it enabled the parts to add up to an operating system.

The rapid success of Linux resulted from a number of factors. First, Linux made it possible for developers to continue at home what they did at work. Instead of buying an expensive UNIX workstation along with an expensive operating system, they could use Linux on an ordinary personal computer. The fact that so many people around the world were working on Linux and talking about it created a buzz. The timing was also right because BSD was tied up in litigation with AT&T over whether the Berkeley Distribution contained proprietary Bell Labs material. And the HURD, however clever its architecture, was not yet ready for release.

The arrival of the Linux system in the early 1990s was also made possible by its Free Software licensing scheme, originated by Stallman. Whether the Linux system would have been as successful if it had been released under the BSD or X licenses (all these licenses are discussed in detail in Part III) will never be known. Torvalds pragmatically chose to use the GPL because it allowed freer source code distribution than did the MINIX license, and because it was the license used for the GNU software and it seemed to do the job; he does not claim to be a particular fan of it.

The GPL does have the virtue of making sure that any software changes or additions incorporated in GPL's software are likewise distributed under the GPL; this gives only one licensing possibility for the Linux kernel. Proprietary material might be loosely linked to the kernel by means of the GNU LGPL (a second license allowing this concession that Stallman later regretted), or proprietary programs could simply run atop the Linux system. Torvalds made an important concession to the use of binary-only driver software by allowing the "kernel-loadable module." Stallman disapproved, but said that because neither he nor the Free Software Foundation held the copyright on the kernel software, Torvalds had the right to see things his way.

In contrast to the pragmatism of Torvalds, Stallman remained fixed on his idea of an entire system distributed solely under the GPL. Implacably hostile to proprietary or closed-source software, he steadfastly continued to promote Free Software and Copyleft as the one true faith. To keep the world's attention focused on GNU, he insisted the system be called GNU/Linux (only the Debian distribution follows this convention), and he finished and released the HURD.

Stallman's licensing vision is developer-centric, or hacker-centric, if we recall the Hacker Ethos. Stallman's motive is to keep the code free for other hackers to use. Eric S. Raymond has explored the social motivations of hackers in freely giving away their code (the GPL merely enforces this custom), but in the dedication of Richard Stallman there is self-confessed religious fervor. On public occasions he is wont to dress up in robe and halo (a large disk-drive platter from some forgotten hardware) as St. IGNUtius of the Church of EMACS, and exorcise all proprietary software from those computers brought to him by the faithful. This is the sort of "ha-ha only serious" self-mockery much appreciated in hacker culture.

The Intersection of Hackers and the Real World

Hacking and its folk-ways grew up in an academic atmosphere where wit and indirection are prized. The business community, established chiefly on trust and taking people at their self-stated face value, confines its humor to telling funny stories rather than exchanging playfully-bent perspectives on the world. The world outside Linux is currently wondering how seriously to take Linux and its promises for the future, and is trying to separate truth from what appears to be absurd boasting.

> Watch and hearken, ye solitary! The winds of the future approach
> on stealthy wingbeats, and to sharp ears come good tidings.
>
> *Zarathustra, Teil II: Von der schenkenden Tugend, 3*

What is Open Source and why does it crave world domination?

Popular accounts of the Linux community (often called a movement) tend to focus on the bizarre; visits to hardcore Linux sites on the Internet turn up a colorful landscape showing traces of all the elements that have shaped the community. If you want to draw a caricature, it's easy enough: What do you get when you mix the antiauthoritarian energy and millenarian idealism of hippies, the competitiveness and arrogance of elite hackers, and the role-playing tastes of technical employees? And if you mix in the ideal of service to the Big Idea, a desire for a final showdown between the Children of Light and the Forces of Evil like that at the end of Tolkien's saga, and a sprinkling of born-again Christians? And all of them speaking a dense technical language? Who have somehow taken a penguin as their totem? And whose undisputed leader is a slender young Finn who combines purpose, rationality, maturity, and political skills with a dry sense of humor?

In earlier days it was easier for an outsider to grab the world of Linux by the wrong handle because colorful, self-promoting types were what attracted the press. There is no organized community, but there are organizations within the community. The inner sanctum might be the actual contributors to the kernel itself. Paul Jones of the University of North Carolina's Open Source Research Team and MetaLab (`http://metalab.unc.edu`) says that that there are fewer than 200 named contributors to the kernel (the majority of them in Germany), although there are thousands of contributors to the software surrounding it (see Figure 1-1). There is a central industry organization, Linux International (`http://li.org/`), nominally supported by the dues of various Open Source vendors, but actually dependent on the energy and dedication of its executive director, Jon "maddog" Hall, a UNIX veteran who was at DEC for many years.

Linux Contributions by Top-Level Domain

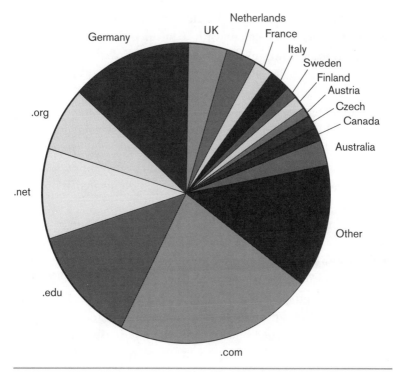

Figure 1-1 *The many Linux contributors are displayed*

The vendors themselves provide further focus points, but the whole community is dispersed around the globe (it originated outside the United States and is probably stronger outside the U.S. than in it), and in constant contact over the Internet. The focus points are generally software development projects. The number of machines running Linux is estimated to be well over ten million worldwide, and while there are probably more machines than users, there must be several million Linux users of varying skill levels as well.

The number of Usenet lists and Web news sites serving these users is endless. One addictive spot is the flamboyant Slashdot (`http://slashdot.org`), which handles more topics than Linux, changes the news several times per hour, and allows all comers to post their comments on that news and on each others' comments. Linux Weekly News (`http://lwn.net`) is more sedate and generally more technical, while LinuxWorld (`http://linuxworld.com`) is stamped by its IDG parent with a blend of commercialism and Linux advocacy. Links to the growing number of news items about Linux are continually posted at Linux Today (`http://linuxtoday.com/`). If the community includes a wide spectrum of personality types and interests, nevertheless people in the community know who is in it, and know who the leaders are and what they are doing. The Open Source world provides a look backwards into the software world of 15 or 20 years ago; in those days, flamboyant personalities were making an industry that is nowadays dominated by blander corporate types.

The Linux community itself has been undergoing changes over the past two or three years. The primary barrier between the community and the rest of the world has been the technical competence needed to deal with Linux. For a long time, many members of the community were not only proud of this difference, but enjoyed its use as a barrier against outsiders. Furthermore, the more juvenile members of the community discouraged outside interest by furiously attacking any journalist who wrote something about Linux and (naturally) got some of the technical details wrong. They would subject the writer to public (at least on the Internet) flaming as clueless and totally unworthy to appreciate, let alone write about the wonderful thing they hugged to their breasts. Proud of their command line interface, many scorned the idea of a graphical user interface (GUI), not just for themselves, but because it might admit the feeble-minded to the sanctuary.

This self-sufficient society, being developer-centric, assumed that all the people who counted could compile their own kernels, and find all the technical help they needed on the Internet. It had the atmosphere of the California of a generation before, when people joined food co-ops and called them "food conspiracies," one more proof of the cleverness of "us" as compared with the others. A number of Linux hackers follow Ayn Rand, and it never occurs to them that not everyone is a Hank Rearden who can invent Rearden Metal. This is a world in which only programmers count.

What has saved Linux from sinking into the navel of its own regarding, is its users' sense of mission. Linux users have always regarded Microsoft code as third-rate technology, and pitied those who are locked into it through their own technical ignorance. Many Linux zealots would like to see Microsoft wiped out, and all would like to see a choice of operating systems for users. At one time most seemed to believe that Linux would eventually dominate because of its technological superiority, but they have come to realize that market forces are stronger than technological excellence. The community accordingly shifted its sights to see what it could do to make World Domination happen.

Some humorless observers seem to misunderstand Linus Torvalds' references to Linux World Domination. This expression of manifest destiny is simply part of the joking that accompanies his technical talks (describing features of the upcoming 2.4 kernel, he said it "will not have a mauve screen of death. . . .Wintel has a lot of patents in that area"). Torvalds soberly says that a 15 percent market share for Linux would be fine — then people would have a choice. Linux fans like the jokey drama implied in World Domination — a secret conspiracy that eventually controls the planet, and they like the deeper irony that if Linux becomes the dominant operating system, users will have choices — freedom — and that freedom is the opposite of World Domination.

The microcomputer world was always a friendly one. In the early days of PCs, nonusers often heard from their friends: "You've got to get one! Don't worry, I'll give you all the software you need. Just get one — you'll love it!" Now, not only have local Linux User Groups (LUGs) been holding Installfests to help beginners past the traditionally difficult, but increasingly easier, installation of Linux, they announce these Installfests as public events to which anyone can bring a computer and have Linux installed on it. Taking the World Liberation/Domination theme seriously meant that the Linux community had to address seriously issues such as ease of installation (the various Linux distributions are making rapid progress) and a graphical user interface (GUI) that would enable former Windows users to function on Linux. As soon as Microsoft pointed out Linux performance problems, developers began to improve the weak points.

This joy in writing good code to earn honor from other hackers fits Eric Raymond's descriptions of the hacker community; the love of good work for itself sounds like Ayn Rand's geniuses, except that these can withhold the products of their genius, and look down on the rest of humanity. A better image of the Open Source community in action is probably Nietzsche's idealization of the perfected person who has evolved beyond humanity, the Highly Evolved or even Super-Evolved *Übermensch*. This person transcends humanity by making himself the pure conduit of the Life Force (der Wille zur Macht) and expresses this transcendence by an endless, bubbling creativity that benefits all humanity. This Virtue of Bestowing (die schenkende Tugend) is the highest virtue.

Free software and Open Source software

The recognition that Linux and Open Source software actually have a chance for World Domination has shifted community focus from inward to outward. Miguel de Icaza, who could respond to a hacker complaint about instability in the prerelease graphical desktop GNOME with a smiling "Linux: it's not for whiners," says that his attitude towards users has changed completely, and that he wants new users to have an easy, comfortable Linux experience. Even the clannish computer games experts are turning their graphics skills to end-user interface development, and it has been a long time since anyone flamed an outsider.

The community has also noticed how resistant many businesses are to the GNU General Public License and to Richard Stallman's insistence that no software can be completely free unless it is issued under the GPL. While Stallman takes this position to defend the freedoms of the user, he sees the user as a competent software developer, not a point-and-click end-user. This developer-centric attitude ignores the vast body of users who are happy with binary-only software, and it defines the only way of making money from Free Software (as it is officially called by the Free Software Foundation) as developer-provided services: program modification or extension, technical support, technical documentation, and training. An end-user who cannot program can hire a developer to make changes in a program, provided the source code and permission to do so are available. This is a hacker-centric view of the world, one that defines computer literacy as programming facility.

To provide a more latitudinarian view of the software world, a group of community leaders met in early 1998 to discuss the situation and to find a way of promoting Free Software to a skeptical business community. The Open Source Initiative (OSI, `http://www.opensource.org/`) was formed to carry the torch of Open Source software. By all accounts, the effort has been successful and can take some of the credit for the rapid rise of interest in Linux and things Open Source. At the same time, the group's touchstone for Open Source software, the Open Source Definition (or OSD, based on the Debian Free Software Guidelines by Bruce Perens) and its interpretation by the OSI, add to the lack of clarity about what constitutes Open Source software.

Who Actually Writes Linux?

Metalab at the University of North Carolina hosts a number of Linux archives, including all major distributions of the kernel, the Linux Documentation project, and the Linux Archive. This latter group contains most of the auxiliary software that has been written around the Linux kernel. Taken together, they form one of the very largest collections of Linux material on the Internet, containing over 30GB of data dating back to 1992. Anyone may send in a piece of code, making Metalab the most open such site on the Web. Submissions of code to the site must include a piece of metadata, called a Linux Software Map (LSM), naming the submitter and giving other information. Recently, several researchers there (Bert Dempsey, Debra Weiss, Paul Jones, and Jane Greenberg) studied the credits inside the Linux kernel and the LSMs for the material around it to form a preliminary picture of who is actually writing the code: *A Quantitative Profile of a Community of Open Source Linux Developers* (http://metalab.unc.edu/osrt/develpro.html).

It is important to remember that LSMs, like the kernel, do not name contributors who submitted patches, regardless of whether these patches were accepted. We can thus assume a larger but unknown pool of Open Source developers.

The Kernel Is a Worldwide Project from a Select Few

The software in the Linux kernel is the result of sifting many contributions and patches from a large number of people; unfortunately, we still do not know how large a group this is. We do know that as contributions pass up the kernel organization (eventually to Linus himself), more are rejected than accepted. The Metalab study shows that there are fewer than 200 accepted contributors to the kernel that is the heart of Linux. The largest single group of contributed code portions (about 40 percent) came from .com addresses, possible evidence that a substantial portion of the kernel contributions are corporate-based. Although we cannot assign nationality to the .com suffix, 42 percent of the contributions using a national suffix were European, and of this

European group, the Germans contributed a dominant share of 32 percent. Thus, there is a substantial international input to the Linux kernel. The educational world (.edu), as might be expected, contributes about 28 percent of the submissions. The total kernel contribution picture is heavily international, especially German, and involving substantial input both from industry and academe.

The Rest of Linux Is a Worldwide Project with Many Contributors

The kernel is useful only when surrounded by a host of auxiliary software that includes drivers, tools, applications, scientific tools, games, libraries, utilities, and the like. The contributors represented in the study are by no means the sum total of all Linux contributors: only those whose contributions were chosen for use by project leaders end up as contributors to the many files in the Archive. An unknown but probably substantial number of contributors had their work declined. The successful contributors number some 2,200 persons. Of these contributors, 75 percent provided one contribution, and 91.4 percent only one or two; only 2.2 percent contributed five or more pieces of code. These figures show that Open Source software is working the way its proponents claim: individual developers scratch their itch, and then contribute their code so that others may benefit from it as well.

Code contributions to the auxiliary archive show that 37 percent came from addresses with European suffixes, 23 percent from .com, 12 percent from .edu, and 7 percent from .org. The suffixes show that this software is more international than the kernel, and less dependent on the academic world.

Although the Metalab study makes the number of Linux developers appear small, there are other indications that a great many developers are capable of working with Linux. Netscape is said to have had 250,000 copies of the Mozilla code downloaded in the first month of its availability in 1998; a study of the Internet addresses of the downloaders would make an interesting study.

Why the Penguin?

Linus Torvalds chose the Linux penguin, commonly known as "Tux," as the badge of Linux. Torvalds shared his vision of the ideal penguin emblem in a parodic mind-concentration exercise eventually posted in many places on the Web (http://www.linux.org/info/penguin.html): "OK, so we should be thinking of a lovable, cuddly, stuffed penguin sitting down after having gorged itself on herring. Still with me?"

Tux was not universally popular at first, and some objectors said that it was hardly an emblem likely to appeal to the business community. Torvalds met the objections by saying that the penguin was much better than the typical corporate emblem designed by an agency because Tux was flexible. Any Linux project or distribution is free to use Tux or its many variations: the bird appears with a policeman's cap and club (security); necktie, briefcase, and cell phone (business); boots and *bierstein* (Linux Bierwanderung, an annual procession through the forests and *bierstuben* of Germany, while packing laptops); wearing a biker t-shirt with "Born to Run UNIX," and also carries national banners. Larry Ewing at Texas A&M created Tux; designs are on file at http://www.isc.tamu.edu/~lewing/linux/.

This does not explain Torvalds' choice of a penguin in the first place. It took a summertime expedition to Helsinki to find the answer. In 1997, Jon "maddog" Hall, executive director of Linux International and eventual godfather of Torvalds' children, went to Finland to gather material on the young man for a Linus Roast scheduled as a benefit dinner at the first Atlanta Linux Showcase. He learned a great deal about Torvalds, including his fondness for cats and ice cream; in fact, nothing could interrupt Torvalds at programming except the bell of the ice cream truck, which would invariably turn him out. As maddog wandered the Helsinki streets, he became aware that he was seeing penguins everywhere: the trademark for a popular ice cream!

The OSI was founded not to commercialize Open Source software (Red Hat and Cygnus had successfully done that), but to promote the commercialization of Open Source software. The Initiative believed that the way to do this most advantageously to the Open Source community would be to issue the Open Source Definition and grant seals of approval to licenses that met the Definition. Although the Initiative carefully replaced the term Free Software with the term Open Source software, and recognized licenses beyond the X License and the GNU GPL, it nevertheless kept the Free Software Foundation's hacker perspective: an individual must be free to modify, reuse, and redistribute the code. Accordingly, its list of approved licenses expanded to include those that favored individual use of the software material, even at the expense of commercial enterprises, while rejecting licenses that served commercial ends, even if they gave developers great latitude but infringed in some small way on an individual developer's freedom with the code. On top of this hacker bias in the Initiative, its powerlessness to control the very term Open Source led a number of parties to describe their own licensing arrangements as Open Source, whether they conformed to the Definition or not; among them are the Sun Microsystems licenses that the community resents for their severe distribution restrictions.

As a result of these controversies, the public is confused about the actual meaning of "Open Source software," and the only common definition seems to be that the term means *"source-inspectable* software," with varying degrees of freedom beyond that, depending on the license. There is a large section in this book dealing with the ins and outs of various licenses and licensing strategies, but the mention of just a few mysteries of the approved license list of the OSI is not out of place here.

- The X License permits a developer to receive source code, modify it, and then to redistribute the derivative product without any accompanying source code at all; it is on the OSI-approved list.

- The license for the Apache Web server, mainstay of the Internet and pride of the Open Source community, does not appear on the approved list.

- The Q Public License (QPL) is an OSI-approved license that does not permit any modification of the source code at all, but only the distribution of patches accompanied by source code. This latter requirement is unlikely to appeal to commercial software distributors, who will then have to buy a commercial license to keep their source code a secret. This restriction is unlikely to bother individual developers who are giving their products away, and because it seems to be there to push commercial users into paid licenses, it appears to violate the OSD restrictions against discriminating on the basis of intended use or groups of persons.

- Sun licenses tend to approve modifications to the code, provided the derivative passes a compatibility test, but none of the Sun licenses has been approved.

- The Zope server is very popular in the community, and permits modification and redistribution of its source code, but its license (the ZPL) does not appear on the approved list either.

- The Mozilla license permits modification to its basic code only in the form of patches, but allows extensions to the basic code to be shipped as binary-only; it is on the approved list.

It doesn't seem possible to draw any firm conclusions from studying the OSD, the licenses on the approved list, and licenses which have been rejected; for that matter, there is no list of rejected licenses. There is no public explanation of acceptance or rejection, nor is there an open process of review. It is not a case of the OSI reckoning that its work as a promoter of Open Source has ended, and fading quietly; it is currently said to be rejecting the most recent of the Sun licenses, and Sun's open challenge to the rejection may possibly open up the process. Unless the OSI clarifies its standards, it runs the risk of becoming irrelevant.

Entering the world of Open Source software, then, means entering a territory with indefinite borders controlled by more or less complex licenses. This should not dismay the adventurer; with care, there are worthwhile commercial opportunities.

Chapter 2

Commercializing Open Source Software

The Linux Community enjoys a popular reputation as a bunch of skylarking juveniles. The previous chapter tried to show where this picture comes from and how much truth might be in it. In this chapter we will look more closely at the Community's ties to a project or set of projects with a much more sober public reputation: the creation of the Internet with public funds.

Open Source Creates Private Wealth

There is still an active community of computer experts who helped start the Internet and who keep it going now. One of their gatherings is USENIX, the meetings of UNIX users that have a club-like atmosphere because so many people have known each other for so many years. Here, the newer Linux Community can look at the founders of the Internet and UNIX, and the UNIX crowd is more than a little aware that Linux is helping to revive UNIX.

When the Open Source Community looks at this side of its origins, it is both awed and emboldened: Open Source worked once and was universal; its time will come again. For the present, the Community is astonished at the sudden wealth it has created, wealth that can be tangibly measured at the Red Hat Wealth Monitor (http://prosthetic-monkey.com/RHWM/). The ostensible motivation for posting the Monitor is to remind Red Hat to reinvest some of its capital in the Community; recently the Monitor's computation showed the values listed in Table 2-1.

Table 2-1 *The Red Hat Wealth Monitor*

Red Hat Market Capitalization	$9,139,700,472
RH Market Capitalization Created by the Community	$7,978,958,512
Your Contribution	$1,595,791

Note

The values listed in Table 2-1 are subject to frequent fluctuation.

The capitalization is updated every quarter-hour while the market is open; the Community share in this wealth is reckoned as the percentage of code in Red Hat 6 not written by Red Hat (~87 percent). The number of contributors in the Community is reckoned at 5,000 persons, including documentation contributors and 1,000 kernel contributors.

Beyond its ostensible purpose, the Monitor operates at several levels. While it has a serious purpose of claiming some or most of Red Hat's wealth as Community property, it is also an imitation or even parody of the Bill Gates Personal Wealth Clock (http://www.webho.com/WealthClock), which tracks Gates's personal fortune and reckons the contributions to it on the basis of the entire U.S. population (some $376 per capita). The Red Hat Wealth Monitor is also awestruck at the size of the money pile measured, and shares in a tiny degree the resentment writ large on the Bill Gates Personal Wealth Clock site. At the same time, every rational Community member understands that the great wealth created by Linux IPOs is still measured in the perilous currency of start-up stocks.

The preoccupation with start-up wealth now rippling through the Community should adjust another popular idea concerning the Open Source Community: that it is a community of selfless or at least nonprofit bestowers, similar to the medieval monks who undertook public works like road repair. Of course there are men like Larry Wall, leader of an important Open Source software project (Perl) but not interested in becoming a CEO; but there are also men like Larry Augustin, founder and CEO of the recently IPO'd VA Linux.

The advantages of the nonprofit model include being able to improve and distribute code from many inspired sources; the advantages of the for-profit model include the ability to continue coding by using resources besides personal motivation. A hacker-centric view leaves out the noncoding part of the population, which includes people who can organize an economic engine to keep the coding going. Open Source software is always a work in progress. Hackers may see a program as an opportunity to become involved and contribute, but software vendors will see it as a deliverable product that must be fully developed to meet a sales deadline. Open Source software can benefit from both points of view.

Origins of the Internet

The Internet goes back to the days of all-software-as-open-source; its origins lie in the national defense research and infrastructure building of the 1950s. It is the virtual parallel to the National Defense Highway System.

One of the early research centers funded by the federal government was at MIT; the technology emerging from the work there helped build the New England computer industry. Government-funded research on the other side of the country at Stanford gave us the early versions of e-mail, word processing, graphical interfaces involving windows and a mouse, and hypertext (the original and still popular form of linking on Web pages).

To tie together the various federal research sites, the Advanced Research Projects Agency of the Department of Defense (ARPA) spun the ARPANET across the country, eventually connecting universities and government research sites. To do so successfully, the network depended on interoperability standards such as TCP/IP and Ethernet. Not only were these standards developed by publicly funded researchers, but they received collaborative input in an Open Source manner as well. To guide standards development, standards bodies were formed. InterNIC, for example, regulated the address system on the network.

The development of open, interoperable standards that could evolve along with the progress in research was paralleled by the invention of an operating system that was not hardware-specific; that is, it was designed so that only a small part of its code would need to be written for the specific hardware on which it was to run. Bell Labs was the home of this new operating system, UNIX. Its wide availability made it popular in universities and research centers, and it was rapidly improved by contributors in many locations.

The version of UNIX called the Berkeley Software Distribution (BSD) demonstrates the two themes of this chapter. First, Open Source software can spread rapidly and undergo development by many hands, while coexisting in a number of different versions. Second, this process does have its commercial application. A 1956 court decision kept AT&T (and with it, Bell Labs) out of the computer business, so that Bell Labs could be liberal in its distribution of UNIX code. In 1982 another court decision brought an about-face in AT&T's attitude towards UNIX, and stiffer control and licensing fees. To telescope a complex story, the version of UNIX that had been developed at Berkeley was offered to the public, source code and all, but missing a few portions of code whose ownership was claimed by AT&T. It did not take many months before the open community of UNIX users supplied the missing code by writing it from scratch. These contributors allowed their work to be distributed under the BSD License.

Commercialization of UNIX had already taken place; the rising minicomputer industry had licensed UNIX to put on their hardware. Because those companies are largely forgotten now, it is interesting to look at one company that decided to put BSD on its hardware and proceeded to attack, not the minicomputer, but the workstation market. That company, Sun Microsystems, is still with us. Because Sun based its original operating system on BSD, it has great affinity with Linux, which is an imitation of the BSD imitation of UNIX.

In the early 1990s, the Internet began to be opened to the public. Originally intended only for researchers in research institutions, its use spread first inside those institutions to all sorts of persons who were not actually science researchers; e-mail was the primary motivation for its spread. Eventually, a few institutions applied for waivers from the "appropriate use" policy of the Internet; that is, outsiders were allowed to connect. The most "inappropriate use" of all, commercial activity, soon followed. A new business was born, the Internet Service Provider (ISP), upon whose back many more Internet-based businesses would be built.

Familiar software of the Internet

The Internet of today not only runs on the protocols developed long ago (such as TCP/IP), a number of the Open Source applications of that period are still with us. In all cases, they are able to evolve because they are open. BIND (Berkeley Internet Naming Daemon) is the service that enables us to type a name instead of a series of numbers to reach a Web site, and Apache is the workhorse of the Internet, driving well over half the Internet servers in existence. The original Web server software was publicly funded; the present Apache project and product was begun by a number of Internet technicians who freely traded their constant tinkerings and improvements to it. Realizing they had a tangle of patches ("a patchy program") on their hands, they decided to organize the project and turn out a new product, Apache.

Apache shows us several ways to build a business based on Open Source software. Although Apache is free and may be used and modified by anyone, much of the development on it is done by private companies. O'Reilly & Associates funds some of the development, making money in its turn by selling books on Apache; IBM funds even more Apache development as a means of extending the life of its legacy computer systems by making their data available. IBM and O'Reilly make their improvements to Apache publicly available. On the other hand, at least two companies have taken the Apache code and put out proprietary versions of the program that include their modifications and improvements, and some Apache experts have started a business that sells Apache support.

Apache and Linux (and many other programs) were made possible by the Internet, which enables rapid cooperation over global distances by an unlimited number of contributors. The Internet was and continues to be a subverter of old standards, today in commerce and yesterday in programming. In place of the carefully planned and sequenced programming of the mainframe ethos, the Internet encourages rough-and-ready improvisation, "No kings, no priests, just a rough consensus and running code." The Internet is based upon cross-platform interoperability standards and encourages this open thinking. The ideal of Java is an Internet ideal.

Privatization of publicly funded technology

Throughout the history of the Internet, however, there were always private firms seeking to take some portion of it into private and proprietary waters. The existence of so much publicly funded code that could be taken private and made proprietary is a rich temptation, and it can be done successfully. SAS Institute, for example, took a statistical analysis product that originated as a Department of Agriculture project and grew it into an enormous privately held corporation.

The Berkeley version of UNIX, BSD, was distributed with its source code and a license that allowed the recipient the options both of altering it and of distributing the altered version without the source code. Sun (for Stanford University Network) Microsystems was one early distributor. Originally the company did not charge for the software, but included it with every machine so that Sun users could run UNIX programs. Other entrepreneurs picked up BSD as well, leading to such varieties as FreeBSD, NetBSD, OpenBSD, and BSD OS. The latter version is never given away, and even charges extra to customers who want to have the source code; the others are available in both paid and unpaid versions.

The crucial difference between paid and unpaid versions is support. Researchers and hackers are delighted with Open Source software that costs nothing; if they have problems, they can always ask user groups on the Internet for assistance. Corporate users, on the other hand, face legal responsibilities to shareholders, and insist on clearly defined support programs and a vendor they can turn to for immediate help. This paid/unpaid split is a constant in Open Source software.

The Browser Wars

If the Apache Web server story has a happy ending as Open Source software, and BSD lives on as both Open Source and closed, the Mosaic Web browser and its descendants sound like a Greek tragedy in midplot. Building on browser code originating at CERN, a research center in Switzerland, the National Center for Supercomputing Applications (NCSA) at the University of Illinois developed its version, the Mosaic browser. According to Netscape founder Jim Clark, Mosaic was not even an official project, just something that some young people at NCSA loved to work on. Made available for free as a download, the Mosaic browser spread across the Web like wildfire. NCSA recognized its commercial potential and licensed Spyglass, Inc. as the exclusive master distributor for the purpose of licensing it to companies who could develop its full commercial value.

Jim Clark also recognized the potential of Mosaic, and hired the original Mosaic development crew to come to California and build an improved version for his new firm, Mosaic Communications (later called Netscape Communications) to market. Although Clark avoided using the NCSA code, which the developers could easily have brought with them, he had the advantage of their expertise, and so duplicated the functionality, if not the code, of Mosaic. Knowing that they had to beat the NCSA Mosaic browser to survive, the company adopted the classic proprietary strategy of product differentiation. The new browser, code-named Mozilla (a monster to destroy Mosaic), would improve and extend the functionality of the browser to take the market away from Spyglass. Deprived of its inventors, the original NCSA Mosaic could not be expected to keep up.

To overcome NCSA Mosaic, Netscape introduced a scripting language into its new browser, and then licensed Java from Sun so that Mozilla could run Java applets. These improvements were de facto extensions of the HTML standard to which browsers were supposed to conform. From a vendor's point of view, the ideal customer lock-up would be a proprietary server whose output could only be read with a proprietary browser and whose content could only be developed with a proprietary tool. This perspective directly opposes the fact that the Internet was successful because of the open standards that govern and support it. These standards are no secret, and they are controlled by cooperative bodies.

There is always a tension between standards bodies and commercial enterprises because enterprises want to differentiate themselves by doing things that their competitors cannot do. If the product does not meet recognized standards, but fills a need, customers will still buy it. Given the speed of entrepreneurial innovation and the deliberate slow pace of standards bodies as they hammer out consensus, it is no surprise that the gap between the two should widen when a technology is hot. Structured Query Language (SQL) is an example; the official standard is less functional than the various versions of it delivered by competing database vendors. Vendors know that control of a de facto standard, that is, a standard accepted by the market in place of an official standard, is the best marketing tool of all.

If Netscape was having these thoughts, so was Microsoft. Microsoft licensed the NCSA Mosaic browser from Spyglass to have a place to start, and eventually produced its own browser on the basis of having studied Mosaic. The Microsoft approach to competition involved packaging the browser with the operating system, thus eliminating browsers as an application category in the Windows world. Netscape, meanwhile, doubled its bets on Java and was developing the Internet Foundations Classes (these were turned over to Sun and emerged as Java Swing) as part of its strategy to have the browser take over the operating system on desktop computers. It was a battle that Netscape could not win. Microsoft's browser, Internet Explorer, developed its own exclusive features, and the Web entered an uneasy era in which developers had to prepare two versions of Web pages to suit whichever browser happened to be visiting.

Netscape had expected an attack by Microsoft from the very beginning; the only question had been how long it would take for Microsoft to field a browser. As part of becoming the de facto browser standard, Netscape planned to have its browser so widely spread across the Web that by the time Microsoft appeared on the scene Netscape would have vanquished Spyglass's NCSA Mosaic and have the lion's share of the market — an advantage they hoped Microsoft would be unable to overcome. Key to the strategy of overwhelming the market with copies of the Netscape browser was the pricing structure. Because Netscape expected to make most of its money from Web servers, the browser was priced nominally at $39.95, but was completely free to educational users and to any other user on a 90-day trial basis. No one seriously expected retail revenues, but the corporate browser market would provide some useful gravy. In fact, browser revenues were far higher than expected.

Microsoft's strategy of bundling Internet Explorer for free with Windows effectively set the price of all sales of the Netscape browser at zero dollars. If Netscape tried to collect money, the user would simply switch to Internet Explorer. Jawboning, elbowing, and copious cash helped Microsoft spread its browser as widely as possible, and the linking of Internet Explorer with Windows was eventually featured in a federal court case against Microsoft. By the time Netscape faced the music and made their browser a giveaway item, the company was failing. This was the moment for the Open Source gesture that caught the world's attention.

Netscape goes Open Source

Seen from a worldly perspective, the opening of the Mozilla source was not a glorious moment: it was simple desperation in the face of overwhelming defeat. Seen in the mythic light that so often seems to shimmer over Open Source events, it was the sad Hebrew slave mother putting the Baby Moses in the basket to be borne downstream to future glory, or Sieglinde dying in childbed as she delivers Siegfried.

The world is slowly coming to reassess the release of software assets as Open Source. Its early reactions to the practice ranged from skepticism to derision. Not so long ago, certain VRML browsers were promised to the world as Open Source, even as they faded from sight, but nothing more has been heard about them. Some observers thought the release of a technology to Open Source by a failing company was an idea sold to management by developers as a public relations stunt, while the developers were planning all the while to pick up the technology once they had left the company. The adoption of Open Source by IBM and other healthy companies has changed public estimates of the practice.

Netscape was the first proprietary corporation to release its technology as Open Source; from the point of view of Marc Andreessen, who had worked with Open Source software at NCSA, it was an obvious move. It was his experience at NCSA that helped shape the Netscape strategy of distributing the browser, not in boxes in retail stores, but over the Web and as freely as possible. Open Source practices were also the inspiration for Netscape to distribute beta software to all comers. While this strategy did not achieve the effect of development by a wide number of people, it did give an opportunity for a wide range of beta feedback.

The Open Source version of the Netscape browser returned to its aggressive internal name of Mozilla; this time Microsoft was the enemy. The only way of keeping a competitor browser alive was to release it as Open Source, so that even if Netscape perished, the browser could live on. Netscape also counted on the enthusiastic hands of a multitude of Microsoft-hating hackers to improve it. Towards the end of this book, we will take a look at what happened to the Mozilla effort, but it is now time to take a brief look at enmity to Microsoft as a motor of the Open Source movement.

Microsoft as "the enemy"

The Open Source movement has its own objectives and ideals and does not need to refer to Microsoft to practice them. Nevertheless, Bill Gates, Microsoft, and Windows appear throughout this book. The three are particular targets for many in the Community. Hackers deride "Windoze" as slow, bloated code that keeps users in a perpetual state of bondage (like the prisoners in the Apple 1984 commercial); software vendors fear the blistering competition, and even the federal government has taken exception to Microsoft business practices.

There is no need to go into details; a partial list of the casualties of the browser wars will do. Netscape's plan was to develop its own browser so it would not have to pay royalties to Spyglass for NCSA Mosaic. This savings, like that achieved by relying on online distribution rather than on stores, was intended to keep Netscape's price below the competition. Microsoft obtained a single-fee, nonroyalty license from Spyglass, negating the first part of Netscape's competitive position. Putting Internet Explorer in the Windows box (and having it preinstalled on most new computers) solved the distribution problem for Microsoft and further undercut Netscape. Making Internet Explorer completely free also made sure that the dwindling number of Netscape users were people willing to take the trouble to download it and (until Netscape finally decided to drop the browser cost to zero) pay for it. Finally, adding to Internet Explorer proprietary extensions that were based on Microsoft's Web development tools meant that loyal Netscape users would find themselves visiting sites that would tell them to get Internet Explorer so they could enjoy the full functionality of the site, or (in the case of at least one site plugging a Hollywood movie) even be allowed to enter the site. By February 2000, site statistics indicated that market shares stood at Internet Explorer 80 percent and Netscape 20 percent.

Incidentally, but not unintentionally, Internet Explorer killed off NCSA Mosaic. Faced with competition from a free browser, Spyglass customers ceased to deliver product and pay royalties. Other browsers and the businesses associated with them failed as well.

The software world is filled with the casualties of Microsoft competition. The return of Open Source provides an opportunity for those of them still able to lift a hand. Ray Noorda, whose Novell was battered by Microsoft, founded two Linux companies, Caldera and Lineo. Borland, now reorganized as Inprise, is converting its tools to Linux and contributing Open Source code. Corel, which assembled an office suite from battered pieces of Microsoft casualties, has decided that Linux is the best way to compete against Microsoft.

SGI has climbed aboard, and Hewlett-Packard is cooperating. Even the twin pillar of the Wintel universe, Intel Corporation, is taking positions in Linux companies. One benefit it may reap is that Linux is likely to be the only operating system ready to run on the new 64-bit Itanium chip when it appears later in 2000.

For many Open Source hackers, an assault on Bill Gates by commercial rivals using Open Source is especially welcome. They remember him as the young "Micro-Soft" executive who warned in his February 1976 "Open Letter to Hobbyists" that folks had better quit stealing (copying and giving away) his software. They also remember his statements in 1980, refusing to lower his profit margins to accommodate hobbyists, and pushing a new argument that the copyright laws also covered computer magnetic media. They find it easy to see him as the guy who invented proprietary software in the first place.

Part II

Open Source Software in Your Business

Chapter 3

Benefits and Cost of Open Source in Your Business

In this chapter we'll look at the ways to use Open Source software inside your company. We'll look at these strategies from the viewpoints of the corporate user, the small-business user, and the sole proprietor. This chapter will spend more time on large firms because the use of Open Source software is more widespread and more complex in them, where Linux is a networking star, particularly among heterogeneous systems.

The Technology Adoption Life Cycle

Open Source software finds its way into businesses by the same process that brought in earlier technologies, including the computer itself. In the technology adoption life cycle, new technologies are first the province of the *innovators*, highly technical people who are distinguished by their love of technological novelty and their lack of budgets. If a business case can be made for the new technology, the visionary leaders, called *early adopters*, will pick it up, first in a pilot project, and then in regular deployment. These visionaries have budgets and are willing to spend substantial sums on a technological advance that will produce a competitive advantage. When enough visionaries have been successful and the technology is sufficiently spread and proven in a number of niches, it may then pass into general use. We will be taking a look at Linux from the perspective of that life cycle. (See Figure 3-1.)

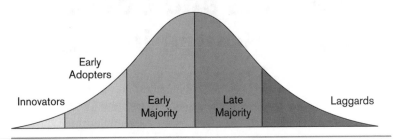

Figure 3-1 *A bell curve for the technology adoption life cycle*

The case for the adoption of Linux (and of BSD, the other major Open Source operating system) has been low cost and high reliability; we will see how these have been the motor for the spread of Open Source through the business world. The only cost for taking advantage of Open Source software is relative to the technical proficiency of the company. The use of open standards by Open Source software is a benefit available to businesses of any size. Open standards allow interchangeability of hardware, software, and of support vendors, so that a user is able to take advantage of competition among all of these. Similarly, open standards enable software vendors to write competing applications using standard protocols open to all users. Probably the most important advantage of Open Source software is the ability of a user to customize an application for its most effective use. You can do the customizing yourself, if you have the skills, or hire whom you please to do the job. No longer does a user have to send begging mail to a software vendor pleading for modifications or enhancements. This flexibility applies at both the operating system and the applications level.

Corporations

In the corporations, Linux first appeared in the hands of technology enthusiasts, innovators who run the systems of corporations and have their own networks set up at home. For those used to working in UNIX, Linux enabled them to run UNIX programs at home on their own inexpensive Intel machines. As corporations became aware of the Internet and wanted to set up e-mail services and Web servers, it was these systems people who figured out how to do it on a minimal budget. All it required was technical know-how (UNIX is found in corporations rather than in small businesses) and any Intel 386 or better machine. Corporations had many surplus Intel 386 and 486 machines, perfectly good, but made obsolete by the growing requirements of Windows software. Thus, a knowledgeable systems administrator could add Internet service to the corporate system by employing an old 386 machine or two, the free Linux operating system, and free e-mail software, such as sendmail, and free Internet server software, such as Apache.

A curious development was that chief information officers (CIOs) tended to be unaware that the Open Source software was actually running in their departments. The mission had been accomplished with a minimum of fuss, expense, and probably no meetings at all. Nor did Linux call attention to itself by crashing. Sendmail, Inc. has recently commercialized the sendmail product, and their method of finding customers for customization and support contracts is to cold-call large corporations where their Internet probing has told them that sendmail is running. Even at this late date, they are surprised and amused by the number of CIOs who deny that they have any Open Source software running.

UNIX companies lead

The use of free software and small desktop machines are insignificant incentives to corporations of a size to run UNIX systems, and these very corporations already had the most expensive resource on the premises: UNIX personnel. Corporations are also the best positioned to benefit from Open Source software because they are Internet- and intranet-oriented and have more direct control over their data pipelines than do smaller businesses. It is no surprise that Open Source has made its greatest progress at this level, which is the natural home of the early adopter. It is interesting, however, to see that in this relatively well-funded environment it was the low cost of Open Source that enabled the innovators themselves to become the visionaries who put the early elements of the systems in place.

It is far easier to introduce a UNIX company to Open Source software primarily because the systems personnel are in place, and because Linux and BSD run many UNIX applications. Burlington Coat Factory, with 260-odd stores, 20,000 employees, and sales of nearly $2 billion, can serve as an example of a successful switch to Linux. The company was always in the forefront of UNIX use, deploying in 1986 and standardizing on TCP/IP the next year.

The objectives of Burlington's conversion included the consolidation of servers, concentrating on large ones to serve applications and to replace the Sun servers; the placement of thin clients onto desktops; and the establishment of a pure system, to avoid mixing Windows NT with Linux. They wanted to use their old software where possible, to write some new applications, such as for a gift registry system, and to accommodate a heterogeneous collection of desktops in Receiving. Significant obstacles to an all-Linux system were the inventory scanners and the fact that several thousand point-of-sale systems could not be replaced until sufficiently depreciated. The original plan was to run Network Computers, but summer interns hired to analyze the job persuaded management to consider using low-level PCs and Linux for the job (another example of the pollinating effect of young systems people).

Hardware had become a commodity by the time the buying decision was made, so the deciding criterion was a commitment by the vendor to support Linux. When Dell committed to shipping machines with complete Linux drivers for all the parts, they won the contract for an initial 250 machines. As for software, the thin clients run Web-based Oracle products and use Applix for the office suite (it can read and write Excel and Word formats). The employees are happy because they have been able to keep their old applications. This helped fulfill the strategic advantage sought by Burlington: low costs with the least disruption. The chief operations officer who had to approve the spending was won over by the fact that the Linux installation represented the least change from the old system.

What about NT companies?

At this time it is far rarer to hear of a company of any size dropping Windows NT for a transition to Linux. On the other hand, there are plenty of NT corporations in which Linux has followed the path of stealthy entry into the Internet niche, with incremental servers running on Linux rather than on NT. Some of the innovators who placed these machines were Linux hobbyists at home, and some were former UNIX systems administrators who found their old skills were still useful. In the NT corporations, as with the UNIX corporations, the progress went from Internet services (mail and Web) to servers for files and printing.

Adoption of Linux for file and print servers in NT companies was helped by yet another piece of free software, Samba, which enables a Linux box to interface with an NT network. The effect is to disguise the Linux server as an NT server. The increasing ability of Linux servers to work with the file directory systems of multiple vendors has made them all the more useful in heterogeneous installations, frequently serving as the middleman in such systems. The original business proposition of Caldera in selling to corporations was that Linux was the glue that would hold everything together and make it work.

Cross-Reference

Chapter 6, "Linux vs. Windows," will deal with the question of Linux vs. NT in more detail.

Some cost comparisons

In the presentations that Jim Geisman (http://www.moreshare.com) and I have made on the issues of Open Source cost and pricing, we have noted the keen interest of IT middle management in the initial cost question. For a manager with a strict headcount and equipment budget, the idea of free software licenses and smaller machines is an appealing argument. Jim and I don't think these cost savings are the greatest that Open Source will achieve, although a manager at a large American-owned auto company recently told me that an evaluation in his division revealed that $50,000 UNIX workstations could be replaced by $10,000 Linux boxes. After looking at out-of-pocket costs, we'll consider the benefits of higher reliability. Upper management in IT finds these benefits the most compelling financial reason to switch.

There are various ways to compare the prices of setting up networks under NT and Linux or BSD; any attempt at laying out the figures will be inexact because it is possible to buy Microsoft products at varying prices, and because filling in $0 for the Open Source side of the equation is not much of a comparison. We will see, however, that the NT packages frequently need supplemental Microsoft software to match the bundle that comes on a typical Open Source disk. Estimates for an NT network range from $15,000 for 50 users to $62,000 for 100 users. Some needed elements are priced at the Shop Microsoft Web site (http://shop.microsoft.com/) as follows:

Product	Client Licenses
Standard NT Server with 5 clients $809	20 for $699
Site Server (for Internet) with 5 clients $1,239	25 for $2,109
Exchange Server (for e-mail) with 5 clients $809	20 for $1,149

Thrifty IT operations businesspersons could forego the client licenses and simply use Win95 or Win98 machines (each about $120) connected to a single Workstation (about $160) for simple networking. Some corporate officers prefer Workstation for all machines because of its limited capacity to run computer games.

On the Linux or BSD side of the equation, each machine is peer networked; each is a server talking to servers. The distributions, which cost from nothing up to $80, include the software necessary for networking, Internet connectivity, and e-mail. Both the NT and Linux prices given here do not include productivity applications, which are extra. The Linux productivity packages are all cheaper than Office 2000 Professional, and some are free.

There is one commercial BSD server package, BSD OS, which has no free version. The pricing is higher than for Linux or other BSD packages: $995 for the binary-only 16-user package (source code $2,995). The 64-user binary-only version costs $1,995 (source code $3,995), and the unlimited-use package costs $2,995 (source code $4,995).

The real savings

Whatever software-cost figures we project over however many users, less than 25 percent of the typical IT budget goes for software (and how much of that is for operating system licenses?). Similarly, hardware costs are less than 25 percent of the budget, and that figure is falling. On the other hand, the corporate personnel sitting at those machines carry a loaded cost of $50,000 to $75,000 on average, or anywhere from five to eight times the cost of the systems they use.

It is the stability and reliability of Linux (and BSD or any other UNIX) that gives a corporation the greatest cost savings. The frequent failure of NT systems (and of ordinary Windows systems) causes lost time and productivity. If we price this at $25 – $50 per hour per employee, and add in the cost of the systems personnel who must bring the systems up again, the cost of unreliability mounts rapidly. The larger the corporation, the more sensitive it is to questions of reliability, and the higher the value it places on high-availability systems. This has been a traditional strength of UNIX. With Linux, that reliability is available at a lower initial cost.

The stability sought by mainstream business users does not mean simply freedom from system crashes or lockups. Businesses are growing resistant to calls for upgrades; the slow penetration of Windows 98 and the light interest in Windows 2000 are an expression of this resistance. Besides this inertia, the growing publicity about continuing security holes in Windows and NT is only slowly beginning to worry businesses with external connections. The fact that these holes, although quickly repaired, are related to the interoperability of the Office package and its macros and thus give documents, spreadsheets, and e-mail—formerly thought to be inert—the power of executables, leaves conservative users wondering whether there isn't an alternative, and whether Linux might be the answer.

Training and support

Beyond hardware and software, Linux can make a strong case for cost savings in training, support, and administration because machines can be remotely configured and administered. Jon "maddog" Hall, executive director of the trade organization Linux International, reports that the University of São Paulo runs Windows, but on machines that can boot either Linux or Windows. When the Windows user reaches the point at which the machine will no longer boot Windows, an administrator can remotely boot the machine in Linux and then use Linux to pull an undamaged copy of Windows across the wire to refresh the machine.

The real issues for an NT-based company are training and support. It may very well be that a Linux aficionado in IT has already begun the process of putting in Linux file and print servers because of their low cost, high capacity, and reliability. In that case, there is some support already on site. Even as Linux has been sliding and creeping into corporations—recently reported by International Data Corporation (IDC, http://idc.com/) as the operating system on 25 percent of new servers—there has been an outcry that the great problem with Linux is lack of official support structures. As Chapter 4, "Available Products (and More to Come)," explains, there are numerous organizations, large and small, stepping into this gap. A large corporation is more likely to have personnel who have a UNIX background and who are also cross-platform trained. Nevertheless, the rapid increase in corporate Linux is likely to cause a shortage of personnel who can use it.

Linux supporters believe the colleges will eventually turn out enough people with Linux experience, but the real test is yet to come. Some estimates say that 25 percent of all Internet servers will be Linux-based within a few years. Linux vendors are meeting the personnel crunch in two ways: Linux software vendors are rapidly improving the operating system's ability to be as self-installing as possible, while hardware vendors are rapidly increasing the number of boxes sold with Linux preconfigured and running. In addition, they are supplying unitary machines such as stand-alone Web servers that can be plugged into the wall and the network and that start running as soon as they are configured by using a simple GUI that asks for IP addresses.

"The Network is the Computer"

As mentioned previously, the desire of corporations to interconnect large numbers of employees and amounts of data across large areas makes them natural beneficiaries of network software such as UNIX and Linux. Although not yet exclusive Linux users, major corporations such as Wells Fargo, Boeing, and Cisco, as well as NASA and the U.S. Postal Service, are all making use of Linux. The auto manufacturer mentioned previously is running a Latin American plant on Linux, and retail chains such as Jay Jacobs are using Linux for point-of-sale machines across hundreds of stores. Cendant Corporation runs some 4,000 servers in its chain-hotel franchises (including Ramada Inn and Day's Inn). Gannett Media Technologies International has stated that it set up its enterprise-wide asset-management servers in 1998 by building its own middleware to its Oracle 8 database. Gannett gives the cost as $300 per server as opposed to the $1,500 it had expected to spend on another solution. Corporate uses of Linux should grow as the operating system improves its capabilities in symmetrical multiprocessing (SMP) and scalability, projects that have gone to the forefront of the Linux development effort since the negative analyst comments on these capabilities in the first half of 1998.

Linux fits nicely into corporate plans to run applications across servers to thin clients. When Sun Microsystems announced its WebTone and DataTone approach to corporate data in 1997 — the idea that all corporate data would be on remote servers accessed not just over internal networks, but over the Web, so that portable thin clients could work anywhere as if at the office — the plan appeared to be a dream suitable for a large corporation. But Sun recently purchased Star Division, makers of StarOffice, the leading office suite in Germany (after Microsoft Office), and able to run on Solaris, OS/2, Windows, and Linux, on which it is most popular in the United States. The product can be run remotely to clients, so Sun is currently giving away the suite to individual users and intending to sell the networked version, called StarPortal.

Small Businesses and Sole Proprietors

At the small end of the scale, all the benefits of Open Source apply, and the low cost may be even more welcome. The fact is, however, that many small businesses do not have the UNIX-type expertise to install and administer these systems. As a consequence, the most likely path of entry into these companies is through the outside integrators who generally serve these companies by installing hardware, software, and providing training and other support. These integrators often serve a particular business niche or domain. Online directories of Linux integrators can be found at (http:// bynari.com/BCG/director.html).

The smaller the business, the more it depends on the technical expertise of its owner. Linux hobbyists will want to apply their skills to their solo businesses, but the rest of us will need the sort of person who got us into computing in the first place: a savvy friend. There are Linux hobbyists who will help you get up to speed, and when you feel you are ready, you can bring Linux into your business operations. Local Linux groups host Linux Installfest events to help anyone who brings in a machine get up and running.

If you have worked out important systems like billing and automated correspondence on Windows and believe this legacy prevents you from moving to an Open Source system, there is a new $299 product that makes possible a stepped transition. VMware, Inc. (`http://www.vmware.inc`) supplies a product that can be installed on a Linux or Windows NT/2000 machine and will run other operating systems concurrently as virtual machines. This way you can take advantage of Linux (or BSD) stability to run the Linux applications you choose and also toggle to a virtual Windows system that will run your Windows applications when you need them. The two systems can share files, and you can cut and paste between them. Through an OEM arrangement, VMware can supply a complete package, including both the Open Source operating systems and a choice of Windows operating system.

Once you feel assured that you will be able to hang onto your vital software that happens to run in Windows, it's time to see what Windows software you can currently replace by adopting equivalents that run on Open Source systems. Because Linux did not attract widespread attention until 1999, there has not been time to match the wide selection of programs that have been written for Windows over the past 15 years or so. But Linux users, particularly if they are willing to look beyond programs with a graphical user interface (GUI), will still find a variety of programs they can use in the office.

Chapter 4

Available Products and More to Come

We often hear that Linux lacks the breadth and depth of applications to make it a successful operating system. Any technology moves forward by first making inroads into niches, where it is appreciated by specialists doing specialized work. Accordingly, Linux has started in the domain of computer programmers and computer network administrators and, from there, it branched out into scientific laboratories. Technical specialists read the same narrow publications, attend the same meetings, and talk to each other, so that what is current among them may be entirely unknown outside their niche. Assuming for the moment that these specialists can find what they need in their fields, what about more general business users? Can you run an office today using Open Source products? And how will users from the Windows world ever adapt to them?

If you are willing to go with an Open Source operating system, such as BSD or Linux, and to run a mixture of Open Source and proprietary software, the number of products is increasing, and there are a number of familiar faces out there. WordPerfect users, for instance, will find that their old favorite is alive and well, and there are also free products that bear uncanny resemblances to Windows products. In this chapter we'll take a look at some of the currently available products that can run a business and look at some of the upcoming products as well.

Office Suites

End-users and managers will be happy to know that there is a choice of office suites already available on Linux, with more to come. Users coming from the Windows world will recognize the Corel package, Office 2000, now fully available on Linux. Law firms and other traditional users of WordPerfect should feel right at home, and reviews indicate that it is only a hair behind Microsoft Office in functionality (which so few of us take full advantage of). Users coming from the UNIX world will recognize an old friend in Applixware Office, which receives increasingly better reviews with each new release. Adventurers who want to try something different (and free!) can install Sun Microsystems' StarOffice, an office suite originating in Germany (it even runs on Windows).

Applixware Office

Applixware for Linux, from Applix, Inc. (`http://www.applix.com/applixware/`), was successful in UNIX as Applixware Office before it extended itself to include a Linux version as well as a version for Windows 95; it currently ships with the Caldera and SuSE Linux distributions. The package includes a word-processor, spreadsheet, drawing program, presentation package, e-mail client, and a set of document filters (file format converters) to ease the job of moving documents — including those created in difficult proprietary formats such as Windows — to and from other formats. The programs are capable of accepting real-time data. Applix recently set up a subsidiary, VistaSource, Inc. (`http://www.vistasource.com`) to deal in Linux products and strengthen its ties to the Open Source community.

For users of Palm Computing's hand-held organizers, there is the Linux Palm Desktop, a Linux-based desktop that integrates the schedule and other Palm data with Applixware Office. The Palm

Desktop was built with the Extension Language Facility (ELF) development tool formerly bundled with the office suite; this has been licensed as Applix SHELF under the GNU LGPL to enable third-party developers to improve Palm Desktop. It is downloadable for free at the Applix site for Open Source projects (http:// applixware.org). Because Open Source users are interested in cross-platform availability, they should note that there is a Sun-certified Java version of Applixware Office called Anyware Office that needs only a Java-enabled browser to run. There are no free versions of the Applixware or Anyware products.

Corel Office

Corel Office 2000 (http://www.corel.com) has just come to Linux, and the reviews are favorable. The Standard Edition includes version 9 of important office software: WordPerfect, Quattro Pro (spreadsheet), Corel Presentations, and CorelCENTRAL (Personal Information Manager and scheduler with Palm connection). The Deluxe Edition adds other software, including the Paradox 9 database.

Accounting Software

If you need accounting software for small and medium businesses, UNIX-proven proprietary packages are available from Appgen Business Software, Inc. (http://www.appgen.com/). There is an Open Source personal accounting package, GNUCash (http:// gnucash.org/), which currently has about 80 percent of the functionality of the basic Quicken package. As it improves, you can watch and see whether Open Source developers will push the project to grow complex and stable enough for small businesses.

StarOffice

Sun Microsystems, Inc. recently startled the world by acquiring Star Division, a German-owned firm that had produced the leading office suite in Germany (after Microsoft Office). The object of making this addition to the product line is not only to add an office suite to the Solaris application line, but also to provide another iteration of the Sun strategy to sell servers by promoting software that is server-intensive. StarOffice originated as a desktop office suite, but Sun intends to rework it into a browser-enabled, server-based application called StarPortal that will once again promote large servers and thin clients. Accordingly, the server version is for sale, but the stand-alone desktop version is available for free to all who care to download it, even if they want to use it in a business (there is optional paid support). Because personal use of StarOffice had been free under Star Division, Sun is making a gesture towards the Open Source community; it is not coincidence, of course, that the Windows stand-alone versions of StarOffice are likewise free. The suite is currently winning high praise from users and reviewers, including *PCWeek* Labs.

Like Applixware, StarOffice has a strong UNIX history, but it also runs on the Windows platforms as well as OS/2 and Linux. Like Applixware's Linux Palm Desktop, StarOffice has a Schedule product that synchronizes data with the Palm hand-held organizer.

In view of the fact that some Microsoft Office users are growing weary of the abundance of features that confuse and hinder, perhaps the relatively light weight (150MB) and flexibility of StarOffice will put it in the position of the emerging product as described in Clayton Christensen's *The Innovator's Dilemma:* When a product becomes too good and too expensive for its intended use, buyers will pick up an emerging technology that manages to do the job, even if it is not so richly-featured.

StarOffice is a workhorse, however, containing a browser and editors for HTML, formulas, and images. In addition, it contains its own desktop, enabling a company that uses it across platforms to have a very similar work interface on all of them. Like other filter sets, the one supplied with StarOffice does a creditable job, but cannot guarantee to take across all the formatting of the original document. Sun says it is working on open standards for document formatting, and the Open Source community hopes that proprietary data format standards will gradually wither away or at least be openly described. The free StarOffice download is 65MB and can be found at `http://www.sun.com/products/staroffice`.

SmartWare 2000 and GoldMedal

SmartWare is probably not a candidate for general office use because it contains only a word processor, spreadsheet, and relational database; it originates in the developer space and contains a Rapid Application Development (RAD) tool. This cross-platform tool (Windows, DOS, and UNIX) is available in a limited-function version for Linux for free. Fifty dollars will purchase the complete Linux version. Angoss Software, Inc. (`http://www.angoss.com`) recently spun off SmartWare Corporation (`http://www.smartware2000.com`) to handle the product.

Like SmartWare, the GoldMedal products for office automation (`http://www.goldmedal.com/gm/index.html`) serve to demonstrate that there is a lot of software originating in niches outside general business purposes (such as software development and scientific applications) that might contain the functionality that you are looking for in Linux. GoldMedal's spreadsheet is three-dimensional, and its relational database is object-oriented. American users who imagine that Microsoft dominates the rest of the world should note that these applications come from abroad.

Emerging suites

At the present time, Lotus is evaluating whether to put its Smart Suite on Linux; the eSuite for Java is already cross-platform.

Although they are not yet finished at the time of this writing, two Open Source suites attract attention with their promises. AbiSuite and GNOME Office both tend to coordinate and incorporate the work of other projects, but each offers a distinctive product at this time. (GNOME stands for GNU Network Object Model Environment.) These are gratis projects under the GNU GPL and even the commercial products discussed previously are cheaper than market leader Microsoft Office. The emergence of Open Source office software is a sign that margins are sure to drop further as these products head into the commodity category.

AbiSuite

AbiSuite is the grand plan of the AbiSource Project (http://www.abisource.com), sponsored by the SourceGear Corporation. SourceGear intends its AbiSuite business to work like other service and support businesses: the product is free under the GNU GPL, and SourceGear plans to make money by selling support, documentation, and packaged versions of the software. For this reason, the code is freely available and modifiable, but the Abi trademarks remain firmly with SourceGear. The first AbiSuite application is AbiWord (described later). It will be followed by AbiFile and AbiShow, all cooperatively developed as Open Source projects. Rather than start an AbiCalc project, AbiSuite will include the GNOME Gnumeric (http://www.gnome.org/gnumeric/) spreadsheet because of its rapid development progress.

GNOME Office

The promising GNOME Office project (formerly GNOME Workshop) is in a very early stage of development (http://www.gnome.org/gnome-office/). The first application, a spreadsheet described later, has not yet advanced as far as AbiWord in version numbering, but it, like the products that follow it, are based on important open standards. By using Common Object Request Broker Architecture (CORBA) standards, the GNOME Office applications will be built in a modular, object-oriented fashion, allowing easy reuse of code. The Bonobo document model used in Workshop will enable easy cross-application data sharing and dynamic updating. More information about GNOME can be found under "Graphical Products and Interfaces" later in this chapter.

The Bonobo Document Model

Miguel de Icaza, the leader of the GNOME Project and founder of Helix Code (`http://helixcode.com/`), a firm that sells and supports GNOME software, likes to name his projects after monkeys.

The Bonobo project (`http://developer.gnome.org/arch/component/bonobo.html`) is building the GNOME architecture for reusable components and compound documents. Although the component framework is based on the open CORBA standard, the intention is to emulate Windows ActiveX. Windows used to call this technology OLE2 (Object Linking and Embedding). The GNOME project is intended for the benefit of all UNIX systems, and Bonobo will enable users to tie applications together and to create compound documents, such as documents containing spreadsheets instantly updated from database changes. Drag-and-drop capability is part of the plan.

Eventually, Bonobo will tie together the GNOME Office applications, but because its architecture is so deep, it will take a long time to pull everything together. The most advanced GNOME Office application is Gnumeric, and it has made the most progress with Bonobo. In the meantime, Helix Code is building a workgroup application called Evolution on top of Bonobo. All its elements are Bonobo components and are fully accessible through CORBA so that applications may be scripted to work automatically together. Because the components include such elements as e-mail, scheduling, task management, and a PIM, Evolution's plans include making it communicate with Lotus Notes servers and Microsoft Exchange. This integration will enable client-by-client infiltration of Linux (or UNIX) software into offices.

Just as AbiSuite has taken on GNOME's Gnumeric as its Open Source spreadsheet, GNOME Office has designated AbiWord as its word processor. Because the two applications are busy cloning Microsoft Word and Excel features, Windows users should feel at home using them.

KOffice

KOffice (http://koffice.kde.org/) is still in the alpha stage of development, but it is based on the more popular Linux desktop, KDE, the K Desktop Environment (http://www.kde.org/). KOffice currently offers early versions of its various components, including KWord, KSpread, KPresenter, and Katabase. All the components of the office suite are embeddable in each other, including the drawing applications: KImage (for bitmaps), KIllustrator (for vector drawings), KImage (the image viewer), and KChart (the chartmaker). The KDE desktop comes installed on several ready-to-run Linux computers, including the NetWinder and systems from VA Linux.

The Windows question

The big question in a business that currently uses Microsoft Office is whether the business will be able to adapt to using the office software that is available on Linux or BSD. The answer will depend on the business and will require careful evaluation of what portions of the business might make the switch, based on existing functionality of available products.

On the whole, the graphical interfaces on the suites just discussed are enough like Windows not to cause undue learning problems; the real issues will be how much users are dependent on templates or macros that they expect to find in documents they use. Against this shortcoming can be balanced the fact that every time there is a new Windows version of Word, its users seem to be unable to bring along their customized interfaces and macros and frequently find that documents are not readable between the versions. Seen this way, it should not be much more of a problem than was moving from Microsoft Word 95 to Word 97.

There is a rumor — or perhaps fantasy — abroad that Microsoft has ported, will port, or is considering a port of its Office suite to Linux. Linux fanatics see this as inevitable, since they expect the imminent demise of Windows and reason that Microsoft will want to salvage its Office suite income from the wreckage. Although Microsoft is always a keen student of competitors (a couple of years ago, people at a major Linux distributor told me that they shipped unbelievable numbers of their product to Redmond), and many people believe that the best thing for Windows and Office would be to rewrite them from the ground up, there are strong reasons for Microsoft not to make the move. For one, the porting of Office to Linux would sharply steepen the curve of Linux adoption. For another, the bringing over of all the products and their underlying machinery in a way that would preserve compatibility with existing documents and applications would require an enormous investment that would be hard to justify, especially because such a move might kill the revenues generated by Windows and Office for Windows.

Corel brought WordPerfect 8 over to Linux as a straight port, but this means that each successive version of WordPerfect will require another port. For the long haul, Corel is investing in the free WINE project (`http://www.winehq.com/`) so that its Windows versions will run on Linux by means of a special layer created by WINE and make successive ports unnecessary. Windows developers are free to use the WINE material to extend the reach of their Windows products to the Linux environment.

Word Processors and Spreadsheets

Although there is no lack of free text editors on Linux (UNIX people can't live without them), the number of graphics-based word processors is smaller. Besides the word processors in the suites mentioned previously, the chief contenders are discussed in this section.

WordPerfect

WordPerfect was the first mainstream office application to come to Linux. It is obvious that Corel had long chafed in a $6 billion Windows office suite market that supported three contenders, one with a 90-percent market share. Corel's attempt to move WordPerfect Office to Java was simply an earlier effort to enter a market not controlled by Microsoft. Corel intends not only to put all its major products on Linux but also to offer its own Linux distribution.

Reviews indicate that the Linux version of WordPerfect works well with Microsoft Word documents, and the TurboLinux distribution includes the free (personal use only) version. Federal agencies can now purchase the Linux WordPerfect from the GSA schedule, and law offices, which are heavily networked and important users of WordPerfect, now have an opportunity to consider moving their operations over to Linux.

AbiWord

There are numerous free graphical word processors available on the Internet but, in practical terms, AbiWord is the leader. While usable, it has not yet reached ready-for-ordinary-folks stage, although it does provide basic functionality. The groundswell behind it eclipsed the only other contender for top free spot, the Maxwell word processor, which was originally designed for commercial release (`http://www.eeyore-mule.demon.co.uk/`). Although also under the GNU GPL, developer interest in the Maxwell died away in 1998, perhaps because it is based on the older Motif widget set, while AbiSource uses the GNOME Tool Kit (GTK) for its graphics.

As part of its Open Source stance, the AbiWord .abw file format is ASCII, marked up with XML. As a result, it is readable in any text editor, and it can output HTML and RTF formats. There are versions for UNIX (including Linux), Windows, and even the BeOS. At this stage, it does not yet support GIF or JPEG graphics file formats, but uses PNG format instead. It handles only Adobe Type 1 fonts, not TrueType.

Currently there is a mailing list to use for support problems; paid support programs will be available for those who want them after AbiWord reaches release 1.0.

Spreadsheets

Xess is a powerful Linux spreadsheet originated by three North Carolina State University (NCSU) faculty members. In its present form, it is a proprietary product published by Applied Information Systems (http://www.ais.com) and marketed by the Business Logic Corporation (http://www.blcorp.com/index2.htm). The full-function Linux version retails for $195, with lesser versions for $39 and $70. Versions for other platforms (UNIX, VMS, and Windows 95), including specialized versions for engineering and finance, sell for considerably more. Its most remarkable feature is the ability to work with real time data feeds, so that values may be changed automatically by outside feeds while the user watches (for instance) the graphing of the results.

The three NCSU professors have allowed the developers of the free Gnumeric spreadsheet, part of the GNOME project, to study the original Xess source code; this help has accounted for rapid development of Gnumeric. In fact, the progress on Gnumeric has been so swift that the AbiSource project has decided not to work immediately on a spreadsheet, since the Gnumeric project should be able to provide one soon. The eventual office suite, called GNOME Office, will be under the GNU GPL, just as the AbiSource suite is expected to be.

Databases

The movement of the large database vendors onto Linux signaled the beginnings of serious interest in the platform by the business community. We can call the roll—Informix (the first), Oracle, Sybase, IBM DB2—in addition, companies like Corel and Computer Associates have said that they will put their entire product lines onto Linux. Corel's Paradox 9 has already arrived.

Oracle likewise has made this commitment. If you are evaluating whether Open Source is here to stay, watch these companies to see whether, after the initial flurry of placing some products there, they keep up the momentum of porting to Linux. It is not a trivial decision to add a platform to a product line, and decision makers in those companies will be watching the market closely to see whether continued investments in the transition make business sense. One place to watch to keep an eye on the availability of databases for Linux is the links page at `http://linas.org/linux/db.html`.

Before the large database vendors noticed what was happening on Linux, a number of smaller vendors had already taken advantage of the need for their products. Many of these were foreign firms, such as ADABAS D (from Software AG); Solid, from Solid Information Technology (`http://www.solidtech.com`); and FlagShip, a Clipper-type product. MySQL has proved very popular on Linux, and UNIX hands will recognize PostgresSQL. Databases you may not have thought about in a while have been here, such as Pick (the entire Pick system was quietly ported to Linux some time ago), Raima, and POET (object-oriented).

Missing Products

So far, we have seen that Linux has basic desktop productivity products (the office suites) and business tools that are more familiar to back-end operations than to end-users (the databases). There is a missing tier of middle-management software that offers obvious opportunities for anyone who wants to enter this space.

- *Personal Information Managers* (PIM) are vital products; they combine schedule and appointment information with contact information. At their simplest, they can be used by everyone; at their most sophisticated, they turn into contact management tools.

- *Sales Management* tools are more sophisticated contact management tools that link to centralized company databases and coordinate the efforts of a sales team and their support personnel to deal with prospects and customers.
- *Decision Support* products can come in many different forms. Often they are spreadsheet add-ons (for that matter, the Linux spreadsheets could use add-ons of all sorts), such as those that go beyond sensitivity analysis to calculating the outcomes of various probabilities and variances inserted by the user. Others use decision models based on decision trees or multiattribute analysis.

There may be Decision Support packages out there among the thousands of scientific packages available for Linux, but it is likely that their use requires expertise in Linux. Similarly, just as Windows users have lots of favorite little utilities that tell the time, print documents as little booklets, track client hours, and compress files, Linux users have their little favorites, but their interfaces are very likely to be command-line driven rather than graphical.

Such *Utilities* might be listed as "semi missing" products. Enterprising developers may very well see the opportunity to take some of these command-line utilities and give them a graphical interface and sell the results to eager users. It should be possible for a Windows brand name to do this, since the utilities themselves would not readily port to Linux, but a familiar interface would be appreciated by customers.

Because application availability is changing so rapidly, you will need to take a look on the Internet for information on what is available, and even then you will have to look carefully. For instance, the good news is that IBM's ViaVoice product is coming to Linux; the bad news (for the end-user) is that it is the software development kit (SDK) containing the voice-recognition technology, not the end-user product; users will have to wait for applications that use the SDK to incorporate speech recognition.

Graphical Products and Interfaces

The biggest gulf between Windows and UNIX users is the interface. Although UNIX does have graphical user interfaces (GUIs), hardcore UNIX users tend to prefer to use the command-line or "console interface." Building programs in UNIX is simply a matter of stringing the right text files together, and the fact that simple text editors evolved into programming tools (and in the case of EMACS, a way of life) only reinforced the preference for the command line (called the "console interface"). The surest way to divide a random group of UNIX developers for some contest is to have them split into EMACS users and vi users (Richard Stallman wrote EMACS, and Linus Torvalds prefers vi).

Many a DOS user moving to Windows felt the same way about the command line: it was quicker and easier to do something by dropping into DOS than by trying to do it in Windows. Windows 95 was fairly unmanageable without DOS, and real control of Windows has always required visits into the text-based Registry to edit it. UNIX users justifiably believe that real power lies in typing text on the screen.

Realistic Linux fans have come to realize that Windows users (and even Windows developers) are so wedded to their GUIs that there is no practical hope of bringing them to Linux without taking this foible into account. Open Source developers have aggressively souped up their GUIs and hope for the day when Windows users will be attracted to Linux by the power and appearance of the many GUIs available for it.

UNIX separates the GUI from the application

An important difference and eventual advantage of UNIX over Windows is that UNIX applications, originating from a command-line or console world, have had their Graphical User Interfaces

(GUI) added at another layer. There are still many Linux and BSD applications for which there is no GUI at all. As a matter of fact, application developers prefer to write pure application code and prefer that graphical people tend to the GUI, although project organization often requires the application developer to provide the GUI interface. The advantages of separating the two layers include the following:

- The application and its graphics can run on one machine, and the application results and the GUI can be sent to a much smaller machine;

- As GUIs make progress, or as fashions in interfaces change, the underlying application need not be completely rewritten;

- Applications that output synthesized speech (for the disabled) work more easily if they are fed the lines of print that characterize the console mode of display; similarly,

- GUIs that emphasize large-print display throughout their menus and the underlying applications can simply be layered atop existing applications.

Linux and BSD applications with a GUI commonly use an X Window server to provide the basic graphics capability. Since any machine may run a number of servers, as well as be connected to other machines or servers, it is usual for a stand-alone machine to run its own X Window server.

In addition, each machine carries a number of software libraries that are called by applications. Not long ago, Motif (and its royalty-free look-alike, Lesstif) was popular; currently the Open Source GNU Tool Kit (GTK) is one of the basic building blocks. The more popular desktop, KDE, is built atop the Qt Toolkit from Troll Tech, while the other popular desktop, GNOME, is built atop the object-oriented version of the GTK, GTK+.

KDE and GNOME

Business users who want a Windows-like interface will pick KDE without any hesitation. You may want to try out GNOME—you can always put it away and go back to KDE after looking at it—but GNOME is currently a less finished and a less stable product than KDE. The smoothest and most stable version of GNOME has just been issued by Helix Code, but the user will have to compile the code to run it. Both desktops are less than three years old but making rapid progress, and both are working towards object-oriented modular design and eventual possible interoperability, so that applications that run on the one will run on the other. Users who choose KDE can still generally run GNOME-based applications, and KDE users should be sure that they include the GNOME libraries when they install their Linux systems.

If you are new to Linux and are coming from Windows, KDE will be easier to adjust to and give fewer problems than GNOME. GNOME probably has a stronger following among technology buffs who can handle its intricacies. It is more customizable than KDE, and its architecture may eventually make it the leading desktop. But if you are getting your Linux help from a GNOME user, you would be better off to go with GNOME.

The chief reason that there is a GNOME is that Open Source developers wanted a desktop in the free tradition of the GNU tools, and KDE is built atop a toolkit that requires royalties for applications that are distributed commercially. GNOME was also inspired by the great graphical progress made by Open Source developers in the GNU Image Manipulation Program (GIMP), an Open Source imitation of Photoshop and the leading Open Source application for photo manipulation, image construction, and similar tasks. GNOME will take a page from the Microsoft Object Linking and Embedding (OLE) book by using the open CORBA standard to achieve the same effect.

Watch for Another GUI

Four of the original Macintosh team have founded a company to produce and support a new interface for Linux, Eazel (http://www.eazel.com/), that will eliminate the need to use the console (command-line) mode. The GNOME project is cooperating in the infrastructure for Eazel. Some people believe that having even two competing interfaces is too many, but Open Source is about choice. Choice, among other benefits, provides opportunities for companies to simplify choices for users – that's how AOL became successful.

The good news from the GUI and desktop front is that Linux developers are embracing the idea that if they are to achieve World Domination, they will have to accommodate the ordinary point-and-click users they formerly dismissed as not part of the real computer population. As their home page (http://www.gnome.org) says, "The GNOME project intends to build a complete, easy-to-use desktop environment for the user, and a powerful application framework for the software developer." The project's leader, Miguel de Icaza, says that his attitude toward ordinary users has improved greatly since he began the project.

KDE, in active competition with GNOME and ahead so far in the race, emphasizes its responsiveness to users by posting a Wish List page where they can state what they want and examine the wishes of other users; votes are held on the relative desirability of the wished-for features (http://homepage.uibk.ac.at/service/wishlist/). As recently as late spring 2000 it read:

> There are currently 1131 wishes and 87 fulfilled wishes (a total of 1218 wishes) from 722 different authors in this list, the last one changed on Friday, May 19th 2000, 20:23:59.

Red Hat, with its heavy emphasis on ease-of-use and ease-of-installation, has become an important sponsor of GNOME by setting up the Red Hat Advanced Development Laboratory (RHAD) and hiring several GNOME developers. The resulting code is issued as Open Source software under the GPL and LGPL. The GNOME project itself sponsors the writing of front-ends to command-line driven applications, as well as the writing of new applications.

Because the different interfaces, like the applications, depend on the presence of certain libraries on the machine, new users should stick with one distribution in which everything needed has been provided. The problem of incompatible libraries is comparable to (Open Source fans will writhe as they read) Microsoft DLLs: having the wrong ones on your machine will keep some of your software from operating. Both the main desktops are working towards providing object-oriented wrappers for the various libraries so that they may be more compatible with each other. Interoperability is a big Open Source goal.

Scientific Products

There are thousands of scientific applications available on Linux, so specialized that there is no point in summarizing them. Most of them depend on a command-line interface, and many are in the semi-finished state often found in software (and hardware, for that matter) developed by researchers for an immediate and specialized use. A good place to look is the page called Scientific Applications on Linux (http://SAL.KachinaTech.COM/index.shtml).

Research scientists are probably running UNIX at this time, if they have not already gone over to Linux. It is business users who are wondering whether they should evaluate Linux systems as possible supplements or replacements for their current computer operations, which are very likely to be Windows NT. The next chapter will take up the Linux vs. Microsoft question and may help some of you decide whether and where to start with an Open Source system.

Chapter 5

Linux vs. Windows

Newspapers and computer magazines love to describe Linux as the Windows killer, but as we have seen in Chapter 5, Linux is not yet ready to cross over into the mass market and find a place on the average desktop. There is little point in comparing it with Windows 3.x (16-bit) or with Windows 95/98 (32-bit). Microsoft is pushing users to the new Windows 2000, is hoping to be able to field a 64-bit Windows for the coming Itanium chip, and is trying to enter the embedded market with Windows CE. Linux will be stiff competition in both the 64-bit and embedded platforms (see Part IV, "Linux is Moving UP... and DOWN.")

For those businesses that are not vendors of 64-bit or embedded systems, the only significant Microsoft versus Linux discussion is about servers (or workstations); that is, Windows NT/2000. Among servers, the Linux displacement threat is probably greater to low-end UNIX rather than to NT, but even if Linux is not displacing NT servers, it is often purchased in place of an incremental NT server. This chapter will look at inroads Linux is making into Microsoft's server market and the countermeasures Microsoft is taking in return.

The Competition with NT

Business users never anticipated a contest between Open Source and NT because for all of the early history of Linux, they were unaware of its existence, even as it was being smuggled into their backroom operations. Rather than wait for an influential visionary to spot the emerging technology, the innovating technologists themselves introduced the pieces they needed, bringing their home hobby into the workplace. Because expenses were low or nil, and because the Open Source software did its work quietly and efficiently, IT managed either to remain ignorant, or preferred not to ask questions. From Web server to file and print server to glue among heterogeneous systems, Open Source software offered inexpensive customizable solutions to the technically proficient.

Web servers

Linux first entered most companies as the platform on which to run the Open Source Apache Web server; we can track its growing use by looking at the Netcraft Web Server Survey (http://www.netcraft.com/survey/). The survey publishes the relative shares of the various servers used on the World Wide Web. Admittedly, this survey is not scientific, as it depends on gathering sites, not by random selection, but by taking URLs entered by visitors and then regularly polling this growing list. The survey is thus skewed by self-selection and by the fact that one server may host multiple polled Web sites, so that a single server may be counted scores of times. For this reason, it does not do much good to worry about fine distinctions; the large picture is interesting enough, however.

Apache (presumably running on Linux or BSD) is on approximately 62 percent of servers surveyed, while Microsoft's IIS server (running on Windows NT) is on about 21 percent. There is also a survey for third-party certified SSL server sites: these commercial sites return the result that about one-third are running Microsoft and something fewer than one-quarter are running Apache. But if we assume that the Stronghold C2 SSL servers are running on Linux, Linux's share rises to slightly more than Microsoft's. In any case, there is serious competition between Linux and NT in this space.

Servers in general

It is always difficult to gather information about the spreading use of Linux. One copy will do for many machines, the copy need not even be paid for, and many Linux users will pay for each new version of the system as it appears. Researchers can count installed systems and the operating systems installed on them, and they can count new systems as they are sold with the operating system already installed. They can also count box sales of Linux distributions.

Sales of New Servers

International Data Corporation (IDC; see http://www.idcresearch.com) studies of unit sales in network operating systems (NOS) provide the figures listed in Table 5-1.

Table 5-1 *Market Shares for Network Operating Systems*

Operating System	1997	1998	1999
Linux	6.8	15.8	25
Windows NT	36.0	38.3	38
NetWare	26.4	22.8	19
UNIX	20.7	18.8	15
OS/2	6.3	3.0	
Other NOS	3.8	1.3	3
Above Totals	100%	100%	100%

From 1997 to 1998, Linux's share of the server market OS sales increased from 6.8 percent to 15.8 percent, more than doubling its share. If we accept a market-size estimate that sets growth at some 26 percent (from 3.5 million to 4.4 million), that means sales of some 695,000 copies of Linux distributions. NT Server weighs in at 38.3 percent (nearly equals 1,685,000) of the 1998 market. In that year, Linux and NT were the only two operating systems to increase their market shares, while UNIX and NetWare were both having their shares cut into by the newer operating systems. By 1999 NT market share was stalled, while Linux nearly doubled its market share and NetWare and UNIX continued to lose ground.

The figures cover only U.S. sales of Linux by the major distributors (Red Hat, SuSE, Caldera, and so on), and they do not cover the free downloading of these distributions over the Web or the purchase of them in inexpensive two and three dollar copies from Linux Mall (http://www.linuxmall.com) or Cheap Bytes (http://www.cheapbytes.com/). Nor do we know how many copies of the distributions were not used for servers, but simply for standalone machines. About all we can tell from the figures is that Linux is a popular new technology and that NT is hardly in danger of disappearance.

Server Installations

The Gartner Group's DataPro Information Services (http://www.gartnerweb.com/public/static/datapro/main.html) published a "User Ratings Survey of Operating Systems" in November 1998, which indicates the installed base of servers among respondents. Most of the respondents were in consulting and professional services, and all were in the United States. Of these, some 67.7 percent had Windows NT installed, some 12.5 percent were using Linux, and 3.9 percent were using BSD. (Of incidental interest are the findings that, on the desktop, some 89 percent had Windows 95 installed, but only 17 percent had Windows 98 installed. The survey also reports that users are buying Windows NT like hotcakes, while not having a high opinion of it as an operating system.)

Respondents indicated their plans for increased or decreased usage over the next three years; the results show that Linux is the UNIX-type operating system most named for increased use among general (that is, including Microsoft) users. Growth in NT is fueled mainly by replacing lower-end Windows systems, by replacing

NetWare, and to a lesser extent by replacing UNIX. The DataPro survey also indicates the uses for Linux. These are summarized in Table 5-2.

Table 5-2 *Uses of Linux in All-Linux Businesses*

Use	Share
Web server	33.3
Applications server	9.9
Scientific and technical workstation	14.8
Networked workstation	9.9
Desktops	6.2
Enterprise	9.9
Total	84%

DataPro explains the 9.9 percent figure for Enterprise use by stating that Linux-only operations tend to be technically oriented smaller enterprises that appreciate the savings that Linux enables.

As for betting on Linux among resellers, the *Computer Reseller News* poll published in October 1999 reported a rising confidence that "Linux would be a viable alternative to Windows in the small and mid-size company markets within the next 12 months," and that the increase in respondents expressing similar confidence in Linux for the enterprise market was even more dramatic. (See Table 5-3.)

Table 5-3 *Computer Reseller News Poll of VARs*

Company Markets	August 1999			September 1999		
	Yes	No	Undecided	Yes	No	Undecided
Viable for small and midsize in next 12 months	45%			52%	37%	11%
Viable for Enterprise in next 12 months	26%	45%	29%	45%	28%	27%

A growing number of VARs are making up their minds (only 11 percent were undecided about Linux for small and midsize businesses), and there was a surprising jump from August to September 1999 in the number of VARs who believed that Linux would be viable for their enterprise in the next 12 months.

Values – Linux vs. NT

There are several Web sites that compare Windows NT and UNIX (including Linux and BSD) in detail, such as the one put up by John Kirch (http://www.unix-vs-nt.org/kirch/). We have already discussed relative costs in Chapter 4, and it is only a question of whether we go into technical matters in greater or in lesser detail. Because both systems are improving, any discussion will quickly become dated, but the larger points of difference include the following:

- Mainly because of stability, cost comparisons are favorable to Linux. Additionally, a typical Linux distribution has everything in one box; for NT, additional products are needed.

- Linux, without a GUI or with a lightweight GUI, will run comfortably on low-end hardware on which NT cannot run.

- Linux can emulate an NT server by using free server software called Samba, enabling integration of Linux and NT without licensing fees, expensive hardware, or instability problems.

- The BSD OSs are older and currently more able to handle high transaction loads than either NT or Linux and may be used to run Linux software and integrate with NT systems.

- Fewer servers are needed to accomplish the same tasks than with NT.

- Linux systems are easier to configure and support than NT.

- Linux runs on many platforms, including 64-bit Alpha from Compaq; NT is now confined to Intel.

- Open Source software may be modified by the user; unneeded portions may be dropped.

On the whole, users of large systems understand that neither Linux nor NT is a neck-and-neck competitor with the older and more functional UNIX systems; the question is which of the two newcomers will close the gap with UNIX more quickly. Microsoft recently announced its determination to bring Windows 2000 up to the mainframe level, and Linux is able to use distributed processing to emulate a supercomputer, but currently neither could safely run a large enterprise such as Sabre, the airlines reservation system.

Microsoft Slaps at Linux

Nineteen ninety-nine was the year of the Linux breakout, and the celebrity and successes of the upstart operating system led Microsoft to tell the Department of Justice that the rise of Linux and office applications for it was proof that Microsoft had genuine competition. In the marketplace, however, Microsoft was finally moved to notice the newcomer and to scoff at it.

Benchmarking

In October 1999, Microsoft struck out at Linux by posting NT/Linux comparisons on a "Linux Myths" page on its Web site (`http://www.microsoft.com/ntserver/nts/news/msnw/linuxmyths.asp`). A number of the alleged shortcomings are related to the usual benchmark problems — Has the problem been set to favor one server over another? Did the tested systems receive the same opportunities for tune-up? — but some of the charges have been heard before, have merit, and the Linux community is on its way to answering them.

The outrage at the Linux Myths page was not nearly so great as the initial outburst at the publication of the April 1999 Mindcraft, Inc. tests of Linux versus NT sponsored by Microsoft. Linus Torvalds initially denounced the tests, but then decided that the better approach was to "Admit it: we sucked," and show the superiority of Open Source development by tackling the shortcomings head-on. At

USENIX in June and at LinuxWorld Expo in August he admitted that too long an interval had been allowed to pass between stable kernel releases and that kernel development was "developer-driven," rather than user-driven. He then allowed that "the anti-Linux group at Microsoft is just a user in disguise," and that such "bug reports are good: they just don't go through normal channels." Finally, Torvalds promised that kernel releases would be more frequent in the future.

Note

Linux releases are odd-numbered for "developer," that is, experimental versions, and even-numbered for stable releases. The gap between 2.0 and 2.2 was two-and-a-half years.

In addition, the summer of 1999 brought a number of Open Source gifts to Linux in the form of donated code to support needed improvements. These contributions demonstrate the increasing interest by large companies in Open Source, and the successful integration of these firms into the Open Source world will demonstrate the viability of the Open Source development model. Among the shortcomings complained of in Linux are the lack of a journalizing file system and the inability to address memory larger than 2GB. A month after the Mindcraft tests, SGI, Inc. announced that it planned to make available the source code for XFS, a 64-bit file system that would also work on 32-bit systems. This will enable a future Linux kernel to access file systems up to 18 million terabytes and file sizes up to 9 million terabytes.

Just before the Linux Myths page hit the Web, Siemens Information and Communication Products and the Linux distribution SuSE announced that they had developed a memory extension allowing Linux to access up to 4GB of memory on Intel servers (Linux could already do this with Alpha servers) and that Torvalds was already planning to include the technology in a future kernel release. Open Source development serves both the community, by making its software stronger, and the hardware manufacturers who donated the code, by growing the Open Source market and enabling the manufacturers to sell their products upward into the more lucrative markets of database-intensive uses.

As Linux moves along to expand its functionality, especially in the fields most often criticized, it will be interesting to see whether the current projects to provide Symmetric Multiprocessing (SMP) and high-availability clustering will also benefit from code donations from large companies.

The Halloween Papers

The Halloween Papers serve as the Pumpkin Papers of the GNU Generation, purloined proofs of a dark plot to destroy the democratic sunshine of Open Source and to bring it and everyone under the power of Microsoft. They are, in fact, two confidential Microsoft memos. There has been heavy discussion of them on the Web, and while there has been less said about them in the press, they hang like background radiation in any discussion of the Open Source future.

The first memo was slipped to Eric S. Raymond a couple of months after it was written. Raymond says that he rushed to write a commentary on it, working into the late hours of Halloween 1998 and publishing the next day on the Web (http://www.opensource. org/halloween/); by adding a commentary he hoped to avoid possible legal action by Microsoft. The second memo, a follow-up to the first, reached Raymond a few days after the publication of the first.

Under the heading "Halloween Documents," Raymond has posted heavily-annotated versions of the two Microsoft memos, links to press coverage, and Microsoft's official responses to the leakage and content, countered with rebuttals in the acid and playful style characteristic of Open Source controversy. The whole collection is worth studying for what it tells us about the perspectives and intentions of both Microsoft and the Open Source community and how they work. From the Microsoft documents, we learn of their high regard for Open Source products, their comparison of Linux to Java as threats, and what weapons they will use to combat this latest enemy.

A Look Into Microsoft's Strategy

The memos' internal praise for Linux and its performance is both surprising and gratifying; there is even a wistful admiration for the Open Source process that produced them, along with the realization that Microsoft will be unable to experiment with it, even internally. There is a fear that the process is so attractive that, particularly when powered by the Internet, it will capture "developer mindshare" and divert interest from Microsoft products. Linux, which within a year Microsoft will publicly deride on its Linux Myths page as based on a 30-year old technology, is here covertly admired as the beneficiary of 25-plus years of UNIX experience, and Open Source applications are recognized as having "commercial quality." While the memo believes that Linux is a more immediate threat to UNIX, it also perceives a near-term threat to NT-server revenues because hardware manufacturers will be able to put out inexpensive special-purpose servers using Open Source software (as indeed Whistle and Cobalt were already doing).

The memos could not go on to discuss the strategy of combating Open Source until they defined the nature of the threat. It was immediately identified as comparable to that of the Java VM (Virtual Machine), but harder to combat because the enemy was a process and not a company. Furthermore, because Open Source code was easily available from multiple sources, Open Source applications could not die easily, and thus enjoyed "long-term credibility." The alarming conclusion was that Open Source could *not* be defeated by FUD. FUD (the sowing of Fear, Uncertainty, and Doubt about competitors' products or their viability) is old stuff in the world of computer competition, and Microsoft has not done anything that IBM did not do in the days when it was mighty in the land. But Open Source developers, as lovers of elegant technologies, loathe the intrusion of sordid sales and marketing practices into what should be purely technical decisions.

The memos did see that Open Source could provide a market-entry advantage by supplying cheap giveaway products that could swamp a competitor, and predicted that cooperative efforts (such as Red Hat

Advanced Development Labs' contributions of Open Source code to the community) would last only as long as vendors felt too weak to compete with each other. Once firmly established, they would introduce proprietary twists to their products. Furthermore, a vendor could use an Open Source project to preempt or forestall competitors' projects by absorbing community talents for its own Open Source project. Thus, the Microsoft analysts managed to see the Open Source process as a continuation of the proprietary wars by other means.

 Note

In the Halloween Papers, Microsoft noticed that "IBM is taking a lead role in optimizing Apache for NT"; among the "Worst case scenarios" covered is "IBM Adopts Linux?" (see Chapter 13, "Companies and Projects").

Further high-level analysis led to Microsoft's assessment of what Open Source developers regard as one of their greatest strengths as, instead, a fatal "core weakness" suitable for direct "attack." This is the use of open standards for protocols that make the Internet possible (HTML, TCP/IP, and many more). The tactics to deal with them had already been tested successfully . . . on Java.

As we will see in Chapter 8, "The Drive Toward the Mainframe," Sun is still smarting from having included Microsoft as both a Java licensee and as appointed developers of the official reference implementation of Java on Windows — "Who could do it better?" they must have asked themselves. The whole point of writing Java code was that it could be interpreted on any platform that had a Java Virtual Machine (JVM) running; although the use of interpreted rather than compiled code made the software run slowly, Java's ideal was "Write Once, Run Many Places." Microsoft decided to "embrace and extend" the Java standard (on Windows, at least) by making available to it all the Visual Basic or ActiveX libraries that developers had already written and that were already running successfully.

This extension was offered, understandably, as a benefit to programmers. The problem was that the resulting Java code would no longer run on a non-Windows JVM; if it ran at all, it could not possibly include all the benefits gained from calling the ActiveX components. Microsoft's vehicle for this hijacking of Java was its J++ development tool, which made calls to the Microsoft Foundation Classes rather than to the Java Foundation Classes. Developers had no warnings about which of the functions they were using were tied to the Microsoft platform, and thus could not count on writing portable Java code when using the tool. J++ has since disappeared, having done its part to drive Java applets from Microsoft clients. Today Java runs very successfully on servers, although few are aware of the fact.

The Halloween Papers talk dismissively of open protocols as commodities. The tactic here is to "change the rules of the game" by inventing new protocols and by extending the functionality of other protocols so that Open Source projects either cannot use them or at least cannot enjoy their extended functionality; the optimal case is to "deny entry" to the Open Source projects. Specific Open Source projects are targeted, and file systems will eventually be included (Linux can read Microsoft File Allocation Tables or FATs, for instance) as the Microsoft operating systems take over middleware functions. The operating system will serve as a barrier to accessing resources.

The other tactic discussed — potential suits over intellectual property — "remains to be investigated." This ominous phrase reeks of FUD. The best use of the threat to sue is not the threat itself; it is the refusal to say whether you will or you won't. Having studied the writings of Eric Raymond (which state that Open Source works best on projects that have some running code that functions and can be tested, even if buggy), the memo writers conclude that Open Source developers are not capable of real innovation and will always be chasing to catch up with superior operating systems (including NT). Further, Open Source developers will be unable to ape their superiors without falling into violations of patent or copyright. No further details are given.

Although Microsoft denies that the Halloween Papers are anything other than a middle-management exercise, Eric Raymond has identified two of their endorsers as members of the highest management team at Microsoft. The Halloween Papers lead the Open Source community to believe that they will have an eventful walk down the road ahead.

How to Close an Open Standard

Microsoft included in Windows 2000 the Kerberos security technology developed at MIT under the X License. This license makes the technology free for all comers to use and modify as they please (`http://web.mit.edu/kerberos/www/`). Microsoft added its own material to a data field left blank for developers to use and did not publish the changes. Although Microsoft acted within its rights, its refusal to document the changes serves to close an open standard and hampers smooth communication between UNIX and Windows 2000 systems via Kerberos security.

The other shoe dropped when Microsoft, responding to public outcry, announced it would publish the standard on the Web in May 2000. Those who responded found themselves downloading a self-extracting compressed file that opened with a non-disclosure agreement (NDA) requiring consent before revealing the information. The NDA warned that Microsoft was imparting a trade secret that might not be published or shared except under NDA. The required secrecy effectively prevented the implementation of the Microsoft standard in open standards or code.

It did not take long for the hotheads at Slashdot to post not only links to Web sites containing the secret, but the secret itself. Microsoft then sent legal notice to Slashdot demanding the removal of the secret and of links to the secret. Slashdot refused and appears to be ready for a long march through the courts.

The trade secret claim is not likely to prevail, since once a trade secret is out on the Web, it is a secret no longer. Microsoft should have taken better care of it than to post it on the Web; a sly developer can easily access the secret directly without passing through the NDA. According to Sam Byassee of Smith, Helms, Mullis & Moore, the copyright claim might not even prevail if a judge rules that the matter is factual, descriptive, and so uncreative as not to merit copyright. If the material turns out to have valid copyright protection, however, then even fair use is no defense for publishing the material, secret or not, on the Web.

Slashdot is invoking the First Amendment, saying that to remove postings on its site would violate free speech rights by forcing them to censor posts by their readers. While copyright would certainly overrule the free speech claim for posting the (former) secret, the case is less clear that merely pointing to another site constitutes a copyright violation. Additionally, Microsoft is demanding removal of readers' posted suggestions on how to access the document while ignoring the NDA (a process probably obvious to most developers). The fact that Microsoft has invoked the new Digital Millennium Copyright Act (DMCA; see Chapter 14, "Intellectual Property") increases the complication because the Act has not yet been tested. Microsoft has at last found a way to go to court with a community it finds a growing threat.

Part III

Open Source Licensing: Does it Have to Be This Hard?

Chapter 6

The GNU GPL and the Open Source Definition

The chief distinguishing feature or unique value of Free or Open Source software lies in the licenses under which it is offered. All parties in the software industry, whether on the Open Source side or the proprietary side, support the idea of copyrighted software and of licenses to control the transfer of those rights in copyright to second and third parties. There are over a dozen licenses in general use in the Open Source software market, and a further couple dozen have been invented, although they are not widely used. Some are tightly crafted by lawyers, and others would make a lawyer laugh. All of them seek to provide just the right measure of freedom and control that accords with the licensors' ideology and (in some cases) business purposes. Unfortunately, the licensing theorists disparage the experiments of the pragmatists, while proposing subtle refinements that serve to discourage business people.

The licenses themselves reflect the engineering minds of the developers who wrote most of them and employ varying degrees of precision and shades of subtlety in differentiating themselves from all the other licenses. Some licenses cause unforeseen (but perhaps not unintended) problems for users and developers, and poorly written ones protect no one. In Open Source software, licensing dependencies have become as important to watch as software dependencies (see Chapter 7, "Unforeseen Complications of Open Source Licensing: Forking and Licensing Dependencies").

A number of large companies have joined the hunt for the perfect license. Netscape was the first, with its Mozilla Public License (MPL), and Sun Microsystems now releases source code for several products under its Sun Community Source License (SCSL). More recently, IBM published its IBM Public License 1.0 (IBM PL).

Any business opened in the Open Source marketplace needs to understand the licenses in use and, in particular, the licenses that affect its own business, whether that business is software development, sales, or support. This chapter will discuss and compare the most important licenses; the texts of some of the licenses are in Appendix A, "Public Software Licenses."

The Copyrighting and Licensing of Software

Independent software vendors (ISVs), like any other business, want to recover their investment in development costs, cover current expenses, and make a profit. Because software is so easily propagated, the most effective means to control its dissemination are legal, not physical. The actual right of ownership in software is traditionally established through copyright, partly by tradition and convenience, and partly because the short life of software technologies rarely justifies the large cost of obtaining a patent on it.

Any author's expression of an idea is automatically copyrighted, whether published or unpublished, regardless of whether the authors mark it as such or take the small trouble to register the copyright. Authors or vendors who take the disposition of their software seriously will both mark it as copyrighted and register that copyright (http://lcweb.loc.gov/copyright/); the registered copyright owner's case will be stronger in any eventual court appearance regarding its ownership.

The copyright itself confers a bundle of rights (so-called, to empha-size that they are separable according to the choices of their owner), which include three that are crucial to software: copying, distribution, and preparation of derivative works. The rights to display and to per-form the work in public apply more to music and representational art than to software, but it is conceivable that someone could violate Microsoft's copyright of *Flight Simulator* by charging admission to watch fly-throughs, thus publicly displaying and performing the work.

Software vendors want their customers to possess and use the copies they have purchased, but vendors also have a financial interest in limiting the users' rights to copying, distribution, and preparation of derivative works. So the user's rights must be carefully defined, accord-ing to the purposes of the copyright holder. Yes, you may make a copy, but only one copy solely for backup; or, yes, you may make three backup copies. No, you may not distribute any copies whatsoever. Yes, you may make derivative works, but only in the sense that the data you prepare in the program's proprietary format is derivative. No, you may not decompile the code, make improvements, and pass on the results to other persons, even if you use only a little of the original code, and charge nothing for copies of the new program. Only a carefully worded license will achieve the goals of the vendor.

Disclaimers

The GNU GPL does not warrant in any way the software it covers; the user simply receives it "as is." Anyone who wishes to, however, is free to sell warranty coverage. All the Open Source licenses dis-claim warranty and liability, including for incidental damages. This practice is not really different from the usual shrinkwrap license, which does not offer more than return of the money paid by the customer.

In Open Source software, which generally allows copying, distribution, and modification, the license is even more critical, since passing along the bundle of rights is not meant merely as conferral of them on the next party, but as a restriction of those rights down the line through successive parties. Prof. Pamela Samuelson of the University of California at Berkeley points out that a license is not simple contract law, which binds only the actual parties to the agreement, but that licenses borrow from real estate law, under which third and successive parties are bound to a contract they had no part in originally making. Thus, a piece of land may have its use restricted according to the original deed of sale, taking the form of a restrictive covenant on the land.

The GNU General Public License

The GNU General Public License (GPL) of the Free Software Foundation (FSF) is the most venerable of the public licenses. Respected for its avowed determination to make all software free, its chief fame is that Linus Torvalds put his Linux kernel under its protection, making it possible for the many contributors to that project to know that their code would remain free for anyone to use, modify, and distribute.

The Linux kernel, in fact, was built largely by tools licensed under the GNU GPL, and the complete Linux operating system consists of many GNU GPL-licensed utilities and applications. The GNU GPL itself often serves as a reference point for discussion of Open Source licenses and makes a good place to begin.

GNU GPL rights

Because freedom for software and its users is the aim of the Free Software Foundation, the GPL, as it is commonly called, places no restrictions at all on most of the rights belonging to copyright. Most importantly, there is no restriction on use, and public display and performance are likewise unfettered. Just as the owner of the software program or code has copyrighted the work to provide it maximum protection, "copylefting" the code under the GPL places strict licensing terms on copying, modification, and distribution of the software. Derivative works are left uncovered, unless the output is a work based on the program. The following sections take these points in order.

Copying and Distribution

There is no restriction on copying and distribution so long as the following conditions are met:

- The source code must either be provided or made easily available to the user.

- The text of the GNU GPL and all notices referring to it must be copied and distributed along with the software, as well as the copyright notice(s) and disclaimer of warranty, unless the distributor provides a warranty.

- Interactive programs must display the notices at startup.

Note

The distributor may charge for the distribution service and for providing warranty service; this concession to commercial activity shows that the FSF is concerned with the free propagation of source code and is not hostile to commercial activity per se in connection with Free Software.

Modification and Derivative Works

Anyone may modify the software but may distribute the modifications only with a notice of what these are, who made them, and when. The modifications must be distributed under the GPL.

The license specifically states that certain output from programs will not be considered derivative works requiring use of the GPL for their distribution: binary output from a GPL-protected compiler or data organized by a GPL-licensed database would be examples of this exemption. Derivative works are any works containing code already covered by the GPL; these can only be distributed under the

GPL. Developers must be careful, however, in how they combine GPL-protected code with code under other licenses. (This is discussed further in the upcoming "The 'Viral' or 'Contaminating' Effect" section).

The hand of an attorney is clearly visible in the closing provisions of the GPL. Third parties who receive the software are considered to have received direct licenses under the GPL. A person who modifies the code may distribute it only under the GPL. The only rights any licensee has are granted in the GPL, and not adhering to the license both terminates the license and is a violation of copyright, which is actionable in court. The termination of a license in the case of one offender does not terminate the licenses of those who received the software from the offender, provided the recipients are in compliance with the GPL. Finally, any copying, modification, sublicensing, or distribution of the software may not take place except under the terms of the GPL.

Effects of the GNU GPL

The GNU GPL has been successful in all its aims. Although the license has never been tested in court, the Free Software Foundation has managed to force every poacher either to back off or to adopt the GPL. The pressure applied consists not only of the threat of copyright suit, but also of the bad publicity attendant on trying to steal the intellectual property of the nonprofit FSF. On the advice of counsel, the Foundation requires that the copyrights to improvements to GNU code be signed over to it before they are incorporated in releases of Foundation software. The concentration of ownership maximizes the standing of the Foundation as the aggrieved party in a lawsuit, as opposed to the collective complaints of hundreds of developers. Linus Torvalds, on the other hand, allows developers to retain their own copyrights in the code submitted to and adopted into the Linux kernel.

Note that just as a developer can hold a copyright on the code and distribute it under the GPL, it is also possible to distribute the code in other ways under other licenses at the same time. The developer could license the code on an OEM basis to a large software firm for incorporation into other software, or even for distribution as a separate product, and still put it out as Open Source software under the GPL. If the developer, however, later incorporates improvements that users have contributed under the GPL, those improvements not only remain under the GPL, but cannot be issued under any license other than one approved by their copyright holders. Thus, although it is theoretically possible for the original developer who likes a certain GPL modification to obtain permission of the contributing copyright holder to distribute the software under a commercial license, the practical effect is to discourage such mixed licensing arrangements owing to the difficulty of securing permission for all the improvements that need to be incorporated in improving the original code. This is an example of what some call the "viral effect" of the GPL.

The "Viral" or "Contaminating" Effect

The unpleasant terms, "viral" and "contaminating," describe what the Free Software Foundation prefers to see as a "liberating" effect. The GPL's terms prevent the incorporation of GPL'd code into software that is not under the GPL. The net effect is to steadily increase the amount of Open Source software made available as developers prefer to take advantage of GPL'd code in building their own products. This situation, while a boon for Open Source, continues to be misunderstood by the business world. The most common myth is that getting too close to GPL'd software will cause proprietary software to be lost forever to its owners. Actually, it takes the compilation of GPL'd software with other software to require that the resultant derivative product be distributed under the GPL. There is no obstacle to distributing GPL'd software on the same disk with proprietary software. Some companies fear that if an employee picks up any GPL'd code into their proprietary product, the company will be forced to GPL the entire product. Worse, they fear that if an employee takes a company's proprietary code and contributes it to a GPL project, the company will not be able to recover it.

These are false fears. An employee who steals property and then brings it to his or her company to use does not make the company liable for his or her actions, nor does an employee who steals company property and pawns it make it impossible for the company to recover its property. In both cases, the employee has acted against company policy and does not have the power to commit the company to his or her unlawful course of action. In all the cases above, the stolen property must be returned to its lawful owners. Companies need to be aware, however, that when they accept GPL'd improvements to their GPL'd software they cannot issue those improvements under a proprietary license without the copyright holders' permission.

Somewhat more legitimate are the fears that somewhere in Linux there may be code that is actually someone's property, and which will be someday detected and reclaimed, crippling Linux systems around the world. There are, in fact, responsible persons who claim to know of such cases, and who believe that the copyright holders are merely biding their time to cause trouble. Linux fans, on the other hand, point out that Linux consists of many small packages or files of code and that any offending code can be rewritten to remove copyright concerns. These Linux defenders allay the even greater fear of patent infringement in the same terms, saying that a workaround is always possible. The super confident believe that any challenge will only be a desperate act by the hidden hand of a weakening Microsoft, unable to resist Linux in any other way.

The Perpetuity Effect

Some cautious companies apparently fear the GNU GPL because it does not provide a perpetual right to the license. Sam Byassee, a partner at Smith, Helms, Mullis & Moore, suggests that these fears are groundless. A termination of the license of one licensee does not terminate the licenses of the others, provided they are not violating the provisions of the GPL. Further, he believes that an argument in equity may be made that an arbitrary "ability to terminate (or revoke) is antithetical to the purpose and intent of the GPL."

The Library General Public License

Richard Stallman actually provided a workaround for the "viral" problem by issuing some software under the Library General Public License (LGPL). Stallman has always been uncomfortable with this stepchild of the Free Software Movement and has recently taken to calling it the Lesser GPL, while urging people not to use it. The original purpose was to spread the popularity of the GNU C libraries by allowing proprietary products to make calls to them, showing that Stallman understands the value of market penetration in the early days of a product. Lately, he believes in using the attraction of the unique properties of some of the GNU libraries such as Readline to compel proprietary software to accept the GPL to use those libraries.

Under the LGPL, the key to the use of proprietary code with GPL'd code is that they not be compiled together, or statically linked. They may instead be dynamically linked; that is, software under one kind of license may make calls to the application programming interface (API) of software distributed under the other kind of license. This way the GPL'd and proprietary software may work together, keeping their separate places and licenses. Some will argue that there is no legal distinction between dynamic and static linking, but the past declarations of Richard Stallman and the customs of the community have laid out the current practices of this useful symbiosis, and it has provided the model for more than one sort of mine-and-thine license down the path of Open Source.

Stallman's growing reservations concerning the use of the LGPL stem from recent changes in technology that increase the complexity of copyright enforcement congruent with GNU licenses. Object-oriented technologies such as CORBA (Common Object Request Broker Architecture) allow the mixing of software components without compiling them together, further muddling the already shaky distinction between dynamic and static linking.

The kernel-loadable module has its origins in the need to add hardware devices to a system without having to recompile the kernel. The problem is solved by having the kernel load a module that carries a list of function names and virtual addresses for these, so that the kernel can make calls to the device driver and manipulate the device (such as a printer, sound card, or graphics card). These modules are in binary format (that is, compiled to work on the system); if they are Open Source software, the source code is available or shipped with the drivers. Linus Torvalds holds that this dynamic linking—the loading of modules into an already-compiled kernel—is covered by the LGPL, making it possible to use proprietary driver software from companies that wish to protect the secrets of the workings of their devices. Although Stallman does not approve of this solution (because his legal advisors tell him there is no distinction between static and dynamic linking), he concedes that the copyrights in question are not his and that he has no say in the matter.

Kernel-loadable modules have done much to extend the reach of Linux to cover many hardware devices because of the ability to use non-Open Source software drivers.

The Open Source Definition

Concerned that the antibusiness ideology of the Free Software Foundation was a barrier to interesting the business community in Linux and other source-available software, a group of leaders, in what came to be called the Open Source Community, met in February 1998 to discuss the situation. The immediate occasion was the recent announcement of Netscape that the source code for their Communicator product, particularly the Navigator browser portion, would soon be available to developers for free. Christine Peterson of the Foresight Institute suggested the group use the term Open Source software in place of Free Software, and the Open Source Initiative (OSI) was born.

As part of its effort to reach accommodation with the business community, the OSI drew up the Open Source Definition (OSD), a guideline to the principles underlying Open Source software licensing. The original document was taken from Bruce Perens' "Debian Free Software Guidelines" (http://www.debian.org/social_contract.html), which stated the principles underlying the distribution of the Debian version of Linux (Debian GNU/Linux). The original intent was to copyright the term Open Source and to certify licenses as Open Source licenses, but the plan proved not to be practical. As a result, the OSI lists certain licenses as "approved," and it also certifies software as being distributed under an Open Source license.

The first difficulty the OSI faced was the wide range of licenses claiming to be Open Source — some of these will be discussed shortly. As a result of the latitudinarian attitude of the Open Source Initiative towards some of the licenses offering themselves as Open Source, Bruce Perens resigned, stating that the OSI had come too far from the principles of the Free Software Movement. Perens is now back in the Stallmanist camp.

The document he left behind, "The Open Source Definition," is now in its seventh revision and provides a guide to the principles of the OSI. There are a wide variety of organizations with licenses that consider themselves Open Source operations; that is, they make source code available and then set rules governing its use. So far, the OSI has approved few licenses and gives no indication of whether this lack of approval stems from limited resources, lack of application by some license authors, or from quiet rejection of some licenses. Because of the broad range of terms of licenses approved by the OSI, there is little to be gained from our examining licenses in terms of their conforming or not to the OSD. It is important, however, that the GNU GPL and LGPL are approved by the OSI, as are the BSD (or X) style licenses, the Mozilla and Netscape Public Licenses, and the IBM Public License.

Some important Open Source licenses

If you are leading an Open Source project, it is usually best to pick a well-known license and use its terms. This will save people from the trouble of having to read a new license and then figure out how it will fit with software distributed under other licenses. Unless a new license (or a variant on a familiar one) is done with great care for a particular purpose, it is more likely to be a hindrance to the project's acceptance. The licenses described in this section have been successful in protecting and promoting the software they cover; it is more than likely that one of them will suit your purposes.

The BSD-Type or X-Type Licenses

When AT&T was broken up by court order, the company undertook an evaluation of all its assets. One of these was the UNIX operating system, popular in universities and research institutions because its cost was low or free, its source code available, and because AT&T was willing to incorporate improvements sent in from all over the world. When AT&T set a high monetary value on UNIX, resulting in their charging large sums of money for a source license, this happy symbiosis came to an end. The sudden disappearance of UNIX source code from the universities particularly rankled programmers because they felt they had developed much of the code for which AT&T was charging such a high price. The resulting movement to clone UNIX centered on the University of California at Berkeley, and thus the Berkeley Software Distribution (BSD) was born.

BSD has a distinguished history, and at this time is probably a stronger and more scalable operating system than Linux. One of the reasons for the rapid growth of Linux was that AT&T tied up BSD in lawsuits for several years, causing some users to fear for its survival. Having successfully purged all AT&T code from its system, BSD today powers such large sites as Yahoo! and was the basis for the original Sun operating system.

Sun's ability to take the BSD source code and turn it into proprietary, binary-only software depended on the very liberal BSD license, of which a number of variants exist, such as those covering FreeBSD, OpenBSD, and NetBSD. These licenses originally varied from the Massachusetts Institute of Technology (MIT) X license (MIT X license), which was developed to cover the X Window graphics system (variants of the MIT X license include the XFree86 and XOpen licenses) by requiring the mention of copyright holder(s) in advertising and other locations, but even that restriction has fallen by the wayside. The FreeBSD license, for example, is short; apart from the disclaimers, the longest of which disclaims warranty, the relevant terms are:

> Redistribution and use in source and binary forms, with or without modification, are permitted provided that the following conditions are met:
>
> 1. Redistributions of source code must retain the above copyright notice, this list of conditions and the following disclaimer.
>
> 2. Redistributions in binary form must reproduce the above copyright notice, this list of conditions and the following disclaimer in the documentation and/or other materials provided with the distribution.

 Cross-Reference

For the complete text of the disclaimer mentioned in the extract, see Appendix A, "Public Software Licenses."

Any recipient of one of the BSD distributions is entitled to take the code, modify it, and to distribute it in either source or binary form; many software vendors choose this type of license because it allows distribution of binary-only versions. Unlike the GNU GPL, there is no programmatic statement of agenda in the BSD-type licenses; BSD providers state that their object is simply to see that the software is distributed as widely as possible and that no person or endeavor is restricted from using, distributing, or even selling it. The result is that Linux contains helpings of BSD code, as do Windows NT and the new Apple operating system, Mac OS X.

The Open Source Initiative approves BSD- and X-type licenses because the original distributor makes the source code available, and does not prohibit modification or further distribution. The license also allows the making and free distribution of derivative works. Although there are many critics of the binary-only privilege, these distributions still receive voluntary modifications from developers, who hope the BSD distributor will incorporate the modifications and thus spare the developer the burden of individually supporting them. Because the BSD distributions themselves always include source code, developers don't believe their contributions will be subsequently unavailable to them.

The Netscape Public License

The Netscape Public License (NPL) covers the source code that Netscape released for its Communicator product, material referred to in the NPL as the "Covered" code. Part of the delay in releasing this code was the time it took either to drop third-party proprietary code from the package or to secure distribution rights for that software. Further hindrances to immediate release were the sharing of some code between Communicator and Netscape's server products that remained proprietary, as well as the existence of obligations to supply source code to third parties for inclusion in proprietary products. Choosing the GNU GPL would have negated the value of exporting code for the community to improve, because the GPL would have prevented the contributed improvements from being used in proprietary products.

Accordingly, Netscape devised a pragmatic license that would protect their proprietary interests while allowing the incorporation of contributed code and, at the same time, enable outside developers both use of the source code and protection for their own proprietary technology. The NPL gives Netscape special privileges in the Covered code for a limited time. By that time, the company will have reengineered its proprietary server products so that they will either no longer be dependent on the Covered files or will use them on the same terms as everyone else. Netscape will then retain only one other special right: that of distributing Covered file code to those customers whose contracts provide for their receiving this client-side code for use under non-NPL terms in proprietary products.

Netscape's released client-side code, called collectively Mozilla, consists of several files, each of which has a header stating its licensing terms: the NPL. Developers can make modifications to these Covered files and distribute them as they please, provided they include the source code for the modifications (it need not be the source code for the entire modified file). The modifications will probably consist of either bug fixes or extensions to the application programming interface (API) that add functionality to the product. Thus, bug fixes and improvements to the Covered code are required to be turned back to the community once these changes are distributed outside the developer's organization.

New code, however, may remain proprietary; it might, for instance, be libraries called by the new API functions inserted in the Covered code as modifications. These new files in the distribution may have their source code included — or not — as the developer chooses. The choice of binary-only distribution and the licensing is up to the developer. But the developer who wishes to contribute them to the Mozilla community can place a header in the files stating that they are distributed under the Mozilla Public License and include the source code.

The Mozilla Public License

The Mozilla Public License (MPL) is just like the Netscape Public License, except that it includes no special privileges for Netscape. The MPL makes it simple and easy for proprietary and Mozilla software to work and be distributed together while protecting the openness of the Mozilla code by requiring that further redistribution of it be under the terms of the MPL.

As an example of how the Covered code and proprietary code could work together, the developer could modify Covered code to call added binary or proprietary software and disclose only the changes to the Covered code needed to enable these calls. The developer's own software that is called by the changes in Mozilla can remain private.

Although the basic concept is simple, the twin licenses add complexity as they add flexibility. Because of potential copyright and patent problems, the license requires that a text file, LEGAL, accompany all distributions of Mozilla code. This file must contain notices and details concerning all software that is subject to intellectual property claims by third parties, including patented software. For this reason, every developer who works with Mozilla software—and particularly with derivative software—must pay attention to the other licensing involved and to the resulting licensing dependencies.

The GNU GPL allows a developer to issue new source code under a particular version of the license, and optionally to allow the code to be distributed under "any later version." A user who receives GPL'd code with no version number specified may pass it on under any version of the GNU GPL. The NPL/MPL, on the other hand, allows users to choose whether to use received code under the license version that covered it when received, or to choose instead to use any later version of the license. Over time, this will be another area that will need watching.

If the GNU GPL is the product of careful lawyering to impose absolutely the will of the Free Software Foundation on Free Software and to force the liberation of as much other software as possible, the MPL is the result of careful consultation among business managers, lawyers, and the Open Source community to balance the interests of all parties. MPL language regarding arbitration, termination, breach, cure, and named jurisdiction for litigation sounds like other business contracts. The MPL pays particular attention to possible patent infringement claims and includes the provision that if any licensee brings an infringement suit against any contributor to Mozilla, that licensee's license in Mozilla and in any patented software of the defendant are subject to termination, with the further provision that anyone who has received Mozilla software from the plaintiff shall continue to hold valid licenses as received from both the plaintiff and the defendant, as appropriate.

Although the MPL cannot prevent patent infringement suits from outside the Mozilla community, the focused weapon of license termination should discourage such suits originating within the community and reflects the Open Source community's aversion to software patents of any kind.

The IBM Public License

Just as Netscape's MPL showed that a large commercial software vendor was willing to experiment with the benefits of Open Source licensing and development, the size of IBM makes the issuing of its Public License an even louder and more public endorsement. Like the MPL, the IBM Public License (IBM PL) separates the code into two types: Contributions (the original IBM-supplied code and that added to it from other contributors), which must be offered with source code, and other — proprietary — software, provided it is in separate modules and is not derivative or a modification of contributor code.

The IBM PL handles potential patent problems in a manner similar to the MPL: Each "Contributor" grants all users ("Recipients") licenses for the Contributor's patented software, which is included in the Contributions. This licensing does not include the right to use the patented software except with the Contributions. If any Recipient brings any software patent infringement suit against any Contributor, the Recipient (but not users downstream from the Recipient) automatically suffers termination of patent licenses of the Contributions as of the date of the suit.

The Sun Community Source License

The best-known Sun license is the Sun Community Source License (SCSL), which has reaped so much criticism from the Open Source Community. Critics should notice that Sun is feeling its way along in Open Source matters and that the company recently issued a basic version of the Forte tool under a recognized Open Source license. Sun distributes Forte for Java, Community Edition, under the Mozilla Public License (MPL). The SCSL, however, continues as the license for picoJava and some other Sun products, most notably for Java itself.

IBM and Mozilla/Netscape, although they are not full Copyleft licenses, at least represent an accommodation to the Open Source community. IBM learned from studying the Netscape licenses and produced its own, only half as long; Sun, on the other hand, produced its own attempt at an Open Source license, twice as long as the Mozilla/Netscape document. The length and obscurity of the SCSL make it difficult to be clear about all its provisions. The version for Java source code, SCSL 2.3, contains many provisions that tightly control the code and its distribution.

The chief restrictive differences of the SCSL from the MPL and the IBM PL are the SCSL requirement of royalties for any deployment, including internal, and the positive duty to return to Sun any error corrections, whether distributed or not, made in the source code, as well as to report any errors found in the specification. Developers may keep private their modifications to the source code and distribute only binaries, but Sun encourages them to share their source code. Persons who develop implementations of the Java specification for internal use will still have to pay royalties to Sun as if they had used Sun's code. The lowest level of license is free and is for research only; any modification in the source code requires the use of the Technology Compatibility Kit (TCK) for testing to ensure that Java functionality remains unbroken by the developer's changes. It is unclear whether the purchase of a paid support contract is necessary to obtain the TCK. The sort of pilot implementation that many developers would regard as part of testing seems to fall under the Deployment category for Sun, requiring paid support and licenses. Finally, it appears from the SCSL that no one would be able to start a third-party business to provide Java Development Kit (JDK) support.

The extreme retentiveness of the SCSL is probably a result of the company's experiences with Java forking; on the positive side it reflects Sun's strong interest in compatibility testing, which it promotes for Solaris by giving away binary compatibility testing tools to anyone who asks.

Are Open Source Licenses Legal?

Even after they understand the provisions of the GPL and how it is applied in practice, businesspeople always ask one question: Is the GPL, or for that matter, are any of the other licenses in the Open Source world, enforceable? Do they have any standing in law?

The short answer is that the GPL is enforceable, but only by virtue of its leaning on copyright law. The license grants no rights in copyright to a violator of the GPL, effectively stymieing copying, modification, and distribution of the copyrighted software. But since the license is enforced by the roundabout means of a copyright suit or a threat to sue, the question follows: Does the license itself have any validity?

Under current commercial codes, as interpreted by courts, the answer is generally no, for several reasons. First, the courts frown on licenses associated with products that are part of mass commerce (Pamela Samuelson points out that Edison shipped his phonograph cylinders with licenses, and that these were held to be invalid). An individual license negotiated between parties is one matter; one that is the same for everyone and comes with every copy of the product will find that it takes a back seat to the laws of the marketplace. A seller takes his goods to market and exposes them for sale; the buyer agrees on a price with the seller and takes the goods away. The transaction is ended. A license that is accessible only after breaking the shrinkwrap on the box is a one-sided amendment to the terms of sale agreed on between buyer and seller and not considered binding.

There is a further licensing problem, taken up in the GNU GPL, but ignored in some of the other Open Source licenses: the binding of third parties who were not part of the original license agreement. The GPL is careful to state that with each transfer of the software according to the GPL, there comes a direct license from the copyright holders (licensor) to each recipient. Although this provision is probably unenforceable by the courts, the Free Software Foundation has taken every legal care to make the GPL as strong as possible.

The question of whether the GNU GPL and other Open Source licenses are legal cannot be given a simple answer. Steve H. Lee, a student at Harvard Law School, has produced an extensive study of Open Source licensing and shows how to construct a legal case for their legality, using both precedents and interpretation of the law. Unfortunately, this study has not been published. Lee believes that Open Source licenses are enforceable as a matter of contract law and cites some evidence to that effect. Whether his arguments would carry in every court is another matter.

There is a change in the wind, however, that might give Open Source licenses more standing in court. The changes to the Universal Commercial Code originally proposed as UCC Article 2B have undergone rewriting and emerged as the model Uniform Computer Information Transactions Act (UCITA; see Chapter 14, "Intellectual Property"). The general effect of the Act when adopted would be to tighten intellectual property law with regard to software and, as a result, give standing to shrinkwrap licenses. This change would automatically give standing to Open Source licenses as well.

That's the good news. The bad news is that UCITA has been rejected by an original sponsor, the American Law Institute (ALI), as a murky work that will come into conflict with current federal copyright law. Although rejected by the ALI, UCITA has nevertheless been approved by the National Conference of Commissioners on Uniform State Laws and will now begin, state by state, to seek legislative adoption across the land.

You now have a sense of the legal issues of the various Open Source licenses. Some of these licenses can be used together. For instance, the GNU GPL can take in BSD code with no problem, but distribution of the final product must be only under the GNU GPL. The NPL/MPL and IBM PL were all devised to enable Open Source code and proprietary code to work together. The next chapter will deal further with this issue of license interaction or licensing dependency.

Chapter 7

Complications of Open Source Licensing

If everyone took Richard Stallman's advice or followed Linus Torvalds's example and used the GNU GPL, there would be fewer licensing problems. We will learn in this chapter that one complaint against the GNU GPL (and the BSD) licenses — possibility of forking — may actually be a virtue instead of a fault. Beyond the GNU GPL we will look at what happens when developers start choosing different software with different licenses and mixing them together.

What Is Forking and What Causes It?

Forking is a natural process in Open Source software development. Because each user receives source code and is free to make alterations, it is only natural that the theoretical number of versions of a product could approach the number of developers who receive it. Accordingly, there is one camp that believes that every bug fix and every improvement is a potential fork and remains unworried by the process. Developers who are unsatisfied with the way Linux works can devise patches to change its behavior, and freely circulate those patches. Until accepted by Linus Torvalds and his inner circle for inclusion into the kernel, this may be the only way these versions circulate, unless someone chooses to compile a kernel with those patches and distribute that instead.

On the other hand, there are those who worry that Linux may be heading toward the same forking that sapped the strength of UNIX, and that eventually we will have as many flavors of Linux as we have of UNIX. This fragmentation turned UNIX from a promising universal operating system to a series of niche markets. The UNIX flavors originated in the tweaking of the code by hardware manufacturers to obtain the fastest and most efficient performance of UNIX on their own hardware; to fight off commoditization, the various vendors also added what they hoped were distinctive features and insisted that their enhanced versions were superior to the products of competitors. Software interoperability was not an issue. The point of the exercise was to lock in customers to a particular hardware vendor; software was just one means to that end.

Today, some worry that the various Linux distributions will head down this same trail and eventually cause customers to pick a particular distribution not only because it is the "leading brand," but also because all the application vendors are trying to maximize sales by optimizing their code to run on this leading brand, putting the other distributions even further behind in the race for market share. To counter this possibility, the new Free Standards Group (recently formed from the Linux Standard Base initiative and the Linux Internationalization Initiative) seeks to define a common Linux base that all distributions will undertake to implement in the same manner, thus preserving software compatibility while allowing some distinctive features among distributions.

To better judge whether Linux is approaching the dreaded fork in its road, we need to know a little more about why projects fork in the first place. The reason most commonly given is politics among developers.

An Open Source project is a voluntary association based on mutual respect for coding prowess, and a developer is free to leave at any time. It goes to say that only a sensitive but disciplined leader can hold a group together for any length of time. The leader can fail the group in only one way: lack of responsiveness to those led. This lack of responsiveness can take two forms. One is the failure to respond personally to the followers in a satisfactory fashion; "personality differences" is a common reason given for the forking of a project. A more important response failure—and probably the cause of the majority of forks— is that the leader does not take a project technically where the followers want it to go, that is, does not satisfy the technical reasons they are working on the software in the first place. Because technical motivation is the large motor for joining a project, technical motivation is a sufficient reason for forking it.

Because you can

It is perfectly possible for developers to voluntarily join or resign from a project. To be a real member, of course, you need to be a contributor of useful code. But if the leadership will not listen to your ideas and adopt your code, you are free to march off and begin your own version of the project. Whether you attract anyone to join you is a matter of how good and useful the results of your fork are. GNU EMACS, for instance, remains a command-line tool; those who wanted an Intel graphics version eventually left EMACS and formed the project resulting in XEmacs.

The role of licenses

To state that forking occurs because the license permits it is to repeat the reason given above: because you can. The BSD-type licenses permit a developer to accept the source code, modify it, and distribute a compiled version, keeping the changes proprietary. As a result, BSD comes in several versions. Linux so far has not forked.

As an exercise, we can undertake a Unified Field Theory of Forking (see Figure 7-1). While it is not perfect, it provides a useful means of examining some of the licenses and forking phenomena around us.

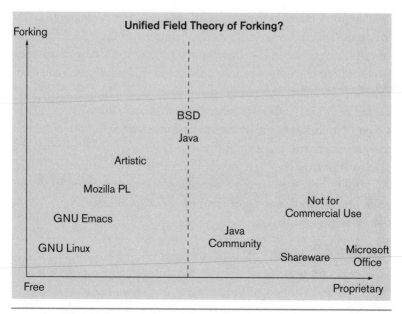

Figure 7-1 *Examining licenses and forking phenomena*

Arrange the various licenses on a two-dimensional grid that measures Free Software versus proprietary software on the horizontal scale, and tendency to fork (or experience of forking) on the vertical scale. On the lower right-hand side, we see that proprietary software such as Microsoft Office is not likely to fork since the source code is unavailable. Shareware may be more freely distributable, but shareware developers keep their hands on the source code. One example of "Not for Commercial Use" software is Aladdin's Ghostscript. The Aladdin Free Public License makes the source code available and distributable with modifications, but commercial distribution is prohibited. Effectively the improvements come from a single source, the copyright holder. There is hardly a forking tendency here.

If we look at the top of the vertical scale, we see BSD with the highest forking tendency (and experience). It sits on the borderline between Free and Proprietary because its source code is freely available, but may be modified and redistributed without the source code. The various BSD versions (BSD OS, FreeBSD, OpenBSD, and NetBSD) attest to its many descendants, or at least to the ones retaining the BSD name. There is a financial incentive to fork here; BSD OS does not have any free versions, only commercial sales.

The other leader of the forking pack is the original Java license. It sits on the borderline between Free and Proprietary because Sun Microsystems gave developers two choices: license the Sun source code for a large fee or implement the Java specification at no charge. Hewlett-Packard, among others, declined to pay the source code fees and instead did its own implementation. While doing all the coding necessary, HP decided to make a few convenient changes. The result of several companies taking the do-it-yourself implementation option was incompatibilities among Java implementations, a real obstacle to the "write once, run many" objective of the project. Microsoft took the path of paying for the code *and* making its own changes to it.

There is an obvious benefit, then, to having a license that requires that modifications to Open Source code remain under an Open Source license. The availability of modified code to all developers takes away much of the technical motivation for forking. Some firms, however, fear that loss of control of the code will result from allowing variant versions. Sun used the Sun Community Source License (SCSL) for its new Java 2. The license requires all bug fixes and externally distributed modifications to its code to be fed back to Sun. The strictness of the compatibility testing shows that revenue is not the sole aim of this difficult license; it intends to prevent the compatibility problems brought on by forking under the earlier license. The SCSL accordingly ends up low on the forking scale and on the proprietary side of the chart.

The Perl Artistic License

At the top of the Free licenses with forking tendencies we find the Perl Artistic License. Larry Wall, the inventor of the Perl scripting language, never intended to write it or to set up a strenuous definition of property rights; he originally used the GNU GPL. He noticed that businesspeople tended to be shy of the GPL, and so he started including an explanation of it in his package. Just as the Perl scripting language offers multiple ways to achieve an end, Wall thought that offering an alternative license to the GPL might suit some users' taste better. Consequently, users can use either the Artistic License or the GPL, and the Artistic License itself offers a number of alternatives to choose from in following it. Among its considerable freedoms, the license allows forking, provided the forking is plainly marked.

Developers who put out an alternative version of Perl must rename the changed packages so that a recipient's standard version of Perl will still work, or instead include a full standard version of Perl with the alternative version, to ensure that the user has ready access to it. These liberties, combined with the inability of the Artistic License to bind downstream parties to the original agreement, provide a large opportunity for forking. Because Perl itself recognizes alternative ways of doing things, and because variant versions are plainly marked as such, forking has not been a problem for Perl. There was a temporary redundancy of Windows versions, but a directed effort under the One Perl campaign managed to unify the code.

The playfulness of the hacker world played its part in the writing of the Artistic License. Larry Wall has pointed out that his following the Perl principle of TMTOWTDI — "There's more than one way to do it" — is in itself a subversion of the licensing process. He is right, of course.

Freedom to fork converges with freedom from forking

We have seen that the BSD-style license encourages forking because it allows developers to take the source code, freely modify it, and then distribute binary-only versions of the result. The source tree then looks like the one shown in Figure 7-2.

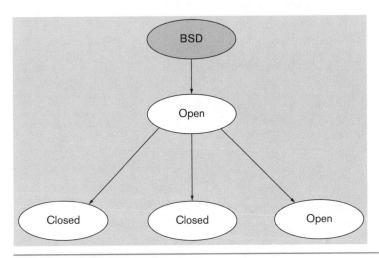

Figure 7-2 *A BSD-type source tree*

There are two unifying centripetal forces working against the unlimited centrifugal forces of dispersion. The first is that because the BSD distributions themselves are Open Source code, the BSD licenses allow each version to borrow improved code from the other versions. The second force returning improvements to the Open Source distributions is that once proprietary innovations have served their market purpose and are subsequently imitated by competitors, the innovators tire of single-handedly maintaining the differences, and seek to return the modifications to the source tree. The BSD distributions do receive freely contributed code from users.

The GNU GPL, on the other hand, mandates openness of source code at all times, with the results shown in Figure 7-3.

Every Open Source project labors to a greater or lesser degree under the possibility of forking. The most conservatively managed projects have licenses that allow only the originator to incorporate changes permanently in the source tree and restrict others to distributing changes only as patches to the code. Projects using licenses like the GPL, on the other hand, live under constant threat of having someone take over the project by producing a better version of the code and doing it faster than the original project owners.

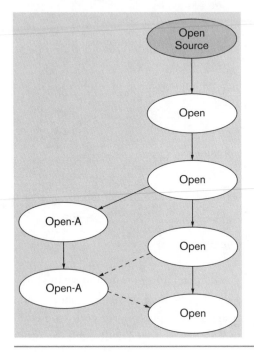

Figure 7-3 *A GPL-type source tree*

Nevertheless, forking seldom happens on GPL-licensed projects because the original project can incorporate the code of variants if it chooses. The original project may not be so advanced as the variants at any given time, but it may, nevertheless, be good enough to be useful, and there may be those who prefer a slower pace of upgrade. Two projects may end up in symbiosis, one advancing the code rapidly, while the other integrates and tests it more slowly and issues more stable releases.

Alternate Licensing and Licensing Dependency

Part V, "Open Source Software AS Your Business," contains a longer discussion of business models and the software licenses that further their goals. The emphasis there is on the use of single licenses. It is important, however, to say a few general words here about how licenses can work together or come into conflict. There is a very limited compatibility among licenses.

The GNU GPL, for instance, is designed to pull into its orbit every piece of software with which it is compiled. It is true, of course, that the copyright holder can issue software under a number of different licenses, but improvements that users submit under the GPL cannot be incorporated directly into versions of the software that are under another license. In such cases, the developer must write new code to achieve the desired functions. Netscape, for instance, did not use the GNU GPL for this reason. On the other hand, code and modifications submitted under a BSD-type or X license can be incorporated into a GPL-licensed product — Linux has enough examples in it.

Subtler and more difficult problems occur when the license does not carry the same terms under all conditions. Some licenses, for instance, say the product may be freely distributed, except as part of a commercial product. This is a particular problem with development tools, since their output is often counted as a derivative work.

The diagram shown in Figure 7-4 illustrates some guidelines regarding licensing dependencies.

The foundation – an operating system under the GNU GPL

In Figure 7-4 diagram, the foundation on which all software rests — the operating system — is shown. The success of Linux demonstrates that this base layer is strongest when it is founded on the GNU GPL, which forces all software to adopt its standard license and thus keeps the system free and open to all developers and likewise free of all closed material. There is not a wide choice of operating systems as there is of applications; an operating system can be seen as a public good or even community property. Certainly Linux users regard Linux as freely available and inalienable community property.

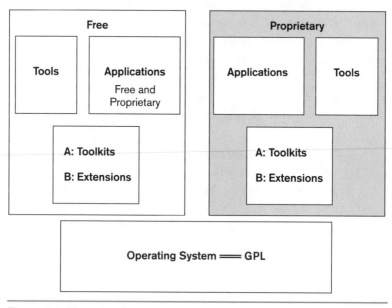

Figure 7-4 *Licensing dependencies*

The middle layer – A: toolkits

In Figure 7-4, the GNU GPL has swept the decks of other licenses at the operating system level, but multiple licenses exist at the next level. While the operating system is free, at this next level there may be either free or commercial software. The licenses for these should be consistent so that the same material may not suddenly come under different distribution restrictions because it has become part of a commercial package. Software that changes state causes problems in licensing dependencies.

The Qt Public License Problem

Because Section 5 in the Open Source Definition (OSD) says that Open Source licenses may not discriminate against persons or groups, we should not expect an OSI-approved license to discriminate against businesspeople. Further, since Section 6 of the OSD says that Open Source licenses may not discriminate against fields of endeavor, we do not expect an OSI-approved license to discriminate against independent software vendors (ISVs).

But this is just what the Qt Public License (QPL) does. Developers can live with its retentive attitude toward code that allows only patches to be distributed, rather than modified files. The real problem with the license is that it allows free distribution of its derivative software (graphical interfaces), except when these are distributed commercially. At that point, the distributor must purchase a special commercial development license from the maker, Troll Tech AS. This problem might have remained a minor nuisance except that the very popular Linux desktop, KDE, was built on the Qt Toolkit. Because KDE is freely distributable, many developers thought that their derivative work built on KDE was free also. But, when these derivative works are commercial software applications depending on KDE for their graphical interface, the commercial license raises its head and the developer discovers that beneath KDE there is a troll awaiting his toll. The fact that the Open Source Initiative has placed the QPL on its approved list does not make licensing any simpler.

A license does not need to forbid commercial distribution in so many words. The QPL, for example, simply requires that distribution of the Troll Tech Qt Toolkit (needed with the derivative applications, such as the graphic interfaces to applications running on the KDE desktop) take place under the QPL, which requires that the source code be made freely available and modifiable. Commercial vendors in a niche market are unlikely to accept this requirement. Although the QPL makes no mention of it, these vendors will find that they can distribute their binary-only code with the Qt Toolkit only under the Qt Professional Edition (commercial) license. To avoid these problems, a firewall should be built between free and proprietary products at this level.

The middle layer – B: extensions and libraries for toolkits

It follows that extensions and libraries for toolkits need to follow the same licenses as the toolkits that use them. This simplifies licensing questions and prevents surprises. Nevertheless, developers must develop the habit of reading the licenses of the toolkits, libraries, and extensions they work with and making sure these match the intended use and distribution of the resulting software. Licensing dependencies are just as important as software dependencies.

The top layer – tools and applications

As we move away from the operating system, there is a larger selection of products and a smaller number of users for each product. Consequently, vendors tend to prefer proprietary licenses and binary distributions to protect their development investment. We can expect the majority of tools to fall into this category. The developer then has the choice of developing proprietary applications with the help of tools that allow either free or commercial applications to be built with them, or to build these applications using tools that limit their derivatives to commercial applications. For simplicity, the tools themselves, like toolkits, should have clear licenses that allow either free and commercial distribution of their derivatives or confine themselves to commercial distribution.

At this level, the GNU LGPL will not always work for proprietary code, but the BSD-type licenses, or an Apache license, will. The Stronghold server is an example of adaptation of Apache code into a proprietary product. The Aladdin Free Public License fits into the category of free-only license, while the Perl Artistic License permits both free and proprietary distributions.

Product segmentation is the art of building a single product into a product line that serves different market segments. Producers can vary size, price, distribution, and many other product characteristics to capture a larger share of the total market. Hard goods from automobiles to breakfast foods have followed these patterns for many years. Intellectual property, that is, software, can likewise be segmented and sized, priced, and distributed in many different ways. The trick is to find the right licensing for the right purpose. Generally, simpler models mean more ease of administration and less confusion, but the right multiple licenses may nevertheless be the best solution to a complex problem.

As Open Source software moves up towards the largest machines, and down into the smallest, licensing will follow it. The next section of this book, Part IV, will deal with these two extremes of the market.

Part IV

Linux Is Moving UP...and DOWN

Chapter 8

The Drive Toward
the Mainframe

The strategy of moving a product upward from modest origins has been successful before. At its beginning, Sun Microsystems took off-the-shelf parts, a freely available operating system (Berkeley UNIX) and set out to overthrow the high-end UNIX workstations of the day. Comparable performance and especially high cost savings were benefits too great for customers to overlook. Apollo perished in the competition with Sun, and Cray, the big name in supercomputers, is no more thanks to competitive pressures in the high-end computing space.

High-end computing focuses on a number of simple problems with complicated solutions. Besides the basic question of *high performance,* there is the problem of *scalability:* How can we keep adding computing power to a system and gain corresponding increases in productivity? How do we manage all the power? Another is the problem of *availability:* How can we maintain a high-power computing system that is available 168 hours a week, that will not stumble or fall when a component fails (whether processor or memory chips, disk drives, network communications, or anything else)?

The Open Source community has attacked these problems in its usual way, with many different projects springing up and then cooperating or fading as the technology as a whole moves forward. The Community has used clustering as the most effective way of dealing with the problems of low-cost high-performance computing, and proprietary software has helped here as well. A few of the projects and successful implementations of them are covered in this chapter; links to many of the others can be found at `http://linas.org/linux/`.

The uses for high-end Open Source systems currently run from weather analysis to encryption cracking to genetic research, and the projects discussed in this chapter may be run on discarded hardware or on workstation or even mainframe processors. Except for the mainframe projects, all of the innovations involve ganging sets of processors in different ways.

High Performance

As ordinary desktop computers have become more powerful, users are discovering that they can join them in clusters to undertake the same computing tasks formerly reserved for the biggest machines. All the hardware of a supercomputer, including its specially designed and enormously expensive high-end chips, is designed to minimize the communications difficulties within the computer, contributing to its great speed. The actual computing power of a supercomputer can now be imitated by clusters of desktop computers; the chief difficulty is getting the desktop computers within these clusters to communicate efficiently so as to approach the speed of the supercomputer. The final result is the raw processing power of a supercomputer, at a lower speed, and at a greatly reduced cost. The Incyte Genomics computer staff estimates that their clustered Linux server farms (described later) do the work of supercomputers at one-hundredth of the cost.

The Linux kernel itself was slow to get started in clustering (see the section "SMP" later in this chapter), partly because Linus Torvalds did not have that many machines around the house. But one element of the Linux community went early and eagerly into *distributed computing*, the use of many different machines for solving a large problem. High-end computer problems tend to sort themselves into two types: one sort of problem, such as cracking encryption, does not require interaction between the various machines as they work on their assigned portions of the work; the other, such as weather prediction, requires a constant manipulation of interacting variables and works best if each processor can communicate directly with all the other processors. The second type of problem will run substantially slower on multiple machines unless some communication arrangements are made. The special hardware design of supercomputers achieved this intercommunication and was responsible for much of their great expense.

Because Linux needed to start at the bottom of cluster computing, a problem involving parallel machines that simply received and executed centrally assigned problems was a natural starting point. It struck many Linux fans and other computing enthusiasts that cracking computer encryption keys would be an exciting development and demonstration ground for distributed computing. In early 1997, a group of hackers (in the good sense, remember!) organized an effort that was to become distributed.net (`http://www.distributed.net/`). The group supplied client pieces for a wide variety of computers (making this a heterogeneous distributed computing project, like the *Titanic* work described later), and invited users to install the clients on their machines to participate. The client software used the *spare* computing power of the local machines as available to do the work of grinding through the possible solutions. A central server organized the division of the work and the checking of results as they came in.

The first challenge was the cracking of a 56-bit key; this took 212 days in 1997. The group immediately took up the much more difficult task of breaking a 64-bit key; the task is still not finished, but the estimated time for the task continues to drop as more powerful computers join the network and the overall project organization and software improve. The client software is Open Source, and anyone is free to submit improvements. In the most recent worldwide demonstration of this method, CS Communication & Systèmes (`http://www.cie-signaux.fr/`), offered a challenge for which distributed.net organized over 38,000 participants in 140 countries to crack the 56-bit key in only 62 days. In the meantime, the Electronic Frontier Foundation (http://www.eff.org/) has demonstrated much faster results using heavy equipment dedicated totally to key-cracking.

From an Open Source point of view, these demonstrations show a) the weakness of the preferred government schemes of encryption, which at that time permitted the export of keys no longer than 56-bits and only to friendly countries; and b) the power of ordinary people to rival the computer power available to governments to address code-cracking. The power to harness dozens of different kinds of computers and their operating systems by using open standards and Open Source software is another demonstration of the limits of the proprietary approach to serious computing.

The dislocations of widely available massive computer power are only beginning to be felt. It is now possible for ambitious secondary schools to collect old i486-based computers and wire them together to get supercomputing power, and the Chinese were not slow to buy up such machines in the U.S. and take them back to China to build their own supercomputers. The Stone Soup Supercomputer at Oak Ridge National Laboratory (http://stonesoup.esd.ornl.gov/) received its name because it cost nothing to build, being made up of donated obsolete computers that had been lying unused around offices at the site. The Beowulf software (discussed later in the section, "Beowulf") with which it was built, makes it easy to add or substitute newer machines as they are donated; Stone Soup has increased its power with the addition of cast-off Alpha-and Pentium-based machines.

From hobbyists and scientific researchers, the technology passed into the commercial world. The expensive film *Titanic* would have cost far more if its producer had not saved money by using computer animation to avoid the hiring of flocks of extras and the building of an enormous ship model and tank to sink it in. Passengers on the ship, waves around the ship, and even the wind's rippling of the lifeboat covers were all depicted with computer-rendered automation. The Render Ranch, as the server farm was called, was built in 1996, and included over 100 Alpha machines running Linux and another 50-odd machines running NT, all coordinated with hundreds of SGI machines and all wired together with a 100Mbps Ethernet.

Beowulf

Beowulf (http://www.beowulf.org/) is the most famous of the Linux distributed computing systems, and its software, continually updated, is often shipped free with Linux distributions. It began at Greenbelt, Maryland, in the laboratories of a NASA contractor, the Center of Excellence in Space Data and Information Sciences (CESDIS) in 1994 as a 16-node cluster. Its design solves one of the problems inherent in regular supercomputers, whose hardware, being designed first, must always race ahead of the software that on which it runs on. Beowulf software is designed to stay ahead of hardware improvements; as newer hardware is added, it is simply plugged into the system. One method that Beowulf uses to increase the speed of communication within the cluster is to use multiple Ethernets.

An important aspect of cost-cutting and ease-of-use in Linux cluster supercomputing is the use of Commercial Off-the-Shelf components (COTS). Their use was a focus of the LoBoS (Lots of Boxes on Shelves) project at the National Institutes of Health (http://www.lobos.nih.gov/) and the Los Lobos project newly announced by IBM and the University of New Mexico. This will cluster 64 servers and a processing speed of 375 GigaFLOPS, which should make it number 24 in the list of the world's 500 fastest supercomputers (http://www.top500.org/), where Linux super-computers regularly appear. The use of machine switches limits the number of computers that can be directly interconnected to 64, but it is possible to use other means, such as clusters of clusters, to join more.

Incyte Genomics, Inc. (http://www.incyte.com/) supposedly has the largest farm of Linux servers, with some 2000 processors linked together for genome mapping. It had been using 4-processor

Alpha 4100 machines costing $140,000 each and decided to save money and increase computing power by switching to Pentium II dual-processor machines at $5,000 each. They found that they could pay a tenth the price in equipment and still manage the same computing power. The large Alpha machines are still used, this time to manage the server farm. The PC equipment may not be so reliable as the more expensive equipment, but the entire system runs without shutdown and at a lower cost, tended by a single system administrator, and porting an application to Linux from UNIX requires very little time. The project is so successful that Incyte plans to keep expanding it.

These savings spur the growing adoption not only of COTS supercomputer systems but also of Open Source software for other massive practices. A large Web site is not actually a supercomputer but does involve the linking of large numbers of hosting machines. A large hosting site for Web pornography, Cave Creek, figures that a $1500 AMD server running BSD on a K-6 processor will deliver 90 percent of the computing power of a $25,000 server from Sun. As in supercomputing, the superior performance of the larger machines cannot justify the large difference in price.

The wide use of Intel chips should not discourage you if you own or prefer the PowerPC processor. Terra Soft Solutions (http://www.terrasoftsolutions.com/), the makers of Yellow Dog Linux for Apple and IBM PowerPC systems, also produces Black Lab Linux (http://www.blacklablinux.com/), both for workstations and for clustering Apple PowerPC G4 chips. It also is possible to buy Linux supercomputing systems as ready-to-run Alpha clusters (http://www.compaq.com/solutions/customsystems/hps/linux.html), and Mission Critical Linux (http://www.missioncriticallinux.com/) supplies enterprise-level Linux systems and support, including on SGI. Intel, however, is the focus of new SGI technology, for the company is developing clustering for the forthcoming Intel Itanium 64-bit processor (IA-64). The IA-64 Linux Project (formerly called the Trillian Project, http://linuxia64.org/), was begun by VA Linux to ensure that Linux will be running on the Itanium when it appears. The effort is supported by the major Linux distributions, but understandably not by Corel, whose specialty is desktop Linux. Indeed, there are signs that Linux will be the first distribution ready-to-run on the new high-powered chip, ahead of Sun and Microsoft. Hewlett-Packard is a member both of the IA-64 project and the Monterey Project, in which it combines with SCO and IBM to produce a 64-bit UNIX for the Itanium.

 Note

The KLAT2 parallel supercomputer at the University of Kentucky was built in April 2000 and uses 64 Athlon chips running at 700MHz. It arranges the connection between the chips in a new configuration called a "flat neighborhood" network. The project cost about $41,000 and points out that the cost of $650 per billion floating point operations per second (GFLOPS) is below a typical Beowulf project cost of $3,000 per GFLOP. KLAT2 can work at more than 64 GFLOPS. The operating system is Linux, and the source code for the networking will be made Open Source.

Don't think that Beowulf Linux systems are confined to users with only a few hundred thousand dollars to spend. The NOAA Forecast Systems Laboratory (FSL) is installing one of the fastest computing systems in the world at a cost of $15 million over three years (http://www-ad.fsl.noaa.gov/ac/HPCS/text0.htm). The first phase of Jet consists of 256 Alpha nodes, stock items supplied by Compaq, and running lightly modified Red Hat Linux for Alpha. Because weather prediction is one of those problems that require each processor to talk to each of the others, the networking is handled by Myrinet from Myricom (http://www.myri.com). High Performance Technologies (http://www.hpti.com/) is organizing the entire project. In late 2000, FSL will double the number of nodes, and two years after that, the 512 nodes will be replaced with newer processors and the number of nodes doubled again to 1024. By then, it will be processing at a rate of about 4 TeraFLOPS (some four trillion computations per second). Even in its initial phase with only a twelfth of its eventual power on tap, the Jet supercomputer will be twenty times faster than the fastest current computer at the Laboratory.

Symmetric Multi-Processing

Symmetric Multi-Processing (SMP) is a clustering method that connects multiple processors on a single server and has them share a single operating system, memory, and input/output devices (the "backplane"). Linux has not shown itself to be particularly strong here, managing only 4 processors in 1999's version 2.2, but large improvements should appear with version 2.4, including 8-processor support. One difficulty with SMP, however, is that if a single processor goes down, the whole system fails. This brings us to the question of availability.

Availability

It is not enough that high-end computers crunch the numbers; for important projects and global businesses to run on them they have to have high availability. In the commercial world, Tandem supplies the famous fault-tolerant computers that have no single point of failure. BSD is the most robust of the Open Source systems, but Linux is improving, and commercial systems that overlay it with high-availability features are becoming available. This is a large market; while high-end high-availability systems are expected to sell only 57,000 units this year, low-end (Linux and SCO) solutions are projected at 1 million units, and 40 percent of those will be in clusters.

High-availability technology includes fault-tolerance. It is not enough to build in redundancy and to avoid single points of failure; the systems must provide for failover, the switching of work to running components when a component fails. Even load-balancing, typically handled by a single front-end server to the cluster (such as in the TurboLinux proprietary solution), must be distributed so that the failure of an entire server (let alone a component of a server) cannot halt the system. Linux is still weak in this regard, but at least one company supplies a commercial system that provides fault tolerance. RSF-1 from High-Availability.com (`http://www.high-availability.com`) is proprietary (although free for non-commercial use); it runs on Solaris (SPARC/Intel), AIX, NT, SGI, Linux, FreeBSD, and HP-UX. The Linux Community is working to build an Open Source High-Availability Linux (`http://linux-ha.org/`).

Linux Virtual Server

One approach to high availability is the Virtual Server, a cluster arrangement that appears to the user as a single machine. This is done by having one machine balance the load among the others and software that both detects and routes around failures and enables the easy addition of additional nodes to the cluster. The network connection among the machines may be a local area network (LAN) or a wide area network (WAN), so that the Virtual Server could be geographically dispersed. The Linux Virtual Server project (`http://www.LinuxVirtualServer.org/`) is directed from China but has considerable help from American and European developers.

Linux on the mainframe

For those who have been waiting for Linux to reach the mainframe itself, the day is already here. The original IBM mainframe port, "Bigfoot" for the S/370, was a Community project; there is also a version for the S/390 (`http://linas.org/linux/i370.html`) downloadable at (`http://oss.software.ibm.com/developerworks/opensource/linux390/index.html`).

One strength of the S/390 is its ability to run multiple virtual machines. A single mainframe, for instance, could easily run 5,000 Linux virtual machines to serve that many users; testing has shown that over 41,000 Linux virtual machines can be run on a single S/390! This approach, however, is hardly cost-effective compared with using smaller machines. IBM is using Linux to keep its older machines, their data, and their users from being stranded. The

S/390 can simultaneously run an older operating system and its applications while also running new operating systems and applications such as Linux. This practice will enable smooth transitioning from old systems to new systems, and also enable spare processor power to be put to use.

The long-range view of IBM may be that the S/390 running Linux will be able to outrun mainframe competitors such as the Sun Enterprise 10000. Sun uses 64 processors to get high performance from this machine, but the Linux kernel, optimized for a single processor and run on the S/390, may very well beat the Sun machine. After all, Linux running on a Sun SPARC chip is reported to outperform Solaris on the same chip.

Actual deployment of Linux on the S/390 so far has been to replace NT servers. The Oklahoma Department of Corrections, for instance, intends to replace 40 such servers with Linux/390; by using existing resources, this will save considerably in system hardware (which would need upgrading to Windows 2000), floor space, and system administration.

Linux and enterprise computing

Cluster computing is only one of a number of technologies that must be tamed for Open Source software to reach enterprise-level computing. At the present time, the most serious piece missing appears to be On-Line Transaction Processing (OLTP), the ability to perform not just enormous numbers of transactions per minute, but to propagate the results through an entire system — airline reservation systems are an example of this sort of computing. With time and the efforts of the large database firms that are embracing Linux, it is possible that OLTP will eventually become a Linux function.

The rapid progress of Linux over the past year came from two salutary shocks delivered in April 1999 by the D.H. Brown Associates report on Linux (http://www.dhbrown.com/dhbrown/linux.html) and by the Mindcraft benchmarking of Linux and NT sponsored by Microsoft (see Chapter 6, "The GNU GPL and the

Open Source Definition"). Linux is now taking SMP seriously, and the Brown criticism concerning the lack of a good file system will soon be met now that SGI has released the Linux source code for its XFS file system. High-end companies watching the rise of Linux like to comfort themselves with the thought that no real innovations can come out of Open Source, but only imitations of continually evolving and superior high-end technology. In this view, Linux is forever doomed to play the dog chasing the tail lights. The Brown report was skeptical that Linux could ever reach the top tier because no one would pay for all the needed improvements. The report did suggest that Intel might have a motivation to do so, since the sale of Intel chips as opposed to mainframe chips would increase. For that matter, why not Compaq as well? When we consider that Linux users and the Open Source GNUPro developers may be the only welcoming committee when Itanium ships, Linux supporters can think a few comforting thoughts themselves. . . . And for now, Linux doesn't have to beat AIX or Solaris; all it has to do is beat Windows.

Chapter 9

The Secret Battlefield: Embedded Systems

Although its progress in small devices is largely unnoticed, Linux is one of the best-suited technologies to take over a space few consumers are aware of. In this chapter you will learn about the strengths of Linux and other Open Source operating systems in this growing market and why it may likely surround you before you are even aware of it.

Background and Advantages

Although a latecomer to the field, Linux has a bright future in embedded systems. From cell phones to household appliances, the number of places in which we find embedded systems in everyday life is growing. The automobile is probably the most widespread intensive user; from brakes to air bags to fuel/air mixture controls, a new model may contain 30 to 50 embedded systems.

Embedded software originated in the late 1960s as "stored program control" in telephone switches; it moved to other devices but was always custom written for a particular piece of equipment. The coming of the microprocessor enabled programmers to write to a particular microprocessor that could be used in different devices and to reuse code from device to device. Originally, this code was machine or assembler language, but by the 1970s, libraries of code appeared, and by the end of the decade there were packaged operating systems intended for embedded use; each operating system was tailored to a particular microprocessor. Eventually, systems began to use C, the portable language that gave rise to UNIX, the portable OS.

Linux has several advantages for embedded systems: a small footprint, ease of use, portability to many processors and platforms, scalability, and its famous stability. A minimal embedded Linux consists of the core kernel and boot utility, along with memory and process management, timing services, and an initialization process. To this we might add hardware drivers, one or more applications, networking, a file system, storage space, and perhaps a simple user interface. Some RAM is needed to hold the kernel and applications; flash memory can be used for file storage, from which the application can load and unload files as needed, saving RAM space. Because Linux is an operating system, it can control all these functions and manage memory as well. Its ability to check and repair itself is useful in case of interruptions, such as a power failure in mid-upgrade.

Although the Linux kernel is small, as full-sized operating systems go, it is not tiny enough for the world of embedded systems. Its size and power suit it to the middle and high end of the embedded systems range; its flexibility and functionality make it large in terms of embedded systems, which are sharply focused on a particular device. For these reasons, part of the skill in deploying Linux for embedded applications is trimming it down to appropriate size and functionality. Linux has the significant advantage of being able to draw on the entire code resources of the Linux Community for faster development and for driver support.

Linux strength in networking is important in modern embedded systems. Hotels, for instance, control electronic keying through console software at the front desk and embedded systems in the door locks; heating and air conditioning are activated or not depending on the remotely sensed presence of guests in their rooms. In any embedded system, networking may be used to manage the embedded software by installing upgrades or by adding or collecting data. The convergence of computers and telephones on digital data, and the growth of communication in embedded devices, particularly over the Internet, calls for an operating system that already implements the new IPv6 communications standard. This standard greatly expands the number of possible network addresses, making it possible to connect many billions more devices to the Internet (a manufacturing plant might need 10,000 addresses for the assembly line; the ESRF laboratory uses some 4,000).

Because current users of embedded Open Source systems are early adopters seeking a proprietary advantage for their enterprises, we hear very little about what they are doing. Nor are we able to track the spread of Linux devices through license counts, because Linux is freely distributable. Only recently are tools for embedded Linux becoming available, along with the associated publicity for them and for embedded Linux.

Many early adopters of Linux are found in scientific research laboratories; an example is the European Synchrotron Radiation Facility (ESRF) in Grenoble, France (http://www.esrf.fr/), home of a gigantic X-ray beam device. The laboratory now runs all its operations on Linux; at the embedded end, the main use of Linux is to control the stepper motors that direct the beams and to control the target samples that the beam bombards. There are 40 beamlines, each operating around the clock seven days a week. Each beamline has over 100 stepper motors. Some of them move independently, and some are moved in coordination with each other.

ESRF chose Linux because it incorporates standards such as POSIX, CORBA, Java, HTTP, and TCP/IP. This enables the embedded Linux software to work with all the other software at the institution, including the Beowulf (Linux) supercomputing installation. Because the controller project is based on a 10-year schedule, the scientists wanted to be sure that they had the source code so that their work would be vendor-independent. They began by cutting down a SuSE Linux distribution to 24MB; they then used a Debian file management system. Finally, they wrote their own device drivers for the equipment and turned these over to the Community, anticipating both that the drivers would be useful to others and that others would in turn contribute maintenance code and additional drivers.

Some Embedded Systems and Tools

Embeddable Linux appeared early in its hobbyist phase. The Embeddable Linux Kernel Subset (ELKS) took the Linux designed for a 386 Intel chip and pared it down to run on the 8086, because at that time the 386 chip was too expensive for embedded uses.

Cross-Reference

Links to other embedded Linux projects can be found at http://emlinux.com/Specialized_linux_projects. html and http://linux-embedded.com/software.php3.

To name just a few, RTLinux, (http://www.rtlinux.org/) is an extension to handle interrupts, so that Linux can be attached to data acquisition and control devices. It is also available in a version for multiple processors (SMP). Linux on a Floppy (LOAF, http://loaf.ecks.org/) is a cut-down Linux that fits on a floppy along with ftp and Lynx browser software. Its main purpose is to enable the user to walk up to any networked computer and turn it into a temporary Linux box; it could also be modified for special purposes. A special-purpose Linux ready for use is the Linux Router Project (LRP, http://www.linuxrouter.org/); it also fits on a floppy and can be used to build and maintain embedded systems, but particularly routers, access servers, thin servers and clients, and network appliances. Its limited functionality increases its security when used for Internet connections.

Cross-Reference

For more information on Community projects, see EmbedLinux.NET (http://www.embedlinux.net/) and LinuxDevices.com (http://www.linuxdevices.com).

Besides these Open Source projects, there are commercial Open Source and proprietary resources for embedded development. Caldera Systems' sister corporation, Lineo (http://www.lineo. com/), provides the Embedix system (based on the Caldera distribution), along with a browser, Embrowser (Caldera's DR WebSpyder). The firm recently bought Zentropix (http://www. zentropix.com/) to add its development tools to the Lineo product line. The rapidly growing start-up MontaVista Software (http://mvista.com/) makes a strong selling point of offering its Hard Hat Linux as royalty-free Open Source software. Lynx Real-Time Systems (http://www.lynx.com/) is now supplying BlueCat, its embedded adaptation of the Red Hat distribution, to interoperate with its own proprietary Lynx embedded OS.

 Note

Open Source embedded systems can offer "real fast," but not "real-time." Despite the use of the term "real-time" in connection with Linux, there is no Linux or BSD system that is a true real-time system. The Open Source systems use timed interrupts that can be assigned different priority levels. BlueCat, for instance, is not real-time, but Lynx is. BlueCat provides the upsell opportunity for Lynx.

Besides selling embedded software, firms can offer the hardware as well: 3iLinux (http://www.3ilinux.com/), part of 3iNET, offers a 386-based Internet appliance with a Linux system already on it, ready for the customer's software. This way customers can invent their appliances and supply the software for them; 3iLinux acts as manufacturer to mount these on their Universal Internet Box (UIB) hardware and software platform. A small 2x16 LCD screen, power supply, two fax modems, and pushbuttons are included in the small device, which has already been cleared by the FCC and EC. All the 3iLinux code is Open Source.

Cygnus Solutions has traditionally been strong in the embedded sector; this capability is the major reason for its purchase by Red Hat

Software. Cygnus has its own embedded operating system, eCos, and has large plans for embedded Linux (see "Standards" later in this chapter), which include an SDK and configuration technology.

Linux may be getting the publicity, but BSD also offers embeddable technology with similar advantages. Free versions include picoBSD, from the FreeBSD project (http://www.FreeBSD.org/~picobsd/); among free real-time systems there is RTEMS (http://www.rtems.army.mil/), which includes FreeBSD material, and you can develop for it using FreeBSD. RTMX/OS from RTMX (http://www.rtmx.com/) has proprietary real-time extensions based on OpenBSD and is POSIX compliant. BSDI offers the proprietary e/BSD (http://www.BSDI.COM/products/eBSD/); it has per-copy licensing fees and a fee for a separate development license.

Business models

Whether any of these companies put out Open Source tools for free, or proprietary tools for money (see Table 9-1), they all face the same economic question of how to make enough money to cover development, distribution, and support of their products, besides making a profit. Lineo and BSDI enforce a per-copy royalty, a model frequently difficult to administer and collect. For companies with a truly open model (that is, the software can be downloaded from the Web and modified and freely distributed), charging for a nice copy of the product (bound manuals, CD, and so forth) will probably not generate much income.

Support, on the other hand, is the natural place to look for revenue. Not only does this represent an attractive exchange of value for the customer, no vendor who is embedding software in a product will want to go without upline support from the tool or operating system supplier. This support may be priced per developer, further stratified by level of support and collected on an annual basis. An alternative model would be to price on the basis of a percentage of revenue from the customer's shipping product. Some of the many ways of slicing the pie are covered in the Guide to OEM Software Licensing at (http://www.stromian.com/guide.htm).

Table 9-1 *Commercial and Proprietary Embedded Systems (Linux and Others)*

Product	System	Acquire for Free?	Modifications Allowed?	Free Distribution of Modifications?
Embedix (Lineo)	Linux	System free; tools and browser not free	Yes	Royalties for proprietary material
Hard Hat (Monta Vista)	Linux	Yes	Yes	Yes
BlueCat (Lynx)	Linux	No	Yes	Yes?
eCos (Red Hat)	Other	Yes	Yes	Yes
picoBSD (FreeBSD)	BSD	Yes	Yes	Yes
e/BSD (BSDI)	BSD	No	Yes	Royalties

An interesting issue has surfaced in the auto industry. Over the years, Detroit automakers have off-loaded many of their costs onto suppliers, letting them carry the inventories, for example, and integrating their information systems into the automakers' own. In recent years, the automakers scrutinized suppliers' costs for the parts supplied. Now that the automakers know how much each screw costs, there is a problem with the suppliers' substituting software for hardware as more embedded systems are built into cars: the automakers don't want to pay for the software. Suppliers are trying to persuade the automakers to accept value pricing based on functionality, not materials costs.

Licensing issues

The embedded market began in fragmentation, with many different pieces of software on many different devices. A trend towards Linux will tend to pull the market together, making more application software available across more devices. Not all of the software needs to be Open Source, but the Linux kernel is covered under the GNU General Public License (GPL), which requires that source code for it be made available to any user who has the binary code.

The average user who has the binary code embedded in a device may not care, let alone know, what the software is or that the source code is available. Nevertheless, anyone who must support the device may have a strong interest in the source code, particularly if modifications to the device's code are still possible in the form of maintenance routines, such as flash upgrades.

There are subtleties to GPL licensing that have not been settled, but they have not slowed down the market. They tend to revolve around the GNU LGPL, a license covering the linking of libraries. Briefly told (details on the LGPL are provided in Chapter 7, "The GNU GPL and the Open Source Definition"), the question is whether the linking of libraries in an embedded device remains dynamic (allowed) or whether, in the confines of a device, they end up statically linked (not allowed). In real-time systems, for instance, all software ends up linked into a single executable.

Another difficulty is the potential conflict between the GNU GPL, the license that covers Linux and asserts the recipient's right to modify received code, and legal constraints. If the software in a device can't be altered after manufacture, few people would claim that limitation as a violation of the GPL, but in a device that could allow the software to be modified (in a PROM, for instance), there may be legal constraints against providing the means of altering the code. FDA-approved medical devices, for example, may not be altered without voiding that approval. In the case of devices not under FDA approval, some people believe that supplying the source code would be a tacit encouragement to modification and that the manufacturer could be liable for damages resulting from such modifications. This is an unfortunate but understandable conflict between the desire to have peer review and improvement of code on which lives depend, such as medical devices and flight control systems, and safety policies that don't want to leave the devices and systems open to tampering of any sort.

Apart from the legal restrictions described previously, you may modify a Linux distribution received in an embedded device, provided there is a way to access it. Vendors who do not want to deal with problems arising from customer modifications might consider using a form of BSD system because the license allows binary-only distribution. In addition, a vendor can freely mix proprietary code with BSD code to build a device; BSD licensing is an important strength in the tight confines of the embedded world. Using BSD will also relieve a vendor of any worry about who in the downstream distribution should be receiving source code or a notice of its availability, as would be the case with Linux.

Standards

Because the embedded world has a large variety of devices and tends to have individually crafted software on each device, it is a highly fragmented world. The Linux world is haunted by the example of the fragmentation that robbed UNIX of much of its influence, and, as they look at the many Linux hacks created for embedding, particularly at the low end, the embedded world seems to some people the most likely spot for that fragmentation to accelerate.

Standards are the logical answer to fragmentation, and some thirty companies have recently formed an Embedded Linux Advisory Board. Lineo, Inc., like its sister firm, Caldera Systems, Inc., is a strong supporter of standards bodies. Such bodies, however, tend to move slowly; the market, on the other hand, likes to follow successful implementations and award them the status of de facto standards. We have already spoken of the advantages of controlling a standard and of Microsoft as a successful example.

We have also looked at de facto standards in the Open Source world, in terms such as forking and project control. Although anyone can begin a new fork of a project, the original project group and its leader, so long as they continue to invest resources in the project and show responsiveness to their public, are unlikely to be bypassed. Cygnus plans to continue to be a leader in the embedded market. Its acquisition by Red Hat led to the Open Sourcing of eCos under an arrangement like the Mozilla Public License and called the Red Hat eCos Public License (`http://sourceware.cygnus.com/ecos/license.html`). This Open Sourcing serves to reinforce the central position of Cygnus in embedded systems, a position that the company intends to extend by promoting the EL/IX interface as a standard.

The Cygnus answer to fragmentation is the EL/IX embedded Linux application program interface (API) based on POSIX real-time standards. The object is to encourage embedded systems to implement this API, as eCos is doing. Then, any tool that writes to the EL/IX API can expect portability across systems that implement it, whether they are Linux, eCos, or any other system that chooses it. This arrangement ensures that eCos, a highly specialized, deeply embedded (that is, not nearly so large as Linux) system will continue to evolve, along with Linux. An Open Source, freely downloadable and distributable eCos is more likely to become widely used and a standard; Cygnus will flourish by providing packaging, support, and consulting.

Cygnus's deep knowledge of eCos and EL/IX will enable it to do a superlative job of incorporating EL/IX support into its own tool, which it also sells to Windows developers. By arranging the pieces properly, Cygnus (and Red Hat) tap into the much larger Windows market. Other Windows development toolmakers may also wish to implement the EL/IX API, especially to take advantage of free eCos. This is great leverage of its resources by a small firm; participation will only make the arrangement stronger and more profitable for everyone. This is the classic Open Source approach; you don't pay for the software, you pay for the support. If you can't afford paid support, you can use free versions of software and look on the Internet for community support.

Although the strategy is very young, it is already bearing fruit. Red Hat/Cygnus has invested the developer effort and made the Open Sourcing commitment on both eCos and EL/IX. A demonstration of the strategy's attractiveness is that the 100 persons attending the Linux Real Time Workshop (http://www.thinkingnerds.com/ projects/rtl-ws/rtl-ws.html) in Vienna in February 2000 (an estimated 20 or 30 Americans attended) voted 99 to 1 to adopt EL/IX as the interface they would write to. They did not legislate anything, but their vote shows the attraction of the EL/IX standard and the worldwide reach of Linux.

Red Hat intends to leverage its new strength in embedded systems even further. Michael Tiemann's persistent talk about "the post-PC world" points to a world of devices with Internet capability rapidly taking over functions now belonging mostly to PCs. This world of intercommunicating autos, appliances, telephones, computers, and other devices will come about much more quickly if there is an open standard of cross-platform development that ranges from high-end systems to embedded systems. Linux can play a large part in this system and may be the eventual winner. Red Hat has two roles to play: it can provide the technology to put the software on all these systems, and it can provide hosting and services and storage in this Internet-based world. If eCos helps bring on this new world and flourishes, that's fine; if all the improvements are gradually imported into the Linux kernel itself, that's fine, too. All Red Hat needs to do is be careful not to point EL/IX too specifically at eCos, as Microsoft pointed its Java tools at ActiveX.

On its way to becoming all things to all people, Red Hat is bound to encounter Sun Microsystems, who began to dream the same dream some years back. The Sun implementation is to use Java, which began as an embedded language and which is also network-enabled. By putting a Java Virtual Machine (or Sun's Jini technology) on your device, you should be able to run Java code written to the proper Java standard. The adoption by developers of the EL/IX standard, providing it is not hijacked by any vendor, would bring Linux closer to this goal than Sun. In its NT version, eCos has the sort of visual interface favored by Microsoft-based developers, as mentioned previously. The strategy here is to milk the Windows market by allowing developers to use NT as a development platform (writing to the EL/IX API) and then to deploy the applications on a free system. Developers at eCos are working on implementing a GNOME-based interface to bring the same sort of graphical interface features to the Linux end of the market. GNOME, by the way, will enable developers to write handsome user interfaces on embedded applications as well.

Microsoft is entering the embedded market by offering a variety of products. Vendors have been slow to adopt Windows CE because it is too cumbersome for its main target, the palm-top market currently dominated by the PalmOS, and so Microsoft will soon enter the market for the larger hand-held computers with a PocketPC device running its own version of Windows. Microsoft also makes an embedded Windows NT product, but it is basically an NT that will run without a monitor and is intended for ISPs and similar sites. In the anonymous space of device software, the Microsoft name is not a strong advantage. The newly announced Microsoft X-Box runs a cut-down version of Windows 2000; it would be interesting to consider Microsoft's position as an embedded device vendor if they were to adopt Linux. There are rumors that one faction within Microsoft wants to Open Source Windows CE. Even if Microsoft did not do so, merely dropping royalty fees on the distribution would be a boost to Microsoft embedded ambitions, and Microsoft could sell its development tools to a larger group of developers.

Over the long haul, however, the Linux and BSD advantages of having a separate operating system and graphics system mean that smaller, simpler interfaces are possible, and the fact that they will interoperate with much larger UNIX machines (or Beowulf clusters) give a strong push into wider adoption.

Some implementations

Embedded software may originally have meant an application with no user interface, hidden deep within a device, but the addition of a button or two does constitute an interface. It is thus common nowadays to talk about "deep embedded" (more like the original embedded) and "high embedded," meaning with quite a lot of interface and functionality — examples would be kiosks or handheld devices, such as the little hand-held computers running Windows CE or PalmOS.

Linux and BSD, because of their size, came late to the embedded market, but they shine in large devices with extended functionality. Internet appliances, for instance, are plug-in servers that require a minimum of configuration, such as the Interceptor firewall from Technologic, Inc. (http://www.tlogic.com/), which uses BSD/OS, or the Cobalt Qube Web server (http://www.cobalt.com/), which uses a BSD variant, or the similar Whistle InterJet (http://www.whistle.com/), which uses FreeBSD. A Linux system forms the basis of the secure server BRICKHouse from Systems Advisory Group Enterprises (http://3rdpig.com/). High-end systems could even have voice interfaces added with the SDKs available for Linux from IBM (http://www.ibm.com/) and Learnout & Hauspie (http://www.lhs.com/).

Note

Samsung has announced a Linux PDA and MP3 player for summer 2000 release (http://www.sem.samsung.co.kr/eng/product/digital/pda/).

Linux is also at the heart of the Philips TiVO personal video recorder, and WebPad, an information appliance platform from National Semiconductor (the WebPad also runs PSOS and Stinger embedded systems). Interestingly, Sun Microsystems gave a demonstration of its digital living room using a WebPad running Linux to substitute for a PC, remarking that the operating system was not "a big issue." Sony's Playstation2 will use Linux; this box will compete against the forthcoming Microsoft entry into the video game console, the X-Box. A French product called Everybook will use Lineo's Embedix and Embrowser, while several companies are using NetBSD for their embedded projects.

Finally, Linus Torvalds's employer, Transmeta Corporation (http://transmeta.com/), has launched what amounts to an embedded computer. The Crusoe chips from Transmeta will have built-in software to enable them to run a number of different operating systems and their applications on one chip.

Part IV of the book has shown you the technical range covered by Open Source, a spectrum running from tiny to huge implementations. Part V, "Open Source Software AS Your Business," will show you a number of the current ways that businesses are making money by writing, supporting, or distributing Open Source software. New businesses are emerging all the time as they find needs and figure out how to fill them. The whole industry is just now getting off the ground, and there is probably room for you, too.

Open Source Databases for Embedded Systems

The larger embedded systems for which Linux and BSD are so well suited frequently need a database to go with them; among available Open Source solutions are the following:

SleepyCat	http://sleepycat.com/	Specializing in embedded
MySQL	http://mysql.com/	Widespread
PostgreSQL	http://postgresql.org/	Object-Relational with commercial support available
db.Linux	http://www.openave.com/db.linux/	Newly-released to Open Source

Part V

Open Source Software AS Your Business

Chapter 10

The Platform: Software and Hardware

If Open Source software were available only from Internet downloads, and installable only by experts, there would not be much of it around. From the beginning, there were services that saved the time and difficulties of downloading and installing the early FreeBSD and Linux by providing coordinated, tested sets of files that worked together. From this beginning, hardware services sprang up that supplied equipment with the systems ready-installed, and paid support systems grew up as well. To these vendors, add custom software developers and systems integrators, and a whole industry is growing up to support Open Source software and users.

This chapter takes a look at software and hardware and service businesses that have been built on Open Source software. Because the market is so new, there are opportunities to spot needs that are not being filled, whether in products or services. This chapter provides some of the categories that have already emerged.

Linux Distributions

Walnut Creek CDROM (http://www.cdrom.com) has been instrumental in getting Open Source distribution going. The company published the earliest widely distributed Linux CD (Yggdrasil) in 1992 and has been distributing Slackware Linux since that same year. In 1993, Walnut Creek began publishing FreeBSD on CD-ROM; recently the FreeBSD organization (http://www. freebsd.org) has begun publishing their own CD-ROM at the FreeBSD Mall (http://www.freebsdmall.com), as have other publishers in the U.S. and abroad. Walnut Creek recently merged with Berkeley Software Design (BSDI), who supply the proprietary BSD OS (http://www.BSDI.COM/).

Besides earning money on distributing CDs of software in which it has no property rights, Walnut Creek maintains one of the largest free software download sites in the world (ftp://ftp.cdrom.com), where many of the same software distributions, ready for use, may be had free for the downloading. The solo server handles 750,000 visitors a day (6,000 may visit at once) and demonstrates the strength of the FreeBSD operating system and the Open Source economics by which free software distribution enlarges the market — where, in turn, an expanding number of CDs are sold. Visitors download nearly a terabyte of software daily over the constantly full pipeline; a one-day test of the maximum demand showed it to be 1.39 terabytes, which were then served.

Distribution, Publisher

A Linux "distribution" or "distro" consists of the Linux kernel and several hundred additional files that together form the Linux operating system or platform. Collecting these files from the various Open Source projects that originate them and make them available on the Internet, tuning and testing all the components so that they work reliably together, and providing a means of installation is the work of projects like Debian and for-profit companies like Red Hat, SuSE, Caldera, TurboLinux, MandrakeSoft, and others.

Walnut Creek CDROM does not prepare the Debian distribution (called Debian GNU/Linux), but does publish it. Anyone is free to take that or any other Linux distribution and publish it as well. This leads to the curious economic model explained in the following pages.

Major Linux distributions such as Red Hat and SuSE show a similar pull on their sites for free downloads of the software that they package and sell on CDs; in addition, other publishers distribute unofficial versions of the major distributions. Neither free downloads nor republished versions make a penny for the originators. At an earlier stage of its growth, it was worth Red Hat's while to cooperate with the publisher Macmillan in issuing an Official Red Hat Linux (as distinguished from an unofficial copy): Macmillan pushed Red Hat into sales channels that it could not otherwise reach. After an initial push for market share, however, it no longer made sense for Red Hat to see Macmillan earning money on boxes of software that Red Hat now had the power to push into the same channels and sell. As a result, the agreement lapsed, and Macmillan picked up the MandrakeSoft Linux distribution in its place.

All the major distributors see organizations like Cheap Bytes (`http://www.cheapbytes.com`) and the Linux Mall (`http://www.linuxmall.com`) and others selling $2 or $3 CDs containing unsupported versions of their software. In the cases of Cheap Bytes and Linux Mall, these are retailers who sell the official versions as well, along with other products such as CD-ROM collections of documentation, but it is possible for any entrepreneur to publish the major distributions for a couple of dollars and figure out another way to make money out of the opportunity, perhaps by selling mailing lists of the customers. If you have followed this model so far, you are ready for the next surprise: some of the major Linux distributions set up mirror sites or send master CDs to the other publishers to encourage them to continue the practice. The rationale is that the cheap CDs provide a way for users to try out the distributions; when the user is ready to take one seriously, the user will naturally want to buy the full distribution, which will include some sort of support and some proprietary applications, such as an office suite that might have to be paid for anyway. Thus, the cheap CDs serve to distribute sample copies of the various distributions at no cost to their originators and at some profit to the publishers.

It is possible to take an existing Linux distribution and piggyback on it to create value in a new distribution. MandrakeSoft (http://www.linux-mandrake.com) began by selling a distribution that added value to the Red Hat 5.1 distribution by adding the KDE desktop. MandrakeSoft has since evolved its own distribution called Linux-Mandrake, tuned especially for the Pentium chip, but the company is keeping the distro compatible with Red Hat, whom it sees as the market leader. In turn, Mandrake has seen its distribution repackaged by various vendors. For instance, NECTEC (http://www.nectec.or.th/home/index.html), a Thai government-sponsored project to improve information technology in Thailand, together with the Thai Linux Working Group (http://linux.thai.net/MaTEL/), has developed a Thai version of Mandrake originally called MaTEL, or Mandrake & Thai Extension-Linux, and since renamed to Linux-TLE. China has its own simplified-character Chinese version, Red Flag Linux, which runs on the Compaq Alpha and Intel chips. Although all this fragmentation makes it appear that Linux will die the death of a thousand distros, the very license that makes it possible (see Chapter 6, "The GNU GPL and the Open Source Initiative") also exerts a centripetal force that tends to iron out the differences among distributions (see Chapter 7, "Complications of Open Source Licensing"). The very improvements that Mandrake adds to the Linux mix can be taken freely by Red Hat for its next distribution, and the same cross-pollination process holds for the other distributions.

Beyond technical distinctions, which may simply be appropriated by competing distributions, marketing prowess determines the viability of distributions. Marketing promotions may also be copied, of course. Red Hat originally positioned itself as cutting-edge Linux technology for developers; as it pushed more into the mainstream it was unwilling to abandon this part of the market, and set up the Raw Hide program to make available on-line the latest technology that was being developed in the Red Hat shop. MandrakeSoft has a similar on-line program, called Cooker. And as a piggyback on the Raw Hide program, there is a Japanese distribution called Kondara MNU/Linux (`http://kondara.sdri.co.jp`), based directly on Raw Hide. Specialization in a niche market can protect a distribution from its larger competitors. Kevin Fenzi's Red Hat Über Distribution (KRUD)—its motto is "We take Red Hat and turn it into KRUD"—collects the latest application errata, system patches, and some useful material not in the Red Hat distribution and builds an updated version of Red Hat Linux every month (`http://www.tummy.com/krud/`). Fenzi is a security expert, and the chief motive for purchasing KRUD is a desire to make a system secure by applying the latest patches. The practice of monthly rebuilds and CD distribution of them, along with the modest price ($5 for a single month's issue, or $55/year), ensure that Fenzi will be able to keep this business for himself until someone comes along who can do a better job cheaper and convince the buyer of this.

As a result of its level playing field, Linux finds itself in the position of a commodity; how could it be otherwise, given its stated goal of giving the most benefit possible to the user (consumer, customer) at the least cost? The biting irony of the situation is that Open Source fans, who tend to disparage Microsoft success as a result of superior marketing, and not of superior technology, find the success of Linux, and particularly of any one distribution of Linux, heavily dependent upon marketing. Accordingly, the Linux distributions have been plying the tools of marketing. They are targeting various market segments (and most are aiming at the largest and most lucrative, the ease-of-use segment), doing their best to understand and respond to the market needs and adding ancillary products (support, training, and such) to make their distributions into a complete product. Services are traditionally one way to differentiate a commodity product from its competitor.

The strongest differentiator, however, is branding, and Red Hat's success among the Linux distributions has been the result of Bob Young's early and deep understanding of marketing and branding. Before there was a Red Hat, he watched the sales of Linux distribution CDs in his own business and noticed that Patrick Volkerding's Slackware distribution sold much better, and at a higher price, than its competitors. To techies! Here was objective (and bankable) proof of the power of branding. The current Red Hat company was born when the man who understood the market found the man with the software to market. Young enjoys using the example of Heinz ketchup as the example of the power of branding and has used the example so often that the current revival in Heinz sales (after a brief eclipse by salsa) might possibly have felt some effect from Young's speeches.

Branding power comes with its own built-in limitations. Knowing when brand extension fades into brand dilution is the mark of a superior product manager. A hardware manufacturer, for instance, wanting to install a branded Linux distribution on his machines might want certain changes made that would result in the brand-owner's refusal to extend the brand name to cover such a version. And Corel Corporation, in the search for a Linux distribution to bundle with its own software application products, eventually settled on launching its own Corel Linux OS distribution (based on Debian).

Custom Software

The business model we have seen previously is that the originators of distributions take publicly available code and package it in some manner for further distribution. Some companies are able to follow this model with software other than the operating system, as the two examples that follow show.

Cygnus Solutions

Cygnus Solutions (http://www.cygnus.com) provides many developers with employment doing what they love: writing Open Source code. Thanks to the recent sale of Cygnus to Red Hat, some of these developers have found that they have become wealthy doing what they love.

Cygnus is the home of some of the most important development tools, both for the Open Source community and for many proprietary vendors. Michael Tiemann and two others founded the business to provide support and customization for the GNU C Compiler (commonly called GCC, or more often, gcc, in the lowercase UNIX manner), and for the GNU C libraries associated with it. Over the years the developers at Cygnus have ported these tools (and others) across many platforms. Most of this work has been paid for by vendors who wanted the tools ported to new languages or chips so that developers would be able to write software for them. All of this GNU-tool related code is delivered with source code under the GNU GPL, and the copyrights are automatically turned over to the Free Software Foundation.

Cygnus sells a state-of-the-art version of the tools called GNUPro, and also a formerly proprietary tool called Source-Navigator, made Open Source after the merger with Red Hat. A third product, Code Fusion, makes use of both the Open Source GNUPro and the closed-source Source-Navigator. Another tool, called Cygwin, is distributed under a license like the Troll Tech QPL: the product is Open Source if the user uses it to develop Open Source products; if the user uses it for proprietary products, a license must be purchased.

Custom projects (such as the ports mentioned above) will have their source code released as part of the GNU tools; this is generally after a delay. The time is used to thoroughly test the customizations on the customer's site. In addition, the source code may be held back for a period until the customer is ready to release the product (such as a new chip), at which time the code is released.

Cygnus has become so successful as the first enterprise founded on developing GPL'd software, that by now it has written about 70 percent of the code in gcc and employs about 80 percent of the gcc developers. Coordinating the continued development of the GNU C tools was too complicated and demanding for the slender resources of the Free Software Foundation, which agreed to place management of the project in the hands of the gcc Steering Committee. Cygnus turns over copyrights for new code to the Free Software Foundation, and no more than 45 percent of Steering Committee members may be Cygnus employees.

Now that Cygnus is owned by Red Hat, the Steering Committee is looking at measures to make sure that Cygnus/Red Hat employees do not dominate it. Red Hat, which likewise turns over copyrights for GNU software improvements to the FSF, proudly states that it employs five of the eight major contributors to the Linux kernel (but only 5 percent of kernel developers work for Red Hat/Cygnus). By acquiring Cygnus, Red Hat gains a reach into non-Linux platforms, as well as the embedded expertise and tools of Cygnus, which has a real time embedded OS called eCos.

Precision Insight (PI)

Just as Cygnus Solutions found a niche with the GNU software development tools, Precision Insight (http://www.precisioninsight.com) has found a niche with drivers for hardware devices, particularly 3D graphics boards. Hardcore Linux developers are devoted to fast video games, and they resented the lack of interest by graphics card companies in writing drivers for Linux. When the firms did supply such drivers, they were never accompanied by source code because the companies sought to protect any clues to their 3D secrets. The Linux community often had to provide their own drivers through laborious reverse engineering.

Several forces worked to change this situation. The growing number of Linux users caught the hardware companies' attention, and Red Hat invested money to provide some of the important laptop graphics cards with Linux drivers, knowing that the ability to run Linux on laptops would help grow the Linux market. Red Hat hired Precision

Insight to write the drivers; the challenge was to produce the drivers along with source code for them under the Open Source X License. In some cases, the Open Source drivers load a 2D driver for the graphics card; this driver is then capable of loading another driver that will handle 3D, and for which source code is not available. A longer-term solution is to persuade the hardware vendors to show enough of their technology so that an Open Source middle layer can be written for 3D applications to call. This Direct Rendering Infrastructure (DRI) will be incorporated into the Linux kernel, and will have the added benefit of directing the rendering to be done by the graphics board, rather than by the software.

Not only does the steady stream of new hardware devices result in work for Precision Insight; the company also optimizes current Open Source drivers for software vendors who want high performance on their particular application. This work is added to the Open Source driver and improves it, since there is a very large set of paths through OpenGL that might be implemented in a driver, but which are unlikely to be implemented unless someone actually has a purpose for the path.

Opportunity

Software drivers for new peripheral hardware have been a problem in the Open Source world for two reasons. Although the drivers themselves must be binaries to function, Open Source users want source code for the driver. The manufacturers, however, seek to protect their proprietary advantages by hiding their interfaces. There is a further problem for Linux because of its ambitions to cover both high-end and low-end markets. While a popular operating system (such as Windows 98) need only cover the lower end of the printer spectrum, and a high-end product such as Solaris needs only to cover the upper end, Linux must cover them all. There may be room in the market for a company to specialize in writing printer drivers, just as Precision Insight has specialized in writing graphics device drivers.

OpenGL itself is a high-performance graphics interface originating at SGI. Because licenses for it are so expensive, an Open Source project called Mesa implemented the interfaces. SGI realized that Mesa could help extend the use of OpenGL in a market that SGI could not serve without lowering prices and foregoing the high income from the upper end of the market. To keep the Open Source market from forking OpenGL, SGI helped fund development on Mesa. The intention is that programs written for the one will run efficiently on the other. OpenGL is not the only standard feeling uneasy in the presence of the popular and free Mesa. Every copy of Linux carries a free version of the X Window graphics software (a graphics server), XFree86. The Open Group, which keeps the standard for X Window, has to take into account the possibility that XFree86 could fork the X standard. As a consequence, they have granted the XFree86 project an "honorary" membership, waiving the usual large fees for vendor membership. For both X Window and OpenGL there are many more free copies than proprietary copies of these important standards.

If it is a sign of the great momentum of Open Source projects that these concessions have been made for Mesa and XFree86, it is likewise a sign of the strength of Precision Insight that both the head of the Mesa project and the head of the XFree86 are Precision Insight employees. As in the case of Cygnus and Red Hat, those who believe that such projects can be influenced by employers should remember how easily top developers can find new positions. PI can't dictate to its Open Source developers, but it can use its knowledge of the market, its financial resources, and their programming expertise to find what the market wants and commit to deliver and support the products. By hiring the developers, PI gains influence over the scheduling of projects (by committing resources to ensure their completion). There is a similar dynamic at work in Red Hat's hiring of so many Open Source developers and in its acquisition of Cygnus. Commitment to delivery and support are necessary to win the corporate market.

sourceXchange and Cosource.com

Cygnus and Precision Insight are also examples of Open Source developers doing the work they love—writing Open Source code—but they do it as employees of corporations. There are many developers who like to work more independently, and there are programs starting up for them, too. The value of the Internet is not so much that it eliminates the middleman, but that the middleman becomes an organizer of information; the selection and organization of that information constitute the middleman's value. In the case of sourceXchange and Cosource.com, these businesses organize the needs of software users and the resources of software developers and create a market in which the parties may meet directly. sourceXchange (`http://www.sourcexchange.com`) and Cosource. com (`http://www.cosource.com`; recently purchased by Applix) operate at the wholesale and retail ends, respectively, of the business model, but, true to their Open Source origins, there is no barrier to their borrowing each other's business practices and entering each other's niches and competing directly.

Tim O'Reilly, having demonstrated that it was possible to build a successful business publishing books on Open Source software, began a venture called Collab.Net to take advantage of business opportunities in the Open Source world. Brian Behlendorf, a veteran of Apache development, has begun its first enterprise, sourceXchange. A client wishing to sponsor the writing of software at the site registers the specification for the software, the price offered, and the Open Source license that will be used for distribution of the finished software. sourceXchange posts the RFP (Request for Proposals), and helps the sponsor select a likely proposal by a developer (or developer group) from among the respondents. Developer and sponsor agree on the work and the payment, and, for a percentage of the fee, sourceXchange provides a project manager or intermediary between the two; this person eventually passes the job as fit for the sponsor and authorizes the payment to the developer. At the end of the project, both developer and sponsor publicly post evaluations of how each found working with the other, and the software is issued under some sort of public license, free to all users. Although the projects are sponsor-driven in the sense that they are sponsor-funded, there is a place on the site for developers to suggest projects they have completed, are working on, or would otherwise like backing for. Under the sourceXchange model, project sponsors tend to be corporations that fund the entire project. Hewlett-Packard was an early sourceXchange sponsor and, as a consequence, has already had a project completed.

In contrast, the Cosource.com approach emphasizes the community as project sponsor. While Cosource.com fills the same managerial and buffer role that sourceXchange provides between sponsor and developer, Cosource.com lets individuals post projects they would like to see coded, and the prices they would be willing to pay for them. These individual desires are aggregated at Cosource.com, and the responding proposals by developers are also tracked there. The sponsors of a project agree on a proposal, and Cosource.com provides a manager/intermediary between the two groups; like sourceXchange, Cosource.com takes a portion of the fee for management. When finished, the project is released under an agreed Open Source license.

A number of interesting economic facts emerges from these two companies. The project sizes, measured in money, are larger at sourceXchange, sponsored as they are by individual firms. At Cosource.com, the amounts are smaller. The sponsors of Cosource.com projects are smaller, of course, but there are two forces likely to drive prices down in this model. The first is that sponsors know that it is very likely that what they are seeking is out there somewhere, and that the developer of it needs only a little financial coaxing to clean it up and make it presentable for public appearance. The second, and more interesting reason, is that because this model for paid software development draws directly on international resources via the

Internet, the pool includes not only highly-paid American programmers, but others from around the world. Russia, for example, contains highly capable programmers for whom small amounts of dollars are significant rewards.

One of the hopes of the Open Source community rests in the global nature of the movement. Linux is already a bigger success overseas than it is in America. Knowing the ability of young people to delve deeply into technology, the Open Source community is eagerly waiting for the Open Source programming power of South America (for example) to be felt. sourceXchange and Cosource.com will serve as funnels or lenses to concentrate that power as it emerges, and the economic power of the auction model of these sites will ensure its long-term viability. The only proviso is that the broker or middleman agents give real value for the share that they receive.

Hardware and Integrated Systems

Although Open Source is thought of as a software movement that uses ordinary Intel machines, it created a hardware market practically from the beginning. The evolving market is growing from specialized hardware (such as disk drives and communications boards) to specialized machines (heavy-duty servers) to general-use machines (laptops and desktops with Linux pre-installed). As Open Source takes root and then passes into wider use, the hardware market will grow along with it. The Open Source hardware market will be much like the hardware current market: vendors will turn increasingly to service to build a viable business.

Hardware

Long before such large companies as Compaq, Dell, Hewlett-Packard, IBM, SGI, and Sun offered Linux on their hardware, there were small companies that hitched their stars to Linux. One was Cyclades Corporation (`http://www.cyclades.com`), which began by offering multiuser serial port cards; Linux users who wanted to set up networks bought them, particularly small ISPs who attached a dial-in modem to each port. Cyclades then moved on into routers for Linux.

Such specialized hardware suited a specialized technical market, but a couple of years later, in 1996, Cosmos Engineering Company (http://www.CosmosEng.com) was the first to offer a hard drive with Linux installed on it, ready to put into a machine and run. Cosmos (and other companies) also offered desktop machines (workstations) and Web servers with Linux on them, ready-to-run. Eventually the Web server aspects of these machines were packaged, minus the peripherals (keyboards, monitors, and the like) as ready-to-use plug-in Web servers, such as the Qube Microserver from Cobalt Microserver (http://www.cobaltmicro.com).

The hardware market is notorious for its low margins, which are a result of its commodity status. If a vendor offers superior quality (high-quality matched parts as the foundation of each system), service (installation, maintenance, guarantees, and such), and expertise, he or she can claim higher margins than competing commodity items. Accordingly, the successful Linux box makers are not merely dropping an operating system onto a screwdriver-assembled box, but are taking advantage of the Open Source nature of Linux or BSD to tweak the system for optimum performance on the hardware. The vendor may also choose a particular distribution of Linux or BSD for its suitability for the intended uses of the hardware.

VA Linux Systems (formerly VA Research; http://www.valinux.com) made staggering first-day gains when its stock first came to market. Part of that value came not just from hardware or software expertise, but from the company's having hired a string of luminaries from the Open Source world, some of them from Red Hat. VA Linux, like Red Hat, employs these experts to improve its products, and like Red Hat, it releases their work to the community under the GPL. VA Linux originally installed the Debian

GNU/Linux distribution on its machines, but found that customer preference ran heavily to Red Hat. Although it has worked to promote the Debian distribution by providing commercial support and helping to push a packaged version of the distro into retail channels, VA Linux listens to its customers and consequently offers all its machines with an optimized Red Hat 6.2 installed.

Some of the other firms having as their main business the building of computer systems with Linux or other Open Source software installed are Penguin Computing (founded by a former VA Research employee, and not to be confused with Penguin Systems, a Linux consulting company; http://www.penguincomputing.com); ASL Workstations; and Atipa Linux Solutions (http://www.atipa.com). Laptops, however, continue to be something of a problem in the Open Source world.

The problems with laptops originate in their hardware, which is always being changed, even while the laptop model number remains the same. The Open Source user wants to be sure the hardware will have drivers that will support Linux. Red Hat had to invest some money to have Open Source drivers written for the NeoMagic graphics boards, which are used in many laptops. Another hardware obstacle is the WinModem. The hardware vendor omits a chip or two that does the usual work of the modem (this makes it fit more easily into a laptop, and lowers its price), and instead passes these functions to the operating system. Since the operating system chosen by the vendor is Windows, Linux is unable to make the hardware calls it expects of a modem and cannot run the Windows software expected to stand in for the missing hardware. A Linux software workaround for this problem may arrive shortly, however — another example of the Open Source community coming up with what it needs.

Of all laptops, the Sony Vaio Z505 is currently high fashion among Open Source coders; it is light and portable and provides no hardware obstacles to running Linux. Nevertheless, it does not come with Linux installed. IBM was the first laptop company to offer factory-installed Linux (on its laptops without WinModems, of course). A new company, Tuxtops (`http://tuxtops.com/`), has just been formed to meet the needs in this market.

Integrators

System integration/value-added reselling is presently a wide-open field in Linux. Competition is tight in established platform markets (such as Windows), particularly because hardware vendors are seeking to increase their margins and bind their customers more tightly to them by supplying integration services. Consequently, the traditional value-added resellers (VARs) and system integrators are under increasing pressure from the very firms that sell them equipment. Because the Linux market is so new, there are few players here, but this does not mean that the same pressures of vertical integration are absent.

In the first place, several Linux hardware manufacturers, such as VA Linux, offer systems integration services. In addition, they offer support. They are probably well down the road to offering not only complete systems to customers, but also installation and financing as well, as some hardware vendors in the established markets already do. Not only are the hardware manufacturers getting into vertical integration, the distro vendors are doing it also. Red Hat, for instance, is helping to wire up the 3,000 terminals in Auto Zone stores with Linux; since the licenses can't really be sold, this is a pure service venture. There are also partnerships between distros and hardware manufacturers, and the major distros are either selling 24-7 support or partnering with third parties to offer it in their name. But these combinations, emulating the DEC or IBM operations that came before them, are not necessarily a threat to the small integrator, because their focus is on large customers, and their services are priced accordingly.

VARs and Systems Integrators

The VAR and integrator categories are often used interchangeably because there has always been some overlap between them, and because distribution channels themselves are becoming more integrated. Traditionally, the integrator is a bidder on a new project, and because government agencies purchase by bids and proposals, and selling to the government is specialized work, the term integrator frequently refers to government contractors who supply everything on a project from software to cabling.

The term "Value Added Reseller" (VAR; sometimes still called "dealers") on the other hand, originates in retail sales; the customer who needs a modem orders it from a local VAR. Because every sale involves some level of service, and because the more service, the better the price and profits the reseller can command, the VAR adds value by suggesting the most appropriate equipment and software, and perhaps helping to install it. From there it is one more step to offering support, and then to supplying complete systems. So the VAR becomes a systems integrator. Although the term generally means someone who sells to private businesses, as opposed to government sales and service, there is a tendency now to refer to the really large firms as "Global Systems Integrators" (GSIs). GSIs are the very large worldwide firms such as Andersen Consulting that deal with both government and private clients.

Systems integrators tend to be larger-scale businesses, able to carry the overhead of government bidding and contracting and employing a wider range of in-house experts. VARs, on the other hand, include many small operations, and may settle down in close relationships with a limited number of customers in a particular business domain or niche. The VAR's particular strength is that the customer may not have much computing expertise and will thus depend on the VAR for guidance.

The term consultant applies to anyone hired for help with a computer system; the consultant may or may not be a dealer or reseller or connected with one.

The spread of Linux will draw new players into both the large-scale and the small-scale spheres of operations. The one critical question is Linux expertise. Until their customers call for it, the high-end operations such as Andersen Consulting cannot be expected to offer Linux services, but they do have the advantage that when the call finally comes, they have UNIX experts on board who will be able to switch easily into Linux. Smaller integrators, on the other hand, are not so likely to have the UNIX or Linux expertise. The potential small integrators on the other hand, that is, the Linux gurus itching to start small businesses, and the recent Linux-loving college graduates, rarely have the business domain expertise or the business experience to start an integration business. Nevertheless, if existing Windows VARs were to decide they could run more profitable and less harried businesses by switching part or all of their customers' operations to Linux, they would be in an excellent position to profit from any coming Linux wave.

At this stage in the cycle of technology adoption, Linux is at the edge of Geoffrey Moore's famous Chasm. Currently used by large-firm visionaries who seek a competitive advantage by undertaking internal Linux projects, Linux itself awaits the forces that will carry it across the Chasm from specialty into general acceptance. These forces will be the niche integrators and resellers who will develop Linux-based products for particular specialized business domains, slowly spreading the adoption and use of the new platform. The highly profitable niches, such as oil exploration or financial broker-age, require extensive business domain knowledge. For that matter, so does selling to doctors' or dentists' offices. You will be able to track this process of crossing the Chasm by watching for the success stories to shift from triumphs of internal projects to accounts of how niche vendors sell specialized products across multiple companies.

Becoming a Dealer or Consultant

Linux experts looking for help in breaking into the VAR/integrating business should look at the Consultants' Resources at the Bynari Systems Web site (`http://www.bynari.com`). By offering this help, Bynari seeks not only to grow the Linux market, but also to add partners to its network of consultants.

Resellers for vendors who are beginning to put out Linux versions of their software represent a particular challenge. Since the earliest independent software vendors (ISVs) to offer Linux or BSD applications already have UNIX versions, it is likely that the resellers also support UNIX. But in the cases in which a non-UNIX company announces a Linux version, some resellers who lack UNIX/Linux resources may resent the need for additional personnel and expertise, and the burden of supporting an additional platform for the product. In this case, they may decide to drop the product, a disincentive that makes software vendors think twice before announcing a Linux product. On the other hand, a reseller who chooses not to support the new Linux versions takes the risk of having the entire business pulled into the vendors' growing consolidation of the sales channel.

Whatever the complexities of the Open Source environment, no reseller or integrator who lives by service and customization can afford to overlook the chief value of Open Source software for such a business and its customers: What the customer saves on the license fees can be spent on customization and support.

Support, training, and certification

For years, every time someone suggested that businesses should take Linux seriously, someone else was there to say, "But Linux can't succeed in business until it has credible support organizations." That day is finally here. Enterprises want 24-7 support and someone to help with problems and to be held accountable.

The original Linux support, asking Linux developers and users via an Internet list how to solve a problem, still provides expert answers, although not necessarily as soon as the question is asked. IT managers do not want to deal with amorphous groups or with many individual outsiders; they want a single point of contact, and they don't see the point in free support: they want a businesslike business relationship.

When you consider that anyone can enter the support business provided he or she can supply answers to problems via FAX, e-mail, or (most expensive of all) telephone, you may ask why there were not more support businesses earlier. The answer is that large corporations would not have taken such small organizations seriously. It is perfectly possible for a company to be built on an Open Source project, manage that project to the satisfaction of the community, and still see the majority of the support revenue for that project go to other, particularly larger, firms. The first Linux support that was credible to the enterprise came from other large corporations: IBM, Hewlett-Packard, and Compaq, for instance. Nortel Information Network now guarantees 99.5 percent uptime to the thousands of customers of its (Linux-based) Internet services.

Just because there are large players in the support game does not mean there is no place for smaller players. IBM uses its own personnel for first-line support and for consulting services but relies on Red Hat for next-level support. Dell offers support for the Red Hat Linux it ships on its systems, but the service is provided through LinuxCare (http://www.linuxcare.com), which supports all of the major Linux distributions. The support market is quite fluid. At one time MandrakeSoft contracted with an American consulting company for support of its own boxed Linux-Mandrake distro in the U.S., while Macmillan contracted with LinuxCare to support the Macmillan version of Linux-Mandrake distro. Now that MandrakeSoft is letting Macmillan handle all Linux-Mandrake boxed sales in the U.S., MandrakeSoft no longer contracts for support of its boxed distro, but it does publicize a network of Linux-Mandrake consulting companies that its users might want to try.

LinuxCare itself is a good example of how Linux enthusiasts can found a company and capitalize on their expertise. Any reseller or integrator who wants to keep a long-term relationship with a customer needs to consider starting a support service, and many do, but LinuxCare started with support services and is branching into consulting and training. The fact that Linux source code is available makes supporting the product easier and more effective. Besides the ability to communicate with customers, a support organization needs a means of tracking bugs and other problems and organizing the solutions into a knowledge base. In the spirit of Open Source sharing, LinuxCare and Red Hat make their knowledge base available on the Web to all comers. Reciprocally, Linux support businesses can harness the help resources of the entire Linux community in a way that individual businesses would find difficult to manage.

A new support company squarely aimed at the enterprise market is Mission Critical Linux (http://www.missioncriticallinux.com), founded by entrepreneurs with enterprise support experience in DEC UNIX and dedicated to support of high-availability, high-performance Linux in the enterprise.

Just as VARs and integrators move naturally into support services, support operations can extend themselves into training. The rapid rise of interest in Linux and the shortage of experienced Linux systems administrators have led to another growth industry: Linux training. The focus of modern computer training is not merely competency, but certification. Because businesses set a value on certified personnel — one of the sneers on the Microsoft Linux Myths site asks "how many certified engineers are there for Linux?" — certification operations have also been developing in the Linux community.

There are at least three current projects giving Linux certification tests, and more are on the way. The community-sponsored certification project is the Linux Professional Institute (http://www.lpi. org), funded by several members of Linux International (http:// www.li.org). Because it functions as a standards body, the LPI moved more slowly in preparing certification requirements and beginning to administer examinations. Red Hat was the first to offer a certification program; it specializes in that distribution. A more general certification program is already up and running at SAIR (http://www.linuxcertification.com), and Caldera's Certified Linux Engineer program is also distribution-neutral. As certification grows, the established computer training businesses will also add Open Source platforms and products to their curriculum to train the personnel necessary to a growing support business.

Chapter 11

The Applications: Non-Traditional Business Models

Richard Stallman's model for how to make money with Free Software (that is, software under the GNU GPL) has always been developer-centric: he regards everyone who gets between the developer and the user as mere middlemen. In the Free Software business model, a developer can earn money by supplying documentation, by supporting a product (that is, by answering questions about problems with its use), by fixing it so that it works the way the user wants it to, and by other services aimed at the software user.

In the previous chapter we had a look at some of the forms those businesses can take when they are based on the platform itself, that is, the operating system and the hardware on which it runs. This is a broad field with new competitors entering all the time. Beyond the platform, an entrepreneur can concentrate either on tools or applications, and thus focus both development and marketing to make these efforts more manageable. The trick is figuring out how to build a business when the basic asset, the source code of the product, may be freely taken, changed, and distributed by anyone. As we will see in this chapter, it is possible to work from straight GPL software and build a business, but the more usual models involve some variation from GPL licensing.

Double-Breasted Applications and Consulting

For years construction companies have dealt with different markets — those requiring union labor and those not requiring it — by splitting into two components, one unionized and one open-shop. In the Open Source applications world, a number of companies are using the same approach with licensing.

Ajuba Solutions

Most of the original Open Source projects are tools aimed at developers, rather than applications aimed at the general user. For this reason, the best track records for products and firms are among the tools. Ajuba Solutions (http://ajubasolutions.com/), formerly Scriptics Corporation, is an example of an enterprise built on an established Open Source tool, Tcl/Tk, rather than founded on a new technology. Tcl/Tk consists of a scripting language (Tool Control Language) and an associated Tool Kit (Tk); over half a million developers use it, including some in large enterprises using it for mission-critical work. John Ousterhout tended it for six years at Berkeley, where it was ported across the various UNIX platforms. In need of funding to port to Windows and the Macintosh, the project moved in 1994 to Sun Microsystems, which supported development for a further three-and-a-half years. In 1998 Sun spun off the project as Scriptics Corporation, still under Ousterhout's leadership; he intended to develop a complete product around the technology.

For Open Source technologies to increase their audience beyond the faithful and highly technical few, they must consider other users. Generally a book about the technology comes first, followed by training, packaging, and support. Development tools and add-ons come next, followed by extensions. These all serve to make it increasingly easy for others to use the new technology. The question is, who will fund these activities? Even if it is ultimately to be the users, there needs to be a means of organizing the financial and technical resources to do the work.

Ajuba's approach is to continue Tcl/Tk as an Open Source product, while adding proprietary extensions to it (such as Ajuba2, formerly Scriptics Connect) and selling those. Additional revenues come from training, support, consulting services, and proprietary tools (TclPro) that make working with Tcl/Tk easier. The trick is to make sure Tcl/Tk not only remains a popular tool among developers, but increases its use among them. The proprietary extensions are one way of achieving that goal, but, specifically, Open Source means must be used as well, so Scriptics uses its own resources to improve the free product. Ajuba intends to attract new users with the free product and to remain the center of gravity of Tcl/Tk users by providing a Web site with the Tcl Resources Center, which is intended to be the most complete source of information about the product. Profits from the proprietary tools and extensions will fund the Open Source side of the enterprise.

The fact that Ajuba uses a BSD-style license makes coordinating across the business much easier than it would be under the GNU GPL. The Tcl/Tk license allows users to change and freely redistribute the product but does not require the disclosure of source code. Ousterhout reckons that there is a substantial class of users who are not interested in the GNU GPL and who are, in fact, leery of it. The possibility of forking keeps Ajuba focused on serving the interests of the Open Source users; they, in turn, are happy to turn over their improvements to the free product because, if these are adopted, their originators will no longer have to maintain these changes in their own copies of Tcl/Tk. Ajuba further improves Tcl/Tk by folding in general improvements originating in proprietary work; it is the specialized or niche improvements (extensions) that Ajuba withholds for proprietary use.

Organization of the Open Source Tcl/Tk project into a corporation has given it an important resource generally missing from Open Source projects: a plan for dealing with the market. For instance, because analysts originally yawned at claims that Tcl/Tk could provide 5 to 10 times faster development than C, C++, or Java, Scriptics shifted the focus to Tcl/Tk as a tool for integrating applications in the enterprise. It is interesting to note that the majority of downloads from the Scriptics Web site are for the Windows version of Tcl/Tk.

Perl

Larry Wall, the originator of the scripting language Perl, did not choose to found a company built on his technology. Instead, he is paid by O'Reilly & Associates to work on books about Perl and on any Perl-related project that interests him. There is, however, at least one company built on Perl, ActiveState Tool Corporation (http:// www.activestate.com); like Scriptics it publishes both Open Source and proprietary software in support of its chosen technology.

Licenses that Help Two Old Standards Go Commercial

Apache and sendmail are two ubiquitous programs that helped build the Internet. The Open Source Apache Web server is the foundation for the proprietary secure-server version from C2Net (http://www.c2net.com) called Stronghold. Covalent Technologies, Inc. (http://www.covalent.com) sells support plans for Apache and other products and has also added SSL to Apache in a proprietary add-on called Raven. Apache itself comes with source code but does not require modifiers of the code to pass on their changes to the source code. The Apache project itself continues to be guided by a cooperative group of developers; the founders of C2Net and Covalent come from this group.

The similar terms of the BSD licenses enabled sendmail's originator to start a company both to furnish support and to provide proprietary add-ons (such as a graphical interface) to the product. Among other strategies, Sendmail, Inc. (http://www2.sendmail.com) will provide OEM versions and also encourage third-party products based on sendmail.

This is not a case of an intruder grabbing an Open Source project away from its originator. Larry Wall is still very much the central figure of Perl, but several important Perl leaders are at ActiveState. These include the chiefs of the two variant versions of Perl on the Windows platform who later combined them under the OnePerl plan (see Chapter 7, "Complications of Open Source Licensing"). ActiveState publishes its own Perl products, both Open Source (like ActivePerl) and proprietary (PerlTools comes only in binary form). O'Reilly is an investor in ActiveState and helped get the company started.

Since Perl runs on servers, the Windows versions are 32-bit, aimed at Windows NT. The ActivePerl project was originally funded by Microsoft to add Windows features to Perl; it is now wholly funded by ActiveState, which has added enhancements such as Unicode support. The product is freely downloadable; users can pay for a CD if they wish. The source code is included with the product. The license in this case is a special Community License (http://www.activestate.com/ActivePerl/docs/Perl-Win32/commlic.txt) that conforms to the requirements of the Artistic License. The notable limitation is that persons wishing to distribute a derivative of ActivePerl must apply to ActiveState for a license to do so; this is primarily to secure agreement from the distributor that ActiveState will be prominently mentioned in the derivative product.

ActivePerl provides ActiveState, an increasing presence in the Windows server market, and generates some revenue from CD sales. Major revenue comes from consulting fees and from support programs such as PerlDirect, which provides subscribers with regular updates of the ActiveState Perl distribution and its extensions, along with a newsletter, support services, and a chance to participate in online discussions with leading Perl developers. The PerlDirect distributions are binary-only and may be distributed only within the subscriber's company.

Scriptics and ActiveState were founded on the basis of supporting and extending existing Open Source technologies. Going in the other direction, it is perfectly possible for an existing firm to begin an Open Source project as part of its corporate strategy. The product serves to advertise and promote the skills of the project sponsor; if the community accepts it and improves it, the company will save some of the development costs that it would otherwise spend on maintaining and improving the software. As a best case, the community and the company will produce a better and more useful product that everyone can use, including the firm that originated and released the Open Source product.

Digital Creations (Zope) and Lutris Technologies (Enhydra)

Digital Creations is known for the Open Source application server it originated. Called Zope (http://www.zope.org), this application server is attracting a variety of Open Source projects to extend it. It is a content management system that stores all the material in an object-oriented database (Zope is built on Python). As an application server, Zope is intended to be the Open Source answer to Cold Fusion, serving one or two million hits per day on a low-end machine.

Digital Creations had originally planned a strategy something like that of Capital Technologies: keep most of the technology proprietary and release some of it as Open Source. The firm attracted attention at the end of 1998 when they announced that their Zope server would be released as Open Source software under their Zope Public License (ZPL, a BSD-type license) and that their venture funding was behind the move. Zope is fortunate to have a funder who understands the Open Source world; in fact, the Digital Creations founder, Paul Everitt, met the VC on a Python Usenet list.

Everitt has given many reasons for making Zope Open Source. Among them:

- Rapid market penetration, which would otherwise be unobtainable without a large marketing budget; there is no financial value in a good package that very few use.

- The present Zope technology (or any proprietary technology) will be overtaken by competitors anyway; a vendor must rapidly and continuously improve and evolve the product. Creativity, not technology, is the asset.

- Loyal users provide free and convincing word-of-mouth publicity.

- Making Zope Open Source and talking about it will ride the coattails of Red Hat and the Open Source buzz; in turn, Digital Creations will ride the coattails of Zope.

- A widely used product will enhance the reputation of Digital Creations; its Open Source nature will give users the confidence to try it because the code continues, even if Digital Creations should disappear.

- Digital Creations' consulting business is based entirely on the Zope platform; the fastest way to get extensive testing and thus higher-quality software is to give it away with source code.

- If the Open Source community likes Zope, they will contribute improvements faster than Digital Creations could make them, and these improvements will be more closely aligned with what the market wants.

- As originators and maintainers of the Zope project, Digital Creations is the obvious source for custom and consulting work, just as Cygnus has built its business on the GNU tools.

- Open Source effectively builds a pool of outside experts who not only provide development and maintenance at low cost to Digital Creations, but also show from their attitudes and quality of contributions which ones would make the best new hires as the firm expands.

Digital Creations began by providing a viable applications server to the community and sponsoring the community effort to maintain and improve it. Response has been good, with developers providing not only patches, but also new features and projects. This outside help has lowered the amount of effort Digital Creations has had to put into porting Zope on different platforms and databases. An additional benefit to Digital Creations is that the Zope project occupies the space for an Open Source Python-based applications server; so long as Digital Creations manages the project to satisfy community expectations, there will be no motivation for developers to fork the project and begin a competitor. Thanks to the BSD-style license, code from a competing Open Source project could be folded back into Zope.

Zope forms the basis of Digital Creations' business by providing a pool of potential clients. These clients come to Digital Creations because they want larger Zope-based Web sites and/or want their projects done as quickly and efficiently as possible. Such projects call for consulting services rather than another piece of software, but because consultants have favorite tools that they have developed for their work, it is logical that Zope comes to assignments armed with ZEO (Zope Enterprise Option), the answer to high-end problems. Unlike Zope, ZEO is not Open Source but "source inspectable"; source code is available to clients, but they may pass along neither it nor the binary code. Because ZEO is essentially a tool for Digital Creations' consulting engagements, it comes with 40 hours of consulting; work beyond that is billable.

ZEO Is Going Open Source, Too

Management at Digital Creations like Open Source so much that they are turning their proprietary upsell product into an Open Source project. Believing that improving Zope by adding ZEO is more important to their long-term business success than keeping ZEO to themselves, Digital Creations is now in the process of moving ZEO from proprietary to Open Source status. As is common with new Open Source projects, they are at first working privately with selected partners. Once they judge that the code is ready, they will turn it into an Open Source project and eventually merge the ZEO code into Zope.

As part of its market penetration strategy, Digital Creations is encouraging businesses built upon Zope; it began by listing providers of hosting services for Zope and has recently added a long page of "Zope Solution Providers": essentially competitors with Digital Creations in providing consulting services associated with building and operating Zope-based Web sites. The BSD-style Zope Public License makes it possible for these businesses to make money from Zope and even to make their changes to the code proprietary (or at least to keep it from their clients if they choose this method of locking them in). It is in the interest of these providers to send back at least patches, if not improvements, to the Zope code tree to build a better product so that they will not have to continually update these fixes as new releases of Zope appear.

Digital Creations believes it can better encourage these Zope-based businesses by keeping a distance between its own Web page and that of the Zope project. The only mention of the company on the Zope project site is as one of the many Solutions Providers. The Digital Creations site, on the other hand, takes credit for having developed Zope, placed it in Open Source, and for managing the Open Source project. It also offers ZEO, which is not mentioned on the Zope project site. Paul Everitt regards this separation as "the perfect distance between the two": if it were too close, Zope would be seen as a shill for Digital Creations; if the connection were more distant, people would suspect Zope of not being viable in the long term. Digital Creations is making all this work together to build a business.

If Zope aims to fill the Python-based Open Source application server space, Enhydra (`http://enhydra.org`) intends to be the Open Source Java/XML-based application server. In contrast to the distance cultivated by Digital Creations, Lutris Technologies (`http://www.lutris.com`) features prominently on the Enhydra project site's front page, besides being listed among those providing services for Enhydra. Lutris believes the close association is reassuring for Enhydra users, demonstrating that there are paid resources and developers devoted to keeping the product current. Lutris also encourages associated Enhydra businesses by offering marketing help, currently a set of Enhydra logos, but with the promise of more material to help promote the product.

The Lutris upsell to Enhydra is more open than ZEO; this is Enhydra Enterprise, which adds high-end features to the basic Enhydra, and which is distributed under a derivative of the Mozilla Public License called the Enhydra Public License (EPL). Unlike the BSD license, the MPL prevents the distribution of binary-only copies of Enhydra Enterprise, requires distribution of source code for modifications, and enables add-on products to keep their source code to themselves, provided they use only the published APIs of Enhydra Enterprise. Lutris chose the MPL model because Java binds code too closely together for it to be perfectly clear which contributions should come under the GPL and which need not. At this time, Lutris has no plans for binary-only add-ons; there may eventually be some for vertical markets.

A unique model?

We can see that it is possible to base businesses on the strict GNU GPL by offering services, or on other Open Source licenses by offering a combination of services and proprietary software. BitMover, with its new license and business model, shows that we are only beginning to try out the many possibilities.

BitMover will soon offer BitKeeper (http://www.bitkeeper.com), a system designed to manage source code submitted by multiple developers in multiple locations. It is particularly apt for the distributed nature of Open Source projects, or for other large development efforts.

The originators say that Linus Torvalds has said he will adopt BitKeeper for the management of the Linux kernel, "If it's the best," and they explain any delays in development as necessary to meet that standard. They believe that adoption by Torvalds would bring the rest of the Open Source community to use the product. Linux kernel source control must deal with the many branches of the code: beneath the two main branches to the source tree are the "stable release" and the "development release," and, under the second, are any number of provisory or experimental branches for trying out different approaches.

When BitKeeper is released, any Open Source project will be able to use it for free and to freely distribute it. The restrictions beyond this level are quite interesting. First, while the source code may be modified by a user, it may not be distributed unless the new version passes a regression test using a free testing tool from BitMover. There is nothing unusual about such restrictions in Open Source licensing: the Apache license says that users may distribute a modified version of Apache but may not call it Apache. The Perl Artistic License forbids the use of the Perl name on modifications that are not designed to coexist peacefully with existing Perl installations on users' systems.

It is the second restriction that draws the line between the worlds of Open Source and proprietary software. BitKeeper produces a source change log, which is automatically posted on the Web so that the developers can easily keep an eye on it. This is a useful feature for any multideveloper software project. Open Source projects can hardly object to a public posting of changes, but proprietary developers will most likely object, even though the log does not post the actual source code being worked on. Developers who don't want the change log publicly posted on the Web (at the BitMover Web site), can buy a license for a special version of the software (BitKeeper/Pro) so that they will be able to keep the log on an internal server, or even suppress it altogether.

The BitKeeper model and license offer the Open Source community the full use of the tool; no feature has been crippled and it is not an older version of the software. Besides the requirement to regression-test modifications, the only restriction is that a useful feature be left undisturbed. The only developers likely to object are those working on proprietary software, so they must pay for their request to have the tool modified. By putting its finger on the one feature that a proprietary developer could object to, and by making that feature a benefit for Open Source developers, BitMover avoids the usual vague attempts to tell users that they must pay if they are using a free product "commercially" or "in business," or that certain software is only for "nonprofit use." As clever as this model is, it seems to have one limitation: can another product come up with a feature that benefits Open Source use but is a liability for non-Open Source users?

The payoff for BitMover, however, is clear. As a free product, it may gain wide use among Open Source projects; if many developers become users, it will be easier to sell the commercial version to corporate development operations.

The Open Source model produces creative answers to many problems, whether in code development or business. In the next chapter we will look at the proprietary software world. If we regard Open Source as the original way of writing and distributing software, and proprietary software as an intrusion into and confinement of that original way, we can see where its limitations come from and what effect the return of Open Source will have upon them.

Chapter 12

The Proprietary Software Business: New Opportunities...and Pressures

No one should be surprised that the shortest chapter in this book deals with proprietary software. The Free Software movement abominates it and is working and waiting for its disappearance from the earth. The Open Source movement, on the other hand, believes that proprietary software has its place in the world and that there ought to be licensing arrangements that permit Open Source and proprietary software to work together.

In its pragmatic fashion, the Open Source movement believes that while some developers may develop and give away their code for purely unselfish reasons (as the Free Software movement teaches), many developers have done their work because they needed to do it, and they have made it freely available because they hope to have the bug-fixes and maintenance contributed by others. Proprietary software is needed in an Open Source world when there is a need for software that no one has the resources or the motivation to tackle. This chapter will look at the commercial distribution model we are used to today, and how that model might change with the arrival of more Open Source software.

Linux Distributions

The Linux distributions (distros) have shown that it is possible to base a business on the distribution of free software, including the free distribution of in-house improvements to a distro. This is possible because they are in a perfectly horizontal market — every user needs an operating system.

Looked at as a shrinkwrap product, the distros have the same economic and marketing model as proprietary software. Although development costs are theoretically nil because the raw Linux product is free on the Internet, the distro houses spend a good deal of effort improving their methods of package loading and installation while testing and tuning the entire ensemble. Even if we were to calculate the research and development costs for an Open Source software product to be less than those of proprietary products (even though UNIX programmers are more costly), we must remember that in any software company only a small fraction of the retail price of a product goes to R&D — the majority of each dollar goes to marketing and distribution costs. There are ways, however, to make money from the intellectual property (IP) that each distro house controls.

The chief IP of each distro house is its brand, which may be licensed; in addition, the sales of advertising on the distro Web site or the inclusion of advertising or software in the distro boxes themselves are revenue opportunities. These opportunities grow in value in proportion to the power of the brand. While consulting and training can be handled effectively by third parties (although the distro house may claim superior experience with its own distro), certification is intimately tied to branding. Third parties or even community projects may certify that a person is knowledgeable about Linux, or even about a certain distribution of Linux, but only Red Hat can create a (trademarked) Certified Red Hat Engineer. The process could be handled in house or franchised.

From Red Hat's brand-centric point of view, anything that causes the market to identify Linux with Red Hat is likely to expand further Red Hat's major share of the Linux distro market. As market leader, Red Hat has a further advantage: anything it does to expand the entire Linux market helps Red Hat more than it does competitors. Red Hat's lead is so great that the only other distro to promote a certification program, Caldera Systems, emphasizes that the people trained and certified in its program have had a "distribution-neutral" training and examination. Caldera branding is achieved by emphasizing that the training and certification program is nevertheless sponsored by Caldera Systems.

Red Hat began its training and certification programs as part of its efforts to qualify Linux for the business user: the standard complaint was that there were no such programs for Linux. Now that the Linux Professional Institute (LPI) has begun to test and certify, we have an overlap of a proprietary program and a community-based program. We are going to see a lot of this in the Open Source world, beginning with the horizontal applications described later in this chapter.

Branding and user loyalty to the brand are important to the distros because these assets enable the distro vendors to sell through the large distributors, such as Ingram Micro (`http://www.ingrammicro.com`) and Tech Data Corporation (`http://www.techdata.com`). These in turn sell down to the retail chains, VARs, and integrators. Only products with substantial established sales and large marketing budgets can provide the customer pull to persuade the distributors to carry the product. Branding is likewise important in signing on resellers to carry the distro and promote it to customers. Red Hat, for instance, has the volumes to be picked up by the distributors, and Corel, another strong brand, has preexisting channels into which it can feed its new Linux products. Caldera, on the other hand, has been aggressively signing up resellers and placing a heavy emphasis on training and certification to address the lack of UNIX experience among them. Caldera has shown the patience, attention, and hand-holding necessary to develop a reseller channel; these skills come much harder to Red Hat, whose resources are strained by the tornado of skyrocketing sales and an IPO.

In the push to extend their markets, Red Hat (and TurboLinux) have become OEM vendors. By purchasing Cygnus, Red Hat is aiming itself at the embedded market, as well. Caldera was already there with the formation of a sister company, Lineo (`http: //www.lineo.com`), to deal exclusively in embedded Linux.

Is it possible to make a proprietary distro? Only in the sense that some proprietary applications or utilities might be put in the box and not be made available to the other distros. Because the Linux kernel code and the packages around it that make up the Linux platform are under the GNU GPL and other Open Source licenses, it is possible for any other distro to take advantage of another's improvements. But it might be possible to make a distro that was specially tweaked to serve a market niche and that introduced changes that were unattractive to the other distros.

An example might be a distro for newbies, a Linux "for the rest of us," as Apple used to say. The majority of potential users will never want to see the source code that comes in the box (nor would their bosses want them experimenting with it) and will cheerfully use the binaries they receive. If an easy-to-use totally enclosed distro won the loyalty of its users, they would not notice or care that upgrades to its hundreds of packages were always handled from the distro's Web site or that, in fact, they could load only applications that came from the distro's vendor. They would be, in essence, Macintosh users and regard it as a benefit, not a limitation. The other distros would have no reason to take advantage of code that was focused on a competitor's Web site. Third-party software vendors would have to come to an accommodation with the distro. Open Source purists might scoff at the results, but they could not deny that the source code was available.

Office Suites and Horizontal Applications

As the first popular applications sold for Linux systems, office suite packages give us a look at the direction any set of horizontal (widely-used, or mass) products will take in the future.

In the first place, prices vary widely, from free (StarOffice in the desktop version) to relatively expensive (Applixware and eventually WordPerfect). In any case, the money paid for any of these is less than for the leading brand for Windows. Needless to say, no paid-for office suite can be freely installed on multiple machines. Although the UNIX market has always been envied by the Windows market for its relatively higher pricing structure, it is clear that mass products for Linux will tend to be cheaper than those for Windows. In addition, as completely free Open Source products like AbiOffice mature, they will add to the downward pricing pressure already exerted by three factors: 1) the original base of Linux among impecunious geeks, 2) the need for products in new markets to take losses to establish market share, and 3) buyers spoiled by a cheaper operating system capable of running on less expensive machines. In the Windows market, the increasing price of software relative to hardware causes frequent complaints and, in the case of the operating system, it invited government attention.

If you go into the large office-supply chains nowadays or visit the mass-merchandisers, you will notice racks of software suitable for office work priced very low relative to products from Microsoft or Symantec. In a couple of years (or even less), there is no reason we will not be seeing office suites in this price category for Open Source systems. This boon for the consumer will not necessarily be good for the independent software vendors (ISVs), although it will result from the answer to their frequent prayers: the arrival of the "level playing field."

For years ISVs have looked on as Microsoft relentlessly winnowed their ranks. Some of this attrition has been a normal function of the proprietary software market. In the days of Lotus 1-2-3 and dBase, each was surrounded by a school of small fish who offered little software products that added features to the hugely successful spreadsheet and database. Those add-ons that the market bought in large numbers because they worked and everyone had a use for them (the ability to print spreadsheets sideways was one such winner), found themselves doomed either to acquisition, or worse, to finding the same functions added to the main product they were supporting.

Microsoft intensified this process by several methods. One was to pull into the operating system itself functions formerly offered by third parties, sharply reducing the market for these ISVs. The Windows applets, for instance, forestall many third-party product sales, and the browser is the most famous example of all. Next, Microsoft aggressively promoted its Office applications. Users could still theoretically exercise their choice of best-of-breed among spreadsheets, word processors, desktop databases, presentation packages, and so forth, but Microsoft offered all of these in a suite that cost about what any two or three applications would cost. Furthermore, the applications were tied increasingly together: Word documents could be updated from changes made to Excel spreadsheets. It was a value proposition that users found irresistible and, as more users switched to Microsoft Office, other users found it harder to justify other choices. This is the network effect that establishes a de facto standard among users: if other people send you Word documents and Excel spreadsheets, the best bet for being able to read them is to own Microsoft Office.

Increasingly, ISVs who introduced a horizontal product found themselves competing directly with an aggressive giant who could either acquire them or acquire their market by the methods mentioned previously. A number of smaller companies ended up being acquired by Symantec, one of the few horizontal ISVs remaining. None of these competitive methods, however, irritated the ISVs as much as did the belief that by knowing the innards of the operating system as no one else could, Microsoft had an enormous advantage in building applications for it. ISVs longed for a level playing field. If Linux fulfills that hope, it will not bring a paradise for the ISVs in Open Source horizontal markets. The biggest barrier to market entry will fall because no one will have privileged knowledge of the innards of the operating system, but the lowered barrier will draw forth many new ISVs, and the increased competition will result in lower prices. Linux will have the same price-depressing effect as Philippe Kahn's offering at low prices of the excellent Borland tools and applications back when Windows was young. Factors beyond the number of competitors will also push prices down. Established products in the UNIX market (like Applixware) have already absorbed the bulk of their development costs. Even proprietary products starting from scratch will be able to lower development costs by taking advantage of Open Source work already done (such as the GNOME graphical interface). And any horizontal proprietary products will likely face both proprietary competitors freely given away to support a marketing purpose (as the desktop StarOffice is given away to promote the Web-based product) and GPL'd competitors like AbiOffice, free for the downloading. Horizontal products will be doomed to low margins.

Niche Products

The only refuge from this maelstrom will be in specialized products sold to niche markets. Here the barriers to entry are knowledge of industries and business practices in the chosen niche ("domain" knowledge) and the necessary investment in developing the software. The relative lack of developer power in any one customer's IT shop further shields the proprietary ISV from competition. All of these barriers promote higher margins in niche markets than can be had in the mass market.

Open Source software practices will nevertheless have some effect on niche markets as well. The ISV may be able to appropriate Open Source code to put in a product (as Apple built chunks of BSD into its newest operating system). Open Source advocates believe that eventually developers within an industry will learn to cooperate across companies, working together to develop Open Source products that will serve the industry generally and leaving to individual companies the addition of private (that is, not distributed) features that will give competitive advantages. In the meantime, there is an opportunity for ISVs to create "less-than-finished" products to be sold to VARs and integrators who will customize them for end-users: either APIs — as is generally done nowadays — or, as Open Source becomes more accepted, portions of proprietary source code could be exposed for customizing. Although niche markets are smaller than mass markets and the revenues are correspondingly smaller, the marketing costs are considerably less, a factor that also contributes to higher margins for the ISV.

The more things change, the more they stay the same. In short, the world after the arrival of the level playing field is going to look almost like the software market we know today. Presently, any ISV with a horizontal product knows that Microsoft is the chief competitor and will fight fiercely if the new product is popular and profitable. Today's ISV also knows that Microsoft is not interested in niche markets and that no one in those markets has a privileged view of the operating system, making the niche a better market for ISVs today. In tomorrow's Open Source software market, the mass market will be disputed by a host of horizontal vendors, rather than by one large one, and will continue to offer low profits for that reason. Even if an ISV offered a killer app to this market, it would have to carry a low price to forestall the community's loving it so much that they clone it. This is what AbiWord is doing (and on the Windows platform as well as for Linux). The niche markets will offer more chance for profitability, and there are plenty of expensive Linux applications available today that cater to scientific and engineering specialties. And just as today, the higher-margin opportunities for ISVs will be in training, support, and product updates, especially when these are offered as subscriptions.

The cloning threat is the most interesting innovation that Open Source brings to the proprietary software market. Sun Microsystems's failure to make Java an open standard, its use of restrictive licensing, and its favoritism in tilting the software towards Sun-manufactured hardware caused a number of Open Source projects to emerge, with the result that the fastest Java Virtual Machine and a number of Java development tools are now Open Source products.

You will have a chance to see how much of this turns out in the next year or two. Part of the speed of the changes will depend on how much progress Linux makes among general users. In the meantime, the next chapter will show you additional developments to watch for.

Part VI

The Future of Open Source

Chapter 13

Companies and Projects

This final part of the book does not try to be predictive — Open Source happens too quickly — but it does point out some themes you should watch over the next year. In Chapter 1 we looked at business and social forces feeding into Open Source; this chapter will look more closely at some of them as they interact.

W.R. Hambrecht + Co. (http://wrhambrecht.com/) estimates the size of the Open Source market in 2000 at nearly two billion dollars and predicts a size of eleven billion dollars in 2003. This market's estimates include hardware, software, services, and even on-line advertising, but omits the embedded market.

Open Source Opportunities

Open Source is bringing the developer and the user closer together. As originally conceived, Free Software's users *were* developers: users compiled the source code themselves, adding tweaks along the way. But all across the business spectrum there is now a tendency for middlemen to be pushed aside, for layers of distribution to be thinned and flattened, and for customers and producers to face each other more directly. The ultimate step is for the customer to buy everything from the manufacturer, but the intermediate step of being the sole middleman is most attractive and lucrative to businesses that can figure out how to take this space. A vertical market, for instance, can be run by the customer (like the auto-manufacturer consortium that GM is setting up to buy from suppliers), or it can be run by a third party in the event that the market is fragmented so that no one or three buyers dominate it. The middleman's essential position in these markets is as supplier of information and guarantor of transactions (something the auction sites are aspiring to).

The Internet makes buyers better able to gather and share information among themselves. Discussion lists and consumer opinion sites are established means. Now new technologies enable users to privately mark up Web sites with their own comments and observations so that other users of the technology can read the remarks while the actual Web page under discussion remains unmarked. The Foresight Institute (http://foresight.org/) provides Web site mark-up software such as CritSuite (http://crit.org/), while a commercial site provides its own technology, Third Voice (http://thirdvoice.com/). The ever-present voice of Web criticism has set up a more traditional form of on-line critique at a counter site, Say No to Third Voice (http://saynotothirdvoice.com/). Both types of commentary are upsetting to traditional markets and marketers. In an unpublished article, Sam Byassee of Smith, Helms, Mullis & Moore argues that the insertion of HTML code into the display stream of a Web site is a violation of the copyright owner's right to display, one of the bundle of rights set up in the Copyright Act of 1976.

Whatever the courts may ultimately say on the subject, these protests and commentary are simply an outgrowth of software developers' on-line conversations that have evolved over the years. When software tool companies learned years ago that developers had set up on-line discussion lists to compare notes on particular tools they were using, the smarter vendors learned to send a diplomatic engineer over to the site to deal with problems and the inevitable flaming complaints. Before long, the vendors provided their own discussion sites and also offered on-line help and patches for the products. These practices were translated to the Web, at first for the developer community and then for customers of any product whose vendor chose to recognize a new way of dealing with customers and turning them into a loyal group. Recognizing customer needs and building communities work just as well if you are trying to build a business in the Open Source world. The product need not even be Open Source, just tied to that market. Someone thought it would be cool if Linux folks could carry a credit card with a penguin on it; an entrepreneur just out of college picked up the idea and with minimal cash and maximum persistence created the Linux Fund (http://linuxfund.org/), which issues the free cards to credit-qualified Penguinistas. From the issuing bank's perspective, the demographic of single young males with high-paying jobs is attractive. The Fund is set up as a nonprofit and selects Open Source software projects to fund with its surplus cash derived from a share in the merchant transaction fees.

Another example of a business with modest origins that is capitalizing on the Open Source community is the Web comic strip User Friendly (http://userfriendly.org/). It is by a geek and for geeks and visited often by a loyal following that has come to be called the Ufie community. The growth of User Friendly shows the value of listening to customers: they asked for a book of the cartoons and got it. They asked for caps and T-shirts and stuffed dolls, and User Friendly has supplied them. The cartoon has its own site now, sells on-line advertising, and continues to cultivate its geek community by providing an employment site and an advisor for the lovelorn.

Besides starting businesses from scratch, existing business can find a way of serving Open Source community needs. Tucows (http://www.tucows.com/) began as a Web site for the distribution of Windows software for Web connectivity. As the Web became an easier place to deal with technically, Tucows added other Windows software, Macintosh software, and more recently Linux software; it has also purchased the Linux Weekly News (http://lwn.net).

All of these examples are part of the growing service sector in our economy. Open Source businesses themselves are service business or, more exactly, based on servicing relationships. Just as VA Linux is expanding beyond the hardware business (where margins are traditionally low), Red Hat is expanding beyond software and software support services into new service territories.

World Domination by Whom?

Whatever the origins of the Open Source movement discussed in Part I of this book, no one should believe that the commercialization of Open Source software is a giveaway program. The successful companies take a pragmatic approach to Open Source, just as the Open Source movement itself tempers the ideology of the Free Software movement by attempting to reconcile Free Software goals with proprietary software. Large companies still clash in the software industry (we will look at IBM and Sun in a moment); Open Source has added new players to the struggle while giving the old players new resources.

Red Hat vs. Sun Microsystems

Red Hat is in a particularly visible position in the Open Source world. It can't take credit for being the most profitable Open Source company, since it is currently not profitable at all, like many a young high-tech company. It is, however, successful at what it does, even to the point of stirring murmurs in the Open Source community about how commercial it is becoming. Part of this murmuring is the natural ill feeling that success attracts, and part of it is a recognition that Red Hat is now a public company with the burden of justifying its enormous market capitalization. Red Hat built its success on the cultivation of good relationships with developers; now it must cultivate good relationships with corporate customers, the only source of sufficient revenue to satisfy the expectations of its investors.

Red Hat is not discouraged that the Linux desktop is currently not so functional as the Windows desktop; it has said for years that it is in the server, not the desktop, business. Bob Young has displayed in his office for years a nineteenth-century still-life of the sort that once decorated dining rooms: a dead turkey suspended by its feet. The picture bears a brass label: *Microsoft*. Red Hat does not intend to attack Microsoft directly on the desktop, but to flank it by moving into a new space that will combine servers, close customer relationships, and large corporate customers: the emerging business of distributed computing.

From the beginning, the natural strength of Linux has been its networking strength (borrowed from BSD, to be fair); Apache and Samba are currently the Linux killer applications. Linux enables many different sorts of systems to talk to each other. Embedded devices, particularly over wireless connections, will be an important extension of this network. The acquisition of Cygnus Solutions gives Red Hat an excellent position in the embedded market. Large corporations want to serve their data not only to remote users (the people on the small devices, such as palmtops), but also to in-house users who have over-the-wire network connections. This latter group will receive not only data, but also many of the applications they use, from servers. It is easier to keep software in tune on a server than on a desktop, and the constant service of Windows desktop systems has been enough of a drain on corporate IT that there is a growing market for application servers. Desktop PCs won't have to be constantly upgraded to keep up with growing software demands.

Red Hat will enter this world not so much as a server to desktops, although the interconnecting powers of Linux make this possible, but as a server to far-flung embedded devices — and not just as a vendor of software for those servers, but as a complete service to run the servers and host the data and the applications. Corporations will be willing to pay a firm like Red Hat to provide these services as a turnkey solution rather than try to find the internal resources to do so, and will necessarily enter into close, long-term, and lucrative relationships. At that point, Microsoft becomes irrelevant. Even if, as is constantly rumored, Microsoft is porting its proprietary technologies to UNIX, the arrival of Microsoft's Office suite on the Linux desktop would not move it any closer to the lead that Linux is developing in the embedded field. Microsoft is developing what it calls its Next Generation Windows Services, based on the extension of Windows APIs to the Web, but customers may not wish to repeat on the Web and in Web devices a lock-in they have already experienced on the desktop.

Red Hat may be bypassing Microsoft, but in the Web services space they are coming up against the people who think they invented the idea some years back when they promoted it as "The Network is the Computer." Sun Microsystems has long thought that the remote serving of applications and data over the Internet was natural for them as a UNIX company, and their plans for revenue from the recently purchased StarOffice depend on an application server model. As for Linux, the upstart has already kicked Sun's shins by eroding their market for Solaris on Intel, and Sun has never come to terms with the idea that it could adopt Linux for its low end while continuing to sell the more powerful Solaris at the high end. Sun may eventually come to this position; they have been feeling their way toward Open Source and recently released the source code to the entry-level product of the Forte IDE suite under a Mozilla-like license.

IBM

If Red Hat is skirting Microsoft and confronting Sun, it has no current problems with IBM, which is actually helping to build a bigger market for Linux. IBM has this advantage over Red Hat: if some see Red Hat as a Linux Community member who is growing too corporate for their tastes, IBM is a former Microsoft, now tamed by the market and welcomed because it is rapidly learning the lessons of Open Source. IBM is cultivating Open Source developers; beyond the obvious step of hiring platoons of them, it has set up Open Source and Linux Zones at its developer Works Web site (`http://www.ibm.com/developer/`) and aggressively seeks to make it an Open Source developers' portal.

IBM is careful to be distro-neutral. Besides winning goodwill from all sides of the Community, this action results from IBM's natural advantage gained from not putting out its own distro: IBM does not have to publish and maintain software that others are perfectly willing to provide. Because there is no reason other than convenience (or to demonstrate that an IBM system will run with a fresh-off-the-shelf boxed distribution), IBM need not purchase more than one copy of GPL-licensed software. IBM can instead concentrate on consulting services and the server and storage business.

Can Hardware Fork the Kernel?

As a hardware vendor IBM, like SGI, could choose to fork the Linux kernel in the interests of optimization for its own hardware. IBM would then have to follow the GNU GPL and ship the source code for these changes with the hardware. This GPL requirement means that third-party software vendors will always have a chance to make their applications run on such a system, preventing customer lock-in. The important decision for a hardware company is whether to make changes that Torvalds refuses to take into the kernel, thus forcing the company to support them on its own. IBM has its own version of Linux optimized for its S/390 mainframe and for its NUMA-Q server, which clusters 64 Intel chips. IBM has more incentive to have its improvements accepted into the Linux kernel than to issue them as a distro because, for IBM, the software is only the means to selling the hardware. The difference from the UNIX wars is that Open Source increases the value of the product for the customer.

Hardware vendors accept the burden of code maintenance when they tweak Open Source software to run better on their hardware. As long as the changes do not ripple upward to interfere with the running of applications, they do not really constitute forks.

IBM began in Open Source by using Apache to open up its legacy hardware to modern connections. Linux became a means to free older applications from their isolation on older hardware (DB2 now runs on Linux) and to put their data in contemporary formats. The liberating of the software likewise means that hardware designs and choices can be more flexible.

IBM had a further purpose in backing Open Source Apache: confrontation with and defeat of Microsoft's mixing its proprietary materials with Web standards, such as Microsoft's HTTPNG (for "New Generation"). IBM did not want an important part of its strategy to end up under control of another company, but preferred to base its Web strategy on open Web standards. Apache contains three components targeted by Microsoft: HTTP server, Java servlets, and XML. IBM helped Apache strengthen its HTTP server implementation to standard and worked with Sun on improving JServ. The result was to make Apache much stronger and to lead on to the Jakarta project (http://jakarta.apache.org/).

IBM worked on strengthening Apache's XML as well, and then built Apache into its WebSphere e-commerce product. By offering WebSphere to important commercial e-commerce players such as Ariba (http://www.ariba.com/corp/home/), IBM was able to blunt Microsoft's BizTalk sales. The fact that Apache runs on Windows NT was important to IBM's plans, and IBM's offer of help in improving Apache's performance on NT was important to the loosely organized Apache Group. Open Source thus became a primary means of moving IBM — both software and hardware — forward, and the commercial firm and Open Source both found mutual profit in the arrangement. Non-Microsoft cross-platform strategies, whether Open Source or Java, are key to IBM's strategy not to be pulled into the Microsoft orbit as Windows tries to work its way upward in the computing world.

Standards in the non-Linux world

The war between Microsoft and Everyone Else is a traditional computer business war about de facto standards. Together, the Wintel duopoly, Windows and Intel, have an enormous desktop (and a significant server) market share. The main survivor of the UNIX wars is Sun Microsystems, a hardware company that sells its own SPARC chips running the proprietary Solaris operating software. We have already seen that Linux, in a pattern once practiced by Sun itself, is attacking the Sun market from the bottom by winning the Intel-based Solaris market from Sun on price and performance and by providing more hardware drivers on Intel systems than Sun does. Sun can tolerate this intrusion and is even adjusting Solaris so that Linux applications can run on it. But Sun is facing a number of limitations, most of them of its own making.

The SPARC chip is no longer the powerhouse attraction it once was; the Solaris operating system is. People are paying premium prices for Sun hardware to run Solaris. This should be a warning to Sun that it has already made the transition from hardware company to software company. Besides climbing into the bottom of the Sun market, Linux is openly trying to move up the scale to rival Solaris. If Sun were to defend its position as a hardware company and simply adopt Linux as its operating system, then it would suffer at the high end because Linux cannot match Solaris there. This inability to take over Linux entirely is the basis of the long-term defense by Sun, which will consist simply of improving Solaris at a pace that it hopes Linux can never reach. Nor need Sun share the secrets of its SPARC chip with Linux developers as Intel has with its Itanium chip. It is Sun's gamble that these strategies will work, and one of the things to watch over the next few years is the success of this strategy. At the end of those few years, Sun may be facing the very large machines of IBM; it will be interesting to see whether those machines will still be running AIX, or whether IBM will have promoted Linux up the ladder.

In the meantime, Sun, which has worked to ensure compatibility between Solaris and the third-party products that run on it, has taken measures to make sure that Linux programs will likewise run smoothly on Solaris. The effect of this measure will be to make software vendors indifferent as to whether their programs are running on Linux or not, and to preserve a market for the SPARC/Solaris machines that might otherwise be running Linux, or, more likely, be put aside in favor of Intel machines for running Linux.

Sun, Java, and Microsoft

Rather than rely on merely defensive measures in its niche, Sun has long been brooding its solution to the Microsoft problem: Java. Like Windows, it is a proprietary standard that Sun hopes to make into a de facto standard. This is classic computer marketing. As a countermeasure, Microsoft tweaked its licensed version of Java into a Microsoft-dependent implementation and later dropped it in favor of the current plan of trying to implement Microsoft-proprietary Internet standards that may become de facto standards, particularly when supported by an 80 percent share of the Web browser market.

Sun, with its similarly proprietary attitude towards Java, has never dared to submit it to a standards body or to release it under an Open Source license. One official reason given is that Sun's control prevents any forking of Java, a caution with some justification, for Sun knows that Microsoft will attempt to take over any standards body in control of the Java standard and, if given a free hand with the source code, would return to its previous stance and mix Java freely with Microsoft technology. Sun would rather see Java become a universal programming language, perhaps even supplanting C++ if users were to move from C++ class libraries to Java class libraries. In that case, Linux support for the Java class libraries would make Java an important player across several platforms.

So far, Sun's attempts to build a community of Java developers have not been successful: and Java developers have complained for years that Sun neither improves Java fast enough nor listens to their suggestions, concentrating instead on perfecting the Java Virtual Machine to run best on Sun equipment to the disadvantage of Intel-based developers. Sun's experiments with Open Source have slowly improved, however, and in one instance include a Mozilla-style license. But instead of a single Java, there are several, depending on who has implemented it; and even Sun itself puts out different versions — including its embedded solution, PicoJava — in the hope of making Java a universal solution. The real way to universalize Java, however, would be to make it Open Source.

Technology markets know that the most important factor in the success of a technology is its rapid and wide dispersal so that it not only blocks any competitors, it also becomes a de facto standard. There is no better way to spread technology than to give it away. Even proprietary vendors admit privately that every unlicensed user is a supporter of their standard and might become a licensed user someday (usually when support becomes vital); Lotus 1-2-3, for example, enjoyed this effect in the days when it was riding high. From what we have seen of forking in the Open Source world, a project leader (and Sun would become the leader of an enormous Java project) need not fear forking so long as the project members are getting what they want. Even the forked BSDs share code, and two of the BSD projects have just announced a planned code merge. The rate of improvement of Open Source Java would no longer be limited by the number of developers that Sun dedicated to it.

Open Source Java?

How would Microsoft respond to a Java made Open Source? Microsoft could ignore Java, having already moved on to building its own distributed object technology and its own Internet standards. Or Microsoft could again combine Java with its own technology, thus forking Java. So far we have seen both choices in action and, while they made Java stumble on its march to becoming a de facto standard, there is still plenty of Java activity: it simply retreated to the server (Microsoft's next target, of course). Microsoft could not make its own Java or anti-Java technology Open Source because it likes to tie everything into the operating system on which it bases its domination of the markets; Microsoft can't afford to reveal its operating system secrets as Open Source. That leaves only this question: Could Microsoft's in-house developers, competing against Sun's developers, plus the enthusiastic Java developers of the world (including many at large corporations, such as IBM), produce a better and more acceptable product than an Open Source Sun Java project could?

Sun's hardware position is probably the chief obstacle to a Java Open Source strategy. So far, Sun's control of Java development has meant that Java has been optimized for Sun machines. All of Sun's software innovations, from Solaris to Java, have been aimed at selling Sun hardware. Sun might well fear that an Open Source Java Windows/Intel project, even under its leadership, would cut into Sun machine sales.

Standards in the Linux world

Meanwhile, Linux is moving rapidly forward on the authority of a single project leader. There are some 100 – 150 distros in circulation, and their number will grow as countries prepare their own national distributions. While Linux was still a developer's hobby, no one gave much thought to its being in English: it was, after all, a UNIX clone and was written by a Swedish-speaking Finn who has no difficulties with English, which has become a universal language among developers. As Linux gains wider use, however, national versions are necessary for any wide use of Linux and its applications. Microsoft, for that matter, has a head start in accommodating other scripts and languages. Not only is there a rising number of localized Linux distros, there are competing localized distros in some countries.

Red Hat and everyone else

The main force in the commercial Linux world right now is Red Hat, with a U.S. market share estimated by IDC (in early 2000) to be 44 percent. Evans Marketing Services surveyed North America and Europe and estimated a 60 percent share. Evans (and some other sources) place the Mandrake-Linux distribution in second place, with 9 percent. SuSE is still the leader in Europe (at the time of Red Hat's IPO, SuSE claimed larger worldwide sales than Red Hat). Whatever the exact figures, Red Hat is clearly the distro leader. The discomfort caused by Red Hat's large influence has caused a rise of interest in the Debian distribution, worked on by a body of volunteers whose only commercial outlet was (until recently) Walnut Creek CD-ROM.

Even in the face of Red Hat's dominance in the distro market, a shoestring start-up can still become an important player. But Mandrake, as we saw earlier, *is* the Red Hat distribution, repackaged with a couple of changes. Because Red Hat refused to include non-Open Source software with its basic distribution, it rejected the proprietary-based KDE desktop in favor of the GPL'd GNOME. The Mandrake distribution moved into the niche that Red Hat opened and came to its initial fame as the Red Hat distro that used KDE (later, Mandrake tuned its distro for the Pentium chip, while Red Hat was still based on the 486, and is currently being praised for its easy installation software). The odd effect of Mandrake's sudden rise to popularity is that it has entrenched Red Hat even further as a de facto standard among the distros; MandrakeSoft makes it clear that it is "compatible with Red Hat Linux." Besides Mandrake, there are at least a dozen distros likewise based on Red Hat, which means that Red Hat, as a standard, dominates probably some two-thirds of the distro market (and by one surprising estimate, 85 percent worldwide).

Before we look at what that de facto standard implies, let's recall the unique value proposition of Red Hat. It is the Red Hat brand, obtainable from no other source. True, there are $2 disks containing the latest Red Hat distribution (seen from the Red Hat point of view as "free" samples, because Red Hat is not paying for them) that only serve to spread the Red Hat standard. Mandrake has in one sense followed Red Hat in this strategy of spreading its technology widely to build its brand: Once Red Hat was firmly seated in the leading place among distributions, it terminated the licensing of its trademarks to Macmillan for Macmillan's Red Hat distribution because the deal was unremunerative. Mandrake-Linux immediately stepped into the Macmillan slot, probably gaining little or no revenue, but having its trademarks and brand spread widely through Macmillan retail channels originally closed to both vendors. Now that Mandrake has gained high market share, the deal has been restructured: Mandrake is dropping its own boxed distro of Linux-Mandrake in the United States and relying solely on Macmillan for boxed sales. One study of retail sales of boxed Linux indicated a 36 percent share for Red Hat, a 31 percent share for Macmillan's Linux-Mandrake, and 0.1 percent share for the original Linux-Mandrake, which is, by the way, a leader among the distros downloaded from the tucows.com software site.

There is one other component to the Red Hat brand and unique value proposition. Red Hat is adamant that its products be Open Source. Red Hat made the Cygnus products it acquired Open Source, and the only part of the recently acquired Hell's Kitchen technology that has not been made Open Source is the portion that processes credit cards, because banking security regulations require that the source code not be exposed. Red Hat used its completely Open Source status as a strategy, particularly with its Red Hat Package Manager (RPM), the software used to load software so that the operating system can find it. Not only did Red Hat freely distribute the source code, it also paid to have a programming book written about the RPM and then placed the book under an Open Source publishing license.

Most of the other major distributions restrict in some manner the (re)distribution of the extra software they include for the convenience of the user; depending on the licensing, this practice can prevent the spread of $2 disks, or even force the buyer to install a purchased box on each machine. Mandrake, notably, follows the Red Hat model in not restricting the distribution of the improvements it makes in its distribution. Red Hat attributes its market share principally to this practice (as well as to branding and aggressive marketing, especially in hardware OEM sales and as a platform for ISVs), and regards the restrictions practiced by other distributions as necessarily limiting them to niche markets, rather than to the total Linux market. By playing the proprietary Microsoft game, these distributions are hurting their own chances for wider use.

This is not to say that niche markets are not viable. Caldera is an example. Originally resented by the Linux Community because it targeted business users, and because its sales message was that Linux was the glue for heterogeneous systems (Linux fans believed that Caldera was selling Linux short), its strategy has been vindicated by the general market assessment of Linux: for business rather than for the general user and most useful for its networking capabilities. Caldera has worked to simplify the usual large Linux distributions by dividing its distros into a workstation product and a server product. It is aiming at smaller businesses rather than large corporations, and at reaching them through small integrators. Interestingly, IDC's recent preliminary figures on where Linux is used show that small businesses use it slightly more than large businesses, although one would expect that large businesses, with their greater UNIX expertise, would be a natural leader. According to IDC, 47 percent of companies with under 100 employees have one or more Linux servers, compared to 42.1 percent of medium and large companies. Nevertheless, Caldera has a far smaller market share than Red Hat.

The Red Hat standard and the Linux standard base

The press likes to discuss the possibility of forking in Linux, but the question is a little misleading. Properly, Linux is a monolithic kernel, controlled by Linus Torvalds. It is true that anyone can take the kernel source code and put out his own version of the kernel, but no one has seen the point to doing this. Surrounding the Linux kernel is a large number of software libraries, utilities, and other useful material referred to as packages, largely borrowed from GNU and BSD; for this reason,Richard Stallman and some others prefer to call the operating system GNU/Linux. The operating system, consisting of selected packages tuned to work with the chosen version of the kernel, constitute a distribution. The choice of the packages in the distribution, and the versions of those various packages, are the choice of the distribution preparer and may vary accordingly. In this sense, Linux has already forked (slightly), and no matter how great the centripetal force of Open Source, there will always be a place for specialized distributions.

The real concern of the Community over "forking" concerns binary applications, particularly those that ship without accompanying source code. The point of Open Source is to provide source code so that users can compile it from source to binary (running) form to suit their own situation, but it is growing increasingly unrealistic to expect this situation as the number of nondeveloper users increases, along with the number of proprietary applications that keep their source code secret.

As a result, the Community frequently mentions the need for a standard Linux—embodied in the Linux Standard Base (LSB) of the Free Standards Group at `http://freestandards.org/`—because of difficulties in making sure that applications install smoothly atop the various Linux distributions. This approach would ensure application portability, not so much by the freedom to recompile, but by the setting of standards for all distributions to (voluntarily) follow. The need for application portability demonstrates the strength of the de facto Red Hat standard in that (a) many applications aim themselves at Red Hat as a platform, and (b) Red Hat, with its large market share, does not worry about Linux forking, nor does it feel an urgent need for the LSB.

In the first place, Red Hat, with its lion's share, knows that other distributions are more likely to have to adjust to it than the other way around, and that the Red Hat way of doing things will have a strong influence on the definition of the Linux Standard Base, which is still a long way from its first release (expected by the end of 2000). In the second place, Red Hat believes that Open Sourcing its innovations such as the Red Hat Package Manager will induce other distributions to adopt them and that it can always pull other Open Source technologies into the Red Hat distribution if it wants them. Related to this powerful argument against forking is the fact that a widely distributed distro creates a network effect for its users, just as Microsoft Windows and Office have done. This is the argument that people will adopt not the best technology, but the one most widely spread because they want to be able to interoperate with the largest number of people. There are plenty of Microsoft Word users who will tell you how much they prefer WordPerfect, but they are not using the product because the network effect of Office is too great. Linux users who prefer Red Hat for its network effect also have the consolation that if they are missing anything really great, Red Hat will eventually include it. People fear forking in Linux because they remember its model, UNIX, but UNIX forked precisely because it was proprietary and subdivided itself into proprietary niches, each presided over by a hostile vendor. UNIX forking is the natural result of a proprietary system, while Linux unity is the natural result of the GNU GPL.

Red Hat, although unconcerned with the potential of forking and not feeling a particular need of the LSB, has nevertheless pledged its cooperation when the LSB standard does finally emerge. Without going into depth on all the technical issues at stake, a look at a couple of simple problems will give you an idea of what the issues are.

The most commonly mentioned disparity among distributions used to be the package-management system, the utility that determines which packages the kernel will be using. There are two main systems, the older one originating in the Debian distribution, and the newer Red Hat Package Manager (RPM); each expects to find the packages prepared in a manner peculiar to their respective distributions. In the days when the market shares of the two distributions were more evenly matched, there used to be more argument about two package managers; now that the RPM is so widely spread among the distributions, one hears mostly sighs about the things that Debian does better and a wish that the RPM would pick them up. There are projects afoot to build a newer, better package manager, but even if one were to be devised, there is no guarantee that Red Hat (or Debian) would adopt it. The most likely solution will be a (necessarily large) package manager that handles both Debian and Red Hat packages.

The distributions most frequently compete on their installation utility: some users prefer more control, and others want a utility that will effortlessly make the right decisions. Mandrake and Corel are currently praised for their ease of installation. There is a tendency for these installation utilities to organize the files in a manner peculiar to the distribution, so that users (or applications) might not find the expected fonts, drivers, or libraries where they were expecting them. As a result, some applications play it safe by establishing their own locations for fonts (for instance), and a user may end up with several sets of the same fonts distributed in different places around his system. In some cases, users may find that newly-installed applications overwrite some system files with variant versions, causing other applications to fail.

Windows users will recognize this as the familiar "DLL Hell," the result of having different versions of identically-named executable libraries (.dll files) overwriting each other as each application stows them where it pleases. Similarly, Linux applications (or even the kernel) looking for particular versions of particular libraries may find themselves defeated and unable to run.

The LSB aims to regulate the interface between the kernel and everything else, that is, the packages and applications, by specifying minimal standards. One specification is the Filesystem Hierarchy Standard (FHS), whose latest release is 2.1. The LSB says that the major distributions have either implemented it or its earlier versions, so some progress is apparently being made along these lines. As with all standards bodies, the progress has been very slow, and there is the continuing tension between rapid technological progress and innovation (born generally of competitive pressure) and the slow setting and adoption of standards. The LSB would do nothing to govern or prevent (for instance) proprietary installation systems, provided their results conformed to the LSB standard; one thing we can look for in the future is to see whether such proprietary innovations confer competitive advantage (since they cannot be picked up by other distributions and, especially, by the market leader) or whether they isolate the proprietor from the larger market. The BSD varieties are feeling market pressure to draw closer together and have begun joint marketing at trade shows under the badge of the red Berkeley Daemon.

The shibboleth of UNIX flavors has always been POSIX and, from the beginning, Linus Torvalds aimed Linux at the POSIX.1 standard because he wanted UNIX applications to run smoothly on Linux (in fact, many UNIX applications run with no problem once they are recompiled for Linux). But he could not afford the expensive testing needed for POSIX certification. This may have been just as well, because there is a faction in the Community that regards POSIX as a relic of UNIX ("This [Linux] is not your father's UNIX"), and a few years back there was a distro (Linux-FT) that did uniquely achieve POSIX certification, but it passed from sight. The technology was acquired by Caldera and incorporated into its Linux products, but (like other distributions) Caldera is POSIX-compliant but not certified. Torvalds himself dislikes the POSIX standard for threading (along with some post-POSIX.1 standards) and has implemented his own native Linux threading; it does, however, allow the POSIX "p-threads" or other threading systems to be used on top of it.

On the whole, the condition of standards in the Linux world is no worse than in any other software orbit and may likely be better. UNIX certainly provided no model for unified naming of files or organizing of file systems because of its proprietary fragmentation; for that matter, even POSIX-certified UNIX flavors differed from each other to the point that applications would not run at all on other systems and needed more than a simple recompiling to make them do so. The mainstream distributions of Linux are much closer than that.

Follow That Lizard!
The Mozilla Project

The large and high-profile Mozilla.org project has served for two years now as an object lesson for commercial firms entering the Open Source world. It is hardly the failure it was called by some (including one of its departing leaders) a year ago, and we now have the opportunity of seeing where it goes from here as it enters its first beta or "pre-release" stage.

Under increasing pressure from Microsoft's Internet Explorer (IE) browser, Netscape decided to call on the resources of the Open Source community to rapidly improve and out-evolve the Microsoft browser. At the time, many called the decision an act of desperation by a company with nothing to lose (less than a year later it was acquired by AOL). Internally, the argument was driven by the usual Open Source arguments and revolved around this premise: At the price of opening up its software and letting outsiders use the technology, Netscape would end up with a world-beating browser. The Internet, after all, was a place of open standards and run on Open Source software; the fact that the Netscape browser revealed to the user the source code of every page it touched, and the heavy use of Java, pushed the argument in the same direction. It is very hard for Java developers to hide what they are doing, and proprietary vendors resort to scrambling the code ("obfuscation") to discourage the curious.

It was fortunate that as an Internet company Netscape had emphasized cross-platform products and had a Linux version (although Linux fans complained that it was difficult to find and that most employees seemed to know nothing about it!). Although Microsoft's Internet Explorer 4 also had a UNIX version, it was very much in Netscape's interest to support a heterogeneous market, just as it was in Microsoft's interest to kill other platforms. Netscape was able to appeal to the Open Source community for help by pointing to the Linux branch of the Mozilla product.

Netscape chose not to release the code of its current Communicator version, but instead to open up the code of the next version then under development, Communicator 5. Because Java is proprietary to Sun, it had to be removed from the source code, along with other proprietary material and the encryption technology (per federal regulations). One difficult job was to clean up the code so that outsiders would find it easier to work with; even more difficult was the job of preparing a license that would protect all the parties involved, even as the code was being opened.

The license itself — the Netscape Public License (NPL), see Chapter 7, "Complications of Open Source Licensing" — came under fire from many in the Open Source community, chiefly because it allowed Netscape to take private any contributed material and to issue it under other licenses (for example, to provide to existing licensees of Netscape source code). As a consequence, Netscape set up a more neutral scheme involving the Mozilla Public License (MPL) to use as an alternative. The strongest reaction of the Community, however, was a lack of interest in participating in the project, whether from the licensing structure or from the complexity of the code itself. Consequently, the Mozilla project remained as it was perceived: principally a Netscape project.

The Community had mixed reactions to the code itself. Some said that it was not the Communicator 4 they were used to working with; in addition, the stripping out of third-party technology, cryptography, and news reader made the code less than interesting, and so these developers stayed away. Other Community members, however, while also rejecting Communicator 5 code, said that what they really liked was another Netscape project, Raptor (today called Gecko), a more standards-compliant HTML layout engine that could form the foundation of a browser. These people urged that the Mozilla project, whose technology was to serve as the basis for the next Communicator release (eventually to appear as Communicator 6), be designed around Gecko and that the underlying technology fully support official World Wide Web Consortium (W3C) standards such as HTML4, XML, CSS, and DOM (http://www.mozilla.org/newlayout/faq.html). Although the Community did little coding, they did contribute some key features, and the architectural expertise and the demand for open standards were benefits that could not have been supplied internally, particularly because the changes required added nearly a year to the length of the project. At the end of the first year, with no released product in sight, Mozilla's best-known project leader and evangelist walked away, convinced of failure.

Some time after his departure, the shape and benefits of the small Gecko engine became more apparent (it was embeddable), and interested corporations began to participate in the project. The number of outside developers grew, but they were not necessarily the midnight hackers of Community legend; many of them came from corporations intending to adopt the technology, and a number of them were put on the work full-time by their employers. Information appliances can embed Gecko on top of an operating system (such as Linux); this is the approach of AOL TV, which will combine Gecko with interactive TV technology from Liberate Technology (the former Network Computer at http://www.liberate.com/). Nokia will also put out a set-top box based on Intel and using Linux and Gecko. Gecko runs on Windows, Linux, and Mac OS; Nexware Corporation (http://www.nexwarecorp.com/) is porting Mozilla technology to the embedded QNX system (http://qnx.com/) and its interface, Photon, and the Mozilla project anticipates other UNIX ports.

Whether embedded in appliances or running on desktop clients, Gecko will make possible advanced Web-based applications. With Gecko as the foundation of the Communicator 6 browser, for instance, developers will be able to build applications on top of the browser, just as they can now atop Microsoft's Internet Explorer.

How Cool Is XUL?

One feature of Mozilla undergoing continuing development is XUL, pronounced "Zool," the XML-based User Interface Language that controls the user interface itself. XUL (http://www.mozilla. org/xpfe/xptoolkit/xulintro.html) is more than a "skin" on a fixed interface; following the UNIX tradition, the interface itself is separate from the engine. By editing XUL, a developer (or very advanced user) can add, subtract, or move controls.

Because the technology underneath is based on Web standards, the application will be able to interoperate with a large variety of software and also take advantage of Internet communications; a hand-held inventory bar-code reader, for instance, could transmit updated inventory material to a distant site and also look up unfamiliar bar codes stored at another distant location. RealNetworks is using Mozilla technology to build a private-label media player for Global Media (http://community.globalmedia.com/) that will also display HTML and Macromedia Flash (http://macromedia. com/). Companies are free to follow their wishes in innovation, and there are no fees or royalties for the use of Gecko.

Anyone is free to build a browser based on Gecko; so far only NeoPlanet (http://neoplanet.com) has done so, as an unsupported product that enables viewers to switch between Netscape and Microsoft views, a practice useful for developers who are trying to develop for both browsers. It is an Open Source hope that proper implementation of open Web standards will make it easier for Web sites to develop a single version of their material, rather than preparing two versions for Netscape and for Internet Explorer, as is so often the case today. Although browser share is currently dominated by Microsoft (80 percent), Gecko's release should refocus attention on supporting open standards and give users a better choice than the current Netscape Communicator. Netscape's owner, AOL, will adopt some of the Mozilla technology but is not expected to substitute Communicator 6 for Internet Explorer in its client software because its current use of IE assures AOL of a preinstalled client in preinstalled Windows systems, including an AOL button on the Windows desktop. This is too good a source of new customers for an aggressively growing company to give up. In addition, the customer base of AOL is hardly the experimental, technology-loving crowd that rushes to download new Netscape betas or eagerly anticipates Mozilla.

Netscape began by pushing technology beyond the standards to gain competitive advantage against Mosaic. Microsoft outdid Netscape at this game by making its browser dependent on proprietary technology and outperforming Communicator 4. Netscape now believes that the new Communicator 6 will be smaller, faster, and more functional than Internet Explorer and will achieve this through supporting open standards. The next year will show which side actually achieves better support and wider acceptance and whether Netscape's faith in Open Source and outside developers was justified.

Chapter 14

Intellectual Property

The first chapter of this book began with a broad look at the origins of the Open Source software movement and its position in the operating system wars; this last chapter will look at its position in the broad context of the intellectual property (IP) wars whose first battles are already being fought, and whose outcome may have important consequences for Open Source and businesses based upon it. Presently, pragmatic Open Source and the ideologically-motivated Free Software are disturbers of the proprietary software status quo; it is not at all certain whether, as some believe, Open Source will one day be the only kind of software around because users won't want anything else. What is more certain is that, faced with the growing restrictions in the IP world and their capacity to stifle software innovation, Open Source will be their deadliest enemy.

Community Power

Although not well organized, the Open Source Community can bring its weight to bear upon problems it believes to be sufficiently threatening. In 1994 an opportunist filed for a trademark on the word "Linux," and, after obtaining it a year later, began to send letters to various Linux companies demanding 10 percent of their revenues for the use of the trademark. The trademark apparently held good, for after bringing suit, a coalition of Linux plaintiffs who had called for its cancellation acquired it in a private settlement on undisclosed terms; they subsequently put it in the hands of Linus Torvalds. The danger was averted, but the Community was upset by the close call.

They consequently descended with all the wrath of public opinion on a set of individuals who presumed in 1998 to set up a "Linux Standards Association" without any discussion of it within the Linux Community. The surprise was followed by rumors that the association was a cat's paw of large computer industry companies plotting to hijack Linux. The association proposed (like many standards bodies) that only fee-paying members could vote on the standards and that the two companies who sponsored the association would be the final arbiters of those standards. The promoters withdrew from public view under withering scorn, and no small part of the outrage was the idea that the perpetrators might give a watching world a picture of a disorganized Community at a time when it was trying very hard for public acceptance. The Community-based Linux Standard Base (LSB) found itself strengthened by the episode as at least one independent-minded Linux company decided to give it more support as a means of filling what was obviously a dangerous vacuum.

Businesses venturing into Open Source waters can draw two lessons from these incidents: first, that it is important to deal carefully with the Community when doing something other than straightforward business under Open Source licenses (some companies appoint ambassadors to the Community, a variation on the Apple use of evangelists to drum up interest and support from developers); and second, that the Community can find resources to use to serve its ends. In the case of the Linux trademark, the Community summoned up the necessary effort, funding, and the pro bono services of attorneys. Sun software has begun experimenting with more open licensing in the face of scornful Community opinion, perhaps aided by pressure from IBM, which wants Java, to which IBM has contributed so much code, finally made an Open

Source product. The osmotic and networked nature of the Community mean that efforts do not necessarily have to be planned or coordinated to be effective.

The Coming IP Struggle

The crusader aspects of Open Source, first seen by the public as David versus Microsoft, have not gone away; this time the Children of Light will be fighting the dark forces of IP lockdown. If modern digital technology has given users unlimited powers to filch copyrighted material (particularly popular music), the holders of copyrights are learning to use digital technology along with legislatures to enlarge their IP rights at the expense of users. Not directly connected, but sharing the same goals, the litigious proprietors of software patents are also spreading their domain.

Each side of the contest has its extreme positions. Although the GNU GPL and the Open Source movement rest on copyright as a means of ensuring the freedoms they seek, there are elements on this side of the struggle that believe that once information is digitized it is free for everyone. A Free Music movement, for instance, regards itself as justified on moral, if not legal grounds, to take and freely disseminate any copyrighted form of digitized music. The other side of the struggle has no such fundamental split; it sees digitized IP as uniquely able to be portioned out for payment and intends to capitalize on this windfall. Extended IP rights will make fair use (loaning or giving your copy of a book to a friend, or selling it to a second-hand shop) disappear, along with making a tape of your copy of a CD to take on a picnic. Instead books and music will be tied to particular devices, and transfers among them will be difficult if licensed or impossible if not provided for.

The polarity between the two sides reflects the natural division between business and the Internet culture. Businesses continually seek to erect barriers to entry to protect themselves and their markets from competition; the best barrier is a government-granted and -enforced monopoly, which is what copyright and patent law confer. Open Source, on the other hand, is partly a product of university research laboratories that are publicly funded and that freely publish the results of research to open those results to question or improvement by others; consequently, Open Source supporters believe that only excellence in execution constitutes a real barrier to entry. They believe this not only as a principle, but as a practical truth: a project that fails to serve its constituency will either fail or be forked.

IP and Scientific Journals

As an example of how widely the open versus IP contest has spread, one of the battles between research and business is the growing consolidation of scientific journals in the hands of IP conglomerates. Professors win tenure and promotion by publication in the leading journals of their fields, which are edited by the senior figures in their field, who are in turn paid for their editorial duties by the journals' publishers. The publishers charge special high prices to university libraries (as opposed to individual subscribers), which have increasing trouble affording them as these prices rise. Faculty insist that the libraries continue to purchase the expensive journals. Articles can take from one to three years to appear in these publications, which can be said to embalm rather than to further scientific knowledge.

In many cases, the publishers forbid the authors to put copies of their articles on their own Web sites. Researchers have long had the practice of mailing each other photocopies of articles they were working on, even after these articles were accepted for (eventual) publication by the journals. The Internet was founded in part to speed such dissemination of research and saves the mailing and photocopying costs and delays. Thus, a parallel, open method of furthering scientific inquiry has grown up, and the latest controversy is about (free) electronic journals to publish these findings. The established journals can fight these electronic upstarts by refusing to accept material that has already appeared in them, and the senior faculty, who enjoy income and prestige from the journals, can point out that the articles in the electronic journals are not "refereed," that is, published under the authority and scrutiny of the senior professors in the field, and thus of little consequence to tenure and promotion.

In the days before electronic dissemination, journal publication remained a guild matter, but once digitization became possible, the consolidation of the journals and the hiking of their prices by such pioneering figures as Robert Maxwell became part of a wider pattern and a cause for more public concern. The total effect is that elements of the public-funded research community ally with businesses to hinder the spread of scientific research that the Internet was funded to promote. It is true that researchers who know each other can send private e-mail containing their research to each other (at least, so far), but this practice neglects a wider forum that could be reached cheaply and effectively by electronic publication.

The Open Source movement, only just now coming into public view, feels that the innovation and spread of knowledge that were originally supposed to be promoted by the limited monopolies of the patent and copyright systems are now becoming victims of broad extensions of these two IP protections. This community, the Open Source community, finds itself trying to defend software users, readers, and music fans by providing arguments and technology to be used against IP conglomerates such as Walt Disney and Time Warner and their trade associations, such as the Motion Picture Association of America (MPAA) and the Recording Industry Association of America (RIAA). Unfortunately, the Open Source community finds its efforts blunted by laws that the IP industry has persuaded the federal government to pass and is currently pressing upon the several states.

Intellectual property law is a hot, high-growth area in high technology; the excitement and high pay are attracting young people in droves. Besides the demand brought on by the new extensions of patents and copyright, it has strong connections to on-line issues in free speech, encryption, and privacy. Silicon Valley is a hotbed of law firms and law schools specializing in these issues, and recently Pamela Samuelson, a law professor at the University of California at Berkeley and an authority on these matters, put her weight on the open side of

IP issues by donating with her husband $2 million to found a law clinic to deal with all these issues from the consumer's side of the fence. The founding and funding of the clinic is another demonstration that Open Source is finding the means to put its views forward.

Coming IP Issues to Look For

The review that follows can hardly cover the legal subtleties of the issues, or begin to list the pending law cases in the issues involved. The subtleties will increase as courts in different jurisdictions continue to render different decisions, and the number of law cases can only grow. The main issues are the Digital Millennium Copyright Act (DMCA) and its extensions to the scope of copyright, even to extinguishing Fair Use as it has been understood up to now; the Uniform Computer Information Transactions Act (UCITA), a change to the Uniform Commercial Code (UCC) now attempting to cover the country by engaging state legislatures one by one; and the extensions to patent law that recognize the patenting of computer algorithms and business processes.

The Digital Millennium Copyright Act of 1998 (DMCA)

The Act originated in a 1994 white paper prepared in the U.S. Department of Commerce and entitled "Intellectual Property and the National Information Infrastructure" (http://www.uspto. gov/web/offices/com/doc/ipnii/). Because Congress refused to pass an administration bill incorporating features of the white paper, the Commerce Department proposed features of it to the World Intellectual Property Organization (WIPO) during the negotiations leading to the 1996 Copyright Treaty, apparently with the thought that an international treaty, if ratified, would bring Congress to pass confirming legislation. The WIPO rejected the U.S. proposals, and so the administration set to work again in

Congress and eventually was able to pass the DMCA (http://
frwebgate.access.gpo.gov/cgi-bin/useftp.cgi?IPaddress=
wais.access.gpo.gov&filename=publ304.105&directory=/diskb/
wais/data/105_cong_public_laws). As a result, IP in the United
States enjoys restrictions on fair use of copyrighted material
unknown elsewhere in the world.

The mechanism for implementing these restrictions is technology, such as encryption, which will prevent the average user from
copying copyrighted material or even accessing it. It is specifically
against the DMCA to circumvent this protection, even if the fair
use clauses in the DMCA allow it (!). It is likewise illegal to make
and to distribute any device for the defeat of the protection devices
for copyrighted matter. The practical result is that the user cannot
make a copy, even if fair use allows it (to make a copy would require
defeating the copy-protection system for the purpose of copying, a
crime); the analysis allowed resembles the "look, don't touch"
licenses that call themselves Open Source but deny the user its
fruits — except that even viewing the material can be blocked by the
protection mechanisms.

A detailed critique of the Act ("Intellectual Property and the
Digital Economy: Why the Anti-Circumvention Regulations
Need to Be Revised" at http://www.sims.berkeley.edu/~pam/
papers/Samuelson_IP_dig_eco_htm.htm) takes up many of the
problems for users that the DMCA will cause. In this chapter we
have only space to talk a little about its special protection of
copyright-protection technology. The public has already noticed
that copyrights now typically extend beyond a century, shutting out
many early twentieth-century works that would otherwise have
passed into the public domain and found their way onto the Web.
And thanks to recent law cases, the public is slowly becoming aware
of the problems that the copyright protection technology is causing.

Many software users are able to remember the days when
software publishers, fearing their works would be circulated for free,
installed copy protection schemes on the distribution disks. Some

hindered all copying, some hindered making more than a couple of copies, and some products required the insertion of a special "key disk" every time the program was run. Users objected to the copy protection and found ways to get around it. Products were even sold for the purpose, and the law allowed them because the purchasers of the software had a fair-use right to make a few copies for their own purposes, such as backup on other disks and even on spare machines. The fact that the licenses might forbid these practices did not matter, for the courts regarded the shrinkwrap licenses as having no power against the usual rules covering buyers and sellers in a mass market. The early phonograph records had tried printing licenses on the record sleeves forbidding their resale, for instance, and these had likewise failed.

DVDs, CSS and DeCSS, and VCRs

The use of a tool to defeat copyright-protection technology will not become illegal until two years after the passage of the DMCA, but the making of such a tool is already illegal. The IP conglomerates have begun to test the waters by using existing laws and beginning to use the DMCA. The DVD format is currently used for putting films on compact disks; a DVD is protected against access or copying by lightweight software called the Content Scrambling System (CSS). Now Open Source fans respect copyright (it is the basis of Open Source licensing), but they also believe in fair use. So when users who had purchased DVD movies wanted to play them on their Linux systems, they were unhappy to discover that there were no drivers available. Mac and Windows users, however, had no problems. To study how to write a Linux driver, it was necessary to defeat the CSS (fair use of reverse engineering for compatibility), and playing your own DVDs on your Linux system is also fair use. But both are violations of the DMCA because they require defeating the CSS. A piece of software to enable DVDs to run (to be viewed) on a Linux system is a device to defeat the protection technology, and likewise prohibited. When a fifteen-year old

Norwegian posted such software to the Web—the DeCSS—the fight was on.

The movie industry began its attack in the courts, for example in California, as a suit by the DVD Copy Control Association (http://www.dvdcca.org/) against persons posting the DeCSS on their Web sites; the software violated the trade secrets of the CSS. A suit was brought in Connecticut against an ISP who had such Web sites on its system. The general complaint of the suits was that the only purpose of DeCSS was to break copy protection and thus enable theft of the movies; any site posting the software or tolerating its posting was an accessory to the crime of copyright violation. Norwegian police rounded up the young Norwegian poster of DeCSS following the request of a U.S. court.

The movie industry is even prosecuting sites that do not post the DeCSS, but which only point to sites where it may be found; are these sites exercising free speech, or are they no better than touts for a speakeasy? There is another free speech question regarding the source code for DeCSS: since at least one court has recognized software code as an expression deserving the protections of free speech, shouldn't the posting of DeCSS source code be protected? Linux fans were outraged to see the prosecution of sites posting not the tool itself (the compiled binary) but the source code, which Linux fans are used to circulating and compiling on their own systems for themselves.

Under the DMCA, any protection scheme that serves to prevent copying will enjoy legal immunity against efforts to defeat it, even though it is put to uses that are not covered in the DMCA. For instance, the CSS technology divides the world into zones: a DVD from one zone cannot play on a device (player) from another zone. This prevents your buying a DVD in India or Africa, where they are (like tickets to American movies) cheaper than they are in the U.S. Yes, there is an obscure software feature that enables you to turn your North American device into a device for another zone, but it can be flipped back and forth only a few times before it becomes unavailable. You cannot build a DVD player without a license from the CSS authorities, and we can expect that someday music will be on DVDs, that CD players will no longer be made, and that CSS will prevent CDs from being played on DVD players, so that CD owners will have to buy their music all over again, this time in DVD format. Present DVD owners have already noticed that they cannot fast-forward through the commercials placed on DVDs; the degree of control over access may one day extend to authorizing only a limited number of plays per disk.

The oddest thing about the DVD suits is that Macrovision (http://www.macrovision.com/index.html), which supplies the copy protection for the DVD format, seems to agree with the DeCSS users that they are only defeating the encryption system on the disks to play the contents. In the first place, the encryption technology is a means of compressing the content, which when decrypted is about twice as large as the disk will hold; it can't be copied to a blank DVD, which in any event costs more in its blank recordable state than it would if sold with a preinstalled licensed movie on it. Because the decrypted movie is 5 – 9 GB in size, it can't be written to any readily-transferable medium, and transmission over the Internet would take many hours: all the decrypter can do is play the decrypted movie on his or her own machine. In addition, the Macrovision copy-protection technology is unaffected by this process, and if an attempt were made to transfer the content to an analog VCR, internal checks in the content would foil the attempt.

Although digital convergence (the reduction to digital form of music, movies, and voice and written communications) called forth the DMCA, its hand gladly reaches back into the analog age. One delayed provision of the Act, just now taking effect eighteen months after its passage, is that all VCRs sold in the U.S. will have to incorporate anticopying technology conforming to a prescribed standard. This technology will take its place among the copyright-protection devices that the DMCA forbids anyone, including fair users, to defeat.

Cyber Patrol, cphack, and the GNU GPL

Another recent case demonstrated the growing power of IP holders over fair use and particularly over free speech and public discourse; the case involves Mattel, Inc.'s "nanny" product (one that governs the Web behavior of juveniles or of adults treated as such), Cyber Patrol. Nanny products are hotly debated by parties that want the schools and libraries to install them and by parties that regard them as censorship, particularly when installed in libraries. One point of criticism is that they inaccurately block harmless sites; another is that there is no list of the sites blocked (said to number 50,000) so that innocent sites cannot be restored to visibility.

To prove these arguments, opponents of Cyber Patrol hacked their way into its interior and found listed not only what they judged to be innocent sites, inadvertently blocked, but strong political biases at work in the blocking of other sites. They noted that sites criticizing nanny software were blocked, thus suppressing discussion of free speech matters. They then published their findings on the Web along with the tool for use in examining the interior of Cyber Patrol, calling the package cphack.

Mattel responded with lawsuits against anyone who posted the material, alleging copyright infringement and trade secret protection (other nanny software packages might crib from their list). It then added the cphack site to Cyber Patrol's blocked sites and for good measure used the courts to demand that ISPs around the world reveal identities of persons who had downloaded cphack. The issue as presented by Mattel was not free speech, but theft of their intellectual property.

The resolution of the cphack case was particularly unsatisfactory for the Open Source community. Cphack was distributed under the GNU GPL, probably with the intention of making it as unstoppable as possible. Although the young authors were in Canada, they felt enough pressure to settle the case on Mattel's terms. Mattel compelled them to surrender the copyright to cphack, and then used ownership of the copyright to revoke distribution under the GNU GPL (because they did not assign the copyright to the Free Software Foundation, the FSF has no standing in the case). At the moment, it does not look as if Open Source advocates will have a chance to test the validity of Mattel's revocation because cphack, as a tool designed to circumvent copyright protection, is contraband anyway. The courts are not really finished with any of these cases yet, and we can look forward to more like them.

Give me music, music, music, music, music

The cases that involve the largest numbers of people and make the most noise are particularly dear to the IP conglomerates, because they involve masses of people in a lucrative market—popular music. While the entertainment industry likes to talk publicly about DeCSS users as "thieves," thereby confusing the public about the issues involved, it is a good bet that the majority of the people who are involved with exchanging music via Napster are indeed copyright violators.

The MP3 format originated as a newer and more advanced compression technology, enabling easier transmission and storage of music. Under fair use, users "ripped" tunes from their CDs and built selected playlists for their computers and stored them on their hard drives. They also sent their favorite tunes to their friends. Soon devices appeared that acted like portable CD players, except that they stored and played back MP3 files. The enormous (and generally infringing) traffic in MP3 music attracted the attention of the music industry; the technologies that the DMCA supports are the result. MP3 is too fungible a format to please the industry, and so the newer standards (like DVD) are intended to end the free music party.

The biggest boost to MP3 swapping has been a piece of software called Napster (http://napster.com/), distributed (like so many music tools) free over the Internet. Napster, Inc. does not believe in copyright infringement and has said it will drop users from the system if they are identified as violators (the Metallica suit names 355,000 users who are distributing the band's music via Napster). But Napster makes it so easy. You install the free client, specify (if you wish) a subdirectory on your computer that will contain the tunes you are willing to share, and then ask Napster what music in your favorite categories is available from fellow fans. Napster gives you access to the shared-music subdirectories of your fellow fans and makes downloading as easy as clicking. The fact that the offerings by fans contain much for which they have not paid, and that their promiscuous offering of it amounts to unlicensed publication, have rightly outraged the RIAA, which has also brought suit against the firm. Napster Inc.'s position that they are a "communications system," and thus exempt under the DMCA for what passes over their lines, may be their only hope to escape punishment. The music-finding aspect of that "communications system," however, might well make them accessories to copyright infringement.

So far several colleges faced with Metallica lawsuits have forced Napster off their systems, and some ISPs are telling their customers they will be booted if they use it. In both cases, the presumption is that the material being passed is infringing, and the threat of lawsuits acts as a "prior restraint" on legitimate activity as well.

Wrapster

If Napster was only good for one thing — transferring MP3 files — and a good share of them likely to be illegal, it might be regarded as a piece of criminal equipment. Enter Wrapster (`http://wrapster.homestead.com/`), an add-on that allows any sort of file to be transferred via Napster, which it tricks into believing they are MP3 files. Wrapster transforms Napster from suspicious software to general purpose software, like FTP. But its inventors, in that self-mocking way of hackers, have included in the Wrapster documentation a guide on to how to transfer a file; the file just happens to be called Windows 2000. Obviously, like the rest of the Internet, Wrapster is one more tool for uncontrollable subversion of the old order.

Gnutella

Napster and Wrapster cannot be blamed upon the Linux Community, since they are Windows products. With Gnutella (http://gnutella.wego.com/), we have one more improvement in Internet file sharing, but in the form of a cross-platform Open Source project (Windows, Linux/UNIX, Mac, Java and others).

Gnutella originated in a little company called Nullsoft, which put out the first popular MP3 player, Winamp. AOL acquired the company, and so people were a little surprised to see, coming from within AOL, a notice of an offer of the new Gnutella file-sharing tool by a start-up called Gnullsoft. AOL acted within hours to shut the site down, but a programmer reverse engineered the protocol and began an Open Source Gnutella project. As a result, Gnutella lives on in multiple embodiments (the address given here is simply one of the projects).

Gnutella's inventors specifically designed it to overcome the shortcomings of Napster, particularly as revealed in its persecution on college campuses. Besides making it a universal file transporter, they decentralized its design so that there is no central server to block or serve papers on. It will work even if one end of the connection is behind a firewall, and it employs bandwidth-shaping to make sure that hosting networks are not overloaded; such overloading was an excuse offered by some colleges for evicting Napster. Gnutella is harder to find and block because it enables the user to select different ports to listen on, and it can limit an internal network's connection to the Internet to a single point.

Once you have installed Gnutella, when your request for a file encounters another Gnutella, it contrives to visit every Gnutella visited by the other Gnutella. The connections formed can be one-to-one or many-to-many ad hoc networks that are constantly shifting as Gnutellas encounter each other or go on- or offline. All of the files on all of the connected Gnutellas are available to each other.

The Free Network Project (Freenet)

The fecundity of the Internet is such that Napster is not the only product of its type; it has at least two competitors, though they are not so famous. Gnutella is not alone either. The Free Network Project (`http://freenet.sourceforge.net/`) works without any permanent IP addresses or domain names and ensures anonymity for persons who transfer information over it. Like Gnutella, it is a distributed network, and one that handles not just requests to send files, but also one that initiates file transfers to build mirror sites of demanded information near locations where that information is frequently demanded. Like Gnutella, it offers no central server as a weak point and claims to be more efficient and scalable than Gnutella.

The ability to choose to move information from site to site around the Web, rather than waiting for requests, enables efficient service and, most importantly, assurance that a file, once put on the Free Network, cannot be completely removed, nor is it possible to tell exactly where a file is stored.

Internet culture and intellectual property

The entertainment industry is bothered by emerging technology and particularly by the properties of the Internet that can eliminate or circumvent intermediaries. While the wealth of these companies consists in their "content," or intellectual property, they are only the middlemen, the distributors of entertainment from the artists to the audience. Modern electronics makes it possible for artists to publish their own work on the net, including high-quality audio files. There are a number who publish on their own Web sites rather than approach the record companies, and occasionally a pop group, although signed to a record company, will put a piece of their work on the Web for their fans.

Rather than regarding such gestures as building a community around a Web site (as other merchants are trying to do on the Web), record companies tend to see such incidents as lost revenue. After watching the MP3s fly around the Internet, the companies have decided to embrace modern technology to better control their products. Where Nero could only wish the Roman people had just one neck, the IP conglomerates see digitization as the perfect choke point in the media distribution channel. Product segmentation starts here.

But like Microsoft trying to take control of the Internet with proprietary protocols, the IP conglomerates (who happen to include Bill Gates's media holdings) on their march to control user rights are encountering the same barrier to lockdown: the original spirit of the Internet. The Internet was designed to move information freely and to be uninterruptible, even by atomic war. It was designed to promote cooperation and innovation and a free spirit of inquiry. It was not intended to cause such incidents as Stephen King's being unable to read his own newly-downloaded e-work, *Riding the Bullet*, because it wouldn't run on his Macintosh, and he didn't have the authorization to make it run there.

 Note

American Libraries, published by the American Library Association, reports in its May 2000 issue that Simon & Schuster refused to sell libraries the e-book novella by Stephen King, *Riding the Bullet*. Doing so would violate their policy of one copy per user, the publisher's explained.

Copyright did not formerly cause problems on the Internet. Researchers who used to photocopy materials and rearrange them with scissors and rubber cement were now able to quickly and easily assemble fair use research libraries of material from the Web and to search the material even more efficiently by computer. When they published, they observed the rules for quotation and attribution and avoided plagiarism. They did not publish someone else's copyrighted work on their own Web sites; they linked to the work on its publisher's site. The publisher posted his or her material on the Web in HTML, knowing it enjoyed the usual protections of copyright, even in cyberspace.

Now researchers face a dawning world in which Web-based information will be so tightly controlled that they will be permitted to observe information, but not to manipulate it; unable to access it with anything but their gaze, they will be reduced to the state of cavemen, staring at paintings on the walls. A picture of a page of text is not nearly so useful or informative as the electronic text itself.

The spirit and freedom of innovation expressed in Open Source are trying to continue their life on the Internet. But restrictions are growing. Under fair use, there should be no objection to a user's possessing a RealAudio or RealVideo file, but RealNetworks technology prevents your saving them to disk. Streambox (`http://www.streambox.com/`) offered technology to capture such streams until hit by a lawsuit from RealNetworks. The LiViD Project (`http://linuxvideo.org/`) for Linux video and DVD appears to be pressing ahead, although it is the object of a DVD Copy Control Association lawsuit. One of its innovative projects was said to be a system of searching a DVD for a line of dialog.

All of these innovators are called thieves by the IP conglomerates, and there is worse name-calling ahead. The distributed computing technologies described previously are not really about teenagers trading pop music. They are capable of keeping Falun Gong alive in China, or exchanging information among repressed factions anywhere. To the authorities and those who have their ear, however, these networks will look more like tools of Kinderporn, one of the sticks used to beat the Internet (does the category include Princeton's collection of Lewis Carroll's nude photographic studies of nine-year old girls?). It is true, of course, that pornography has been a technology leader for some time now, playing a role in the rapid spread of VCRs, CDs, and AOL. *Wired* and the *Wall Street Journal* alike have marvelled at the enormous and smoothly running server farms of the porn kings (who happen to prefer BSD). But pornography is simply part of a larger and more important picture.

The extraordinary freedom of the Internet is exhilarating to some and horrifying to others. It exerts a fatal attraction on the repressive mind, who, rather than wanting to share in its marvelous powers, seeks to arrogate them to itself.

Open Source is capable of bringing together some curious allies. The Chinese government has expressed a great interest in Linux based on national defense needs: the code is available and can be inspected for bugs, viruses, and other traps; the Linux-using nation cannot be held hostage by a proprietary firm on the other side of the world. The EC has adopted a policy of seeking Open Source software to use in its operations, and the U.S. Government's Los Alamos laboratories has funded the Software Carpentry Project (http://www.software-carpentry.com) with nearly a million dollars, including prize money, to encourage the building of a new generation of Open Source software tools; the first-round winners have just been chosen.

The Uniform Computer Information Transactions Act (UCITA)

The proposed legislation now known as UCITA was originally proposed as Article 2B to be added to the Uniform Commercial Code (UCC), a joint project of the American Law Institute (ALI) and the National Conference of Commissioners on Uniform State Laws (NCCUSL). The ALI believed the proposal needed much more work, and refused to approve it, whereupon the NCCUSL changed the name from 2B to UCITA and decided to carry on alone.

UCITA is now seeking passage, state by state. Without the backing it needed to become an official UCC model for uniform adoption, however, each state now feels freer to tinker with the admittedly dodgy contents. Some states will do more than others, and even if UCITA eventually passes in all the states (rather than in just some of them), it will still create a national patchwork of laws governing computer transactions.

Perhaps because the law is represented as a magnet to attract high-tech companies eager to flourish under its protection, that aggressively high-tech Commonwealth, Virginia, was the first to pass it, followed by Maryland, who was perhaps wary of any advantage accruing to its first-moving neighbor. Iowa is now the third, perhaps also for reasons of high-tech ambition.

Because the laws vary as they are passed by the several states, it will do to mention only generally some of the provisions of UCITA. On the whole, the law substitutes software licensing for the usual buyer/seller commercial relationship that used to govern buying a box of software; the net effect is to put buyers at a disadvantage. While Open Source fans can be happy that their licenses will now be taken more seriously, so will every other shrinkwrap license that comes in a box. You may be forbidden to pass along (or sell) your copy of the software, for instance, and to be sure of just what the shrinkwrap license says, you will have to read every one of them carefully.

Among the privileges UCITA now allows software vendors is the right to plant a software bomb in their product, just in case you don't live up to the license. In general the vendor is not liable for any damage done by this "self-help," not even if it goes off accidentally, and not even if a visiting cracker decides to activate it. A law like this could be good for Open Source if it stampedes users into buying Open Source so they can check it for self-help code.

Supposedly the law aids the buyer because "mass-market" transactions are supposed to carry a warranty; a look at the Maryland version reveals a definition of "mass-market" so restrictive that few will actually be covered by this warranty. Open Source software, of course, comes with no warranty, and should be able to find a way of disclaiming any, although this will vary state by state. In the meantime, the software business continues as usual: both Open Source and shrinkwrap licenses warn the user to expect nothing.

One interesting feature of the law is that it claims to apply the laws of the adopting state to customers who are out of the state; in Iowa this provision was altered to state that any party in another

UCITA state attempting to apply its laws to a transaction with an Iowan will be subject to the laws of Iowa.

Finally, UCITA bans reverse engineering of software.

Patents

Patent infringement is the monster hiding under every software developer's bed, whether Open Source or not. As Open Source software grows in power, it grows (in theory at least) increasingly likely to infringe some lurking patent.

Up until fewer than ten years ago, business processes and software algorithms could not be patented. Ever since the courts recognized patents in these areas, however, there has been an arms race among software vendors to accumulate as many patents as possible. While everyone protests that these patent arsenals are purely defense, every now and then somebody sets off a missile: Jeff Bezos of Amazon.com shocked online merchants when he used a patent to force BarnesandNoble.com to quit offering one-click ordering; B&N had to add an extra click to the process. Amazon's recent patent on affiliate relationships (having links on your site that send people to do business on your partners' sites) has people wondering when the next litigation will begin: the affiliate practice is common enough on the Internet.

Even the public has begun to notice how absurd the situation has become. Besides the new power to grant patents on business processes and software algorithms, the Patent Office seems to have weakened powers to refuse patents. The shortage of personnel to do thorough research on prior art and the strong possibility that a rejected applicant will simply sue and be granted the patent by court order, combine to make sure that most patents do get approved — even those like US 5443036 *Method of exercising a cat* (http://www.patents.ibm.com/details?&pn=US05443036__) by means of a laser pointer. To a patent attorney, such patents hold no interest because they will obviously never be used against anyone. This one, in fact, might be an office joke, since the inventors have addresses in Virginia suburbs not very far from the Patent Office.

There have been some attempts to adjust to a patent-dominated world in the Open Source area, but not many. The Mozilla Public License (MPL) says that any contributor suing another for patent infringement on the basis of a contribution will lose the right to exercise any license held from that contributor; the IBM Public License increases the penalty by having the plaintiff lose the patent license for the defendant contributor's software, and in the entire program, if the contributor alleges patent infringement against the program itself.

We're All Geeks Now

In the first centuries of our national existence, everyday life involved knowledge of agriculture and mechanics, for the people were largely farmers and artisans and often both. This way of life involved its own politics and political decisions. For the past two centuries technology has grown increasingly important to the way we live and work, and, over the past hundred years, Americans have grown increasingly knowledgeable about such topics as automobiles and business practices and the politics and decisions that surround these fields in turn.

Computers are growing in importance in all of our lives, not just because they are nearly universal in the workplace or because they are increasingly coming into our homes. The PC is only part of the question. Around the world, people's first experience on the Internet will more likely to be through a device than through a PC. The issue is not that Linux wants to be on these devices or that geeks are struggling over a pecking order. The IP issues we have touched on in this chapter will affect every user and every reader of books, newspapers, and magazines, every TV and video viewer, every music listener, and every researcher or library user because our lives will increasingly be pulled into these Internet and computing devices.

These issues are already political, and the proprietary software vendors and IP conglomerates have already structured their own political answers — the DMCA and UCITA — to questions that most citizens scarcely realize exist. For the moment it is the Open Source community that is facing them, but it is time for everyone to become better informed and more deeply involved, whatever opinions they may form on the subject. You may even find yourself joining the Open Source community.

Appendix A

Public Software Licenses

This appendix contains the complete text of the following public software licenses: GNU General Public License, GNU Lesser General Public License, QT Free Edition License, Apache License, Mozilla Public License, IBM Public License, and BitKeeper.

GNU General Public License

`http://www.gnu.org/copyleft/lgpl.html`

Version 2, June 1991

Copyright (©) 1989, 1991 Free Software Foundation, Inc.

59 Temple Place - Suite 330, Boston, MA 02111-1307, USA

Everyone is permitted to copy and distribute verbatim copies of this license document, but changing it is not allowed.

Preamble

The licenses for most software are designed to take away your freedom to share and change it. By contrast, the GNU General Public License is intended to guarantee your freedom to share and change free software — to make sure the software is free for all its users. This General Public License applies to most of the Free Software Foundation's software and to any other program whose authors commit to using it. (Some other Free Software Foundation software is covered by the GNU Library General Public License instead.) You can apply it to your programs, too.

When we speak of free software, we are referring to freedom, not price. Our General Public Licenses are designed to make sure that you have the freedom to distribute copies of free software (and charge for this service if you wish), that you receive source code or can get it if you want it, that you can change the software or use pieces of it in new free programs; and that you know you can do these things.

To protect your rights, we need to make restrictions that forbid anyone to deny you these rights or to ask you to surrender the rights. These restrictions translate to certain responsibilities for you if you distribute copies of the software, or if you modify it.

For example, if you distribute copies of such a program, whether gratis or for a fee, you must give the recipients all the rights that you have. You must make sure that they, too, receive or can get the source code. And you must show them these terms so they know their rights.

We protect your rights with two steps: (1) copyright the software, and (2) offer you this license which gives you legal permission to copy, distribute and/or modify the software.

Also, for each author's protection and ours, we want to make certain that everyone understands that there is no warranty for this free software. If the software is modified by someone else and passed on, we want its recipients to know that what they have is not the original, so that any problems introduced by others will not reflect on the original authors' reputations.

Finally, any free program is threatened constantly by software patents. We wish to avoid the danger that redistributors of a free program will individually obtain patent licenses, in effect making the program proprietary. To prevent this, we have made it clear that any patent must be licensed for everyone's free use or not licensed at all.

The precise terms and conditions for copying, distribution and modification follow.

TERMS AND CONDITIONS FOR COPYING, DISTRIBUTION AND MODIFICATION

0. This License applies to any program or other work which contains a notice placed by the copyright holder saying it may be distributed under the terms of this General Public License. The "Program", below, refers to any such program or work, and a "work based on the Program" means either the Program or any derivative work under copyright law: that is to say, a work containing the Program or a portion of it, either verbatim or with modifications and/or translated into another language. (Hereinafter, translation is included without limitation in the term "modification.") Each licensee is addressed as "you."

Activities other than copying, distribution, and modification are not covered by this License; they are outside its scope. The act of running the Program is not restricted, and the output from the Program is covered only if its contents constitute a work based on the Program (independent of having been made by running the Program). Whether that is true depends on what the Program does.

1. You may copy and distribute verbatim copies of the Program's source code as you receive it, in any medium, provided that you conspicuously and appropriately publish on each copy an appropriate copyright notice and disclaimer of warranty; keep intact all the notices that refer to this License and to the absence of any warranty; and give any other recipients of the Program a copy of this License along with the Program.

You may charge a fee for the physical act of transferring a copy, and you may at your option offer warranty protection in exchange for a fee.

2. You may modify your copy or copies of the Program or any portion of it, thus forming a work based on the Program, and copy and distribute such modifications or work under the terms of Section 1 above, provided that you also meet all of these conditions:

a) You must cause the modified files to carry prominent notices stating that you changed the files and the date of any change.

b) You must cause any work that you distribute or publish, that in whole or in part contains or is derived from the Program or any part thereof, to be licensed as a whole at no charge to all third parties under the terms of this License.

c) If the modified program normally reads commands interactively when run, you must cause it, when started running for such interactive use in the most ordinary way, to print or display an announcement including an appropriate copyright notice and a notice that there is no warranty (or else, saying that you provide a warranty) and that users may redistribute the program under these conditions, and telling the user how to view a copy of this License. (Exception: if the Program itself is interactive but does not normally print such an announcement, your work based on the Program is not required to print an announcement.)

These requirements apply to the modified work as a whole. If identifiable sections of that work are not derived from the Program, and can be reasonably considered independent and separate works in themselves, then this License, and its terms, do not apply to those sections when you distribute them as separate works. But when you distribute the same sections as part of a whole which is a work based on the Program, the distribution of the whole must be on the terms of this License, whose permissions for other licensees extend to the entire whole, and thus to each and every part regardless of who wrote it.

Thus, it is not the intent of this section to claim rights or contest your rights to work written entirely by you; rather, the intent is to exercise the right to control the distribution of derivative or collective works based on the Program.

In addition, mere aggregation of another work not based on the Program with the Program (or with a work based on the Program) on a volume of a storage or distribution medium does not bring the other work under the scope of this License.

3. You may copy and distribute the Program (or a work based on it, under Section 2) in object code or executable form under the terms of Sections 1 and 2 above provided that you also do one of the following:

   a) Accompany it with the complete corresponding machine-readable source code, which must be distributed under the terms of Sections 1 and 2 above on a medium customarily used for software interchange; or,

   b) Accompany it with a written offer, valid for at least three years, to give any third party, for a charge no more than your cost of physically performing source distribution, a complete machine-readable copy of the corresponding source code, to be distributed under the terms of Sections 1 and 2 above on a medium customarily used for software interchange; or,

   c) Accompany it with the information you received as to the offer to distribute corresponding source code. (This alternative is allowed only for noncommercial distribution and only if you received the program in object code or executable form with such an offer, in accord with Subsection b above.)

The source code for a work means the preferred form of the work for making modifications to it. For an executable work, complete source code means all the source code for all modules it contains, plus any associated interface definition files, plus the scripts used to control compilation and installation of the executable. However, as a special exception, the source code distributed need not include anything that is normally distributed (in either source or binary form) with the major components (compiler, kernel, and so on) of the operating system on which the executable runs, unless that component itself accompanies the executable.

If distribution of executable or object code is made by offering access to copy from a designated place, then offering equivalent access to copy the source code from the same place counts as distribution of the source code, even though third parties are not compelled to copy the source along with the object code.

4. You may not copy, modify, sublicense, or distribute the Program except as expressly provided under this License. Any attempt otherwise to copy, modify, sublicense or distribute the Program is void, and will automatically terminate your rights under this License. However, parties who have received copies, or rights, from you under this License will not have their licenses terminated so long as such parties remain in full compliance.

5. You are not required to accept this License, since you have not signed it. However, nothing else grants you permission to modify or distribute the Program or its derivative works. These actions are prohibited by law if you do not accept this License. Therefore, by modifying or distributing the Program (or any work based on the Program), you indicate your acceptance of this License to do so, and all its terms and conditions for copying, distributing or modifying the Program or works based on it.

6. Each time you redistribute the Program (or any work based on the Program), the recipient automatically receives a license from the original licensor to copy, distribute or modify the Program subject to these terms and conditions. You may not impose any further restrictions on the recipients' exercise of

the rights granted herein. You are not responsible for enforcing compliance by third parties to this License.

7. If, as a consequence of a court judgment or allegation of patent infringement or for any other reason (not limited to patent issues), conditions are imposed on you (whether by court order, agreement or otherwise) that contradict the conditions of this License, they do not excuse you from the conditions of this License. If you cannot distribute so as to satisfy simultaneously your obligations under this License and any other pertinent obligations, then as a consequence you may not distribute the Program at all. For example, if a patent license would not permit royalty-free redistribution of the Program by all those who receive copies directly or indirectly through you, then the only way you could satisfy both it and this License would be to refrain entirely from distribution of the Program.

If any portion of this section is held invalid or unenforceable under any particular circumstance, the balance of the section is intended to apply and the section as a whole is intended to apply in other circumstances.

It is not the purpose of this section to induce you to infringe any patents or other property right claims or to contest validity of any such claims; this section has the sole purpose of protecting the integrity of the free software distribution system, which is implemented by public license practices. Many people have made generous contributions to the wide range of software distributed through that system in reliance on consistent application of that system; it is up to the author/donor to decide if he or she is willing to distribute software through any other system and a licensee cannot impose that choice.

This section is intended to make thoroughly clear what is believed to be a consequence of the rest of this License.

8. If the distribution and/or use of the Program is restricted in certain countries either by patents or by copyrighted interfaces, the original copyright holder who places the Program under this License may add an explicit geographical distribution limitation excluding those countries, so that distribution is permitted only in or among countries not thus excluded. In such case, this License incorporates the limitation as if written in the body of this License.

9. The Free Software Foundation may publish revised and/or new versions of the General Public License from time to time. Such new versions will be similar in spirit to the present version, but may differ in detail to address new problems or concerns.

Each version is given a distinguishing version number. If the Program specifies a version number of this License which applies to it and "any later version," you have the option of following the terms and conditions either of that version or of any later version published by the Free Software Foundation. If the Program does not specify a version number of this License, you may choose any version ever published by the Free Software Foundation.

10. If you wish to incorporate parts of the Program into other free programs whose distribution conditions are different, write to the author to ask for permission. For software which is copyrighted by the Free Software Foundation, write to the Free Software Foundation; we sometimes make exceptions for this. Our decision will be guided by the two goals of preserving the free status of all derivatives of our free software and of promoting the sharing and reuse of software generally.

NO WARRANTY

11. BECAUSE THE PROGRAM IS LICENSED FREE OF CHARGE, THERE IS NO WARRANTY FOR THE PROGRAM, TO THE EXTENT PERMITTED BY APPLICABLE LAW. EXCEPT WHEN OTHERWISE STATED IN WRITING THE COPYRIGHT HOLDERS AND/OR OTHER PARTIES PROVIDE THE PROGRAM "AS IS" WITHOUT WARRANTY OF ANY KIND, EITHER EXPRESSED OR IMPLIED, INCLUDING, BUT NOT LIMITED TO, THE IMPLIED WARRANTIES OF MERCHANTABILITY AND FITNESS FOR A PARTICULAR PURPOSE. THE ENTIRE RISK AS TO THE QUALITY AND PERFORMANCE OF THE PROGRAM IS WITH YOU. SHOULD THE PROGRAM PROVE DEFECTIVE, YOU ASSUME THE COST OF ALL NECESSARY SERVICING, REPAIR OR CORRECTION.

12. IN NO EVENT UNLESS REQUIRED BY APPLICABLE LAW OR AGREED TO IN WRITING WILL ANY COPYRIGHT HOLDER, OR ANY OTHER PARTY WHO MAY MODIFY AND/OR REDISTRIBUTE THE PROGRAM AS PERMITTED ABOVE, BE LIABLE TO YOU FOR DAMAGES, INCLUDING ANY GENERAL, SPECIAL, INCIDENTAL OR CONSEQUENTIAL DAMAGES ARISING OUT OF THE USE OR INABILITY TO USE THE PROGRAM (INCLUDING BUT NOT LIMITED TO LOSS OF DATA OR DATA BEING RENDERED INACCURATE OR LOSSES SUSTAINED BY YOU OR THIRD PARTIES OR A FAILURE OF THE PROGRAM TO OPERATE WITH ANY OTHER PROGRAMS), EVEN IF SUCH HOLDER OR OTHER PARTY HAS BEEN ADVISED OF THE POSSIBILITY OF SUCH DAMAGES.

END OF TERMS AND CONDITIONS

How to Apply These Terms to Your New Programs

If you develop a new program, and you want it to be of the greatest possible use to the public, the best way to achieve this is to make it free software which everyone can redistribute and change under these terms.

To do so, attach the following notices to the program. It is safest to attach them to the start of each source file to most effectively convey the exclusion of warranty; and each file should have at least the "copyright" line and a pointer to where the full notice is found.

```
one line to give the program's name and an idea of what it does.

Copyright (C) yyyy  name of author

This program is free software; you can redistribute it and/or modify it under

the terms of the GNU General Public License as published by the Free Software

Foundation; either version 2 of the License, or (at your option) any later

version.

This program is distributed in the hope that it will be useful, but WITHOUT ANY

WARRANTY; without even the implied warranty of MERCHANTABILITY or FITNESS FOR A

PARTICULAR PURPOSE. See the GNU General Public License for more details.

You should have received a copy of the GNU General Public License along with

this program; if not, write to the Free Software Foundation, Inc., 59 Temple

Place - Suite 330, Boston, MA  02111-1307, USA.
```

Also add information on how to contact you by electronic and paper mail.

If the program is interactive, make it output a short notice like this when it starts in an interactive mode:

```
Gnomovision version 69, Copyright (C) yyyy name of author

Gnomovision comes with ABSOLUTELY NO WARRANTY; for details type 'show w'. This

is free software, and you are welcome to redistribute it under certain

conditions; type `show c' for details.
```

The hypothetical commands 'show w' and 'show c' should show the appropriate parts of the General Public License.

Of course, the commands you use may be called something other than `show w' and `show c'; they could even be mouse-clicks or menu items--whatever suits your program.

You should also get your employer (if you work as a programmer) or your school, if any, to sign a "copyright disclaimer" for the program, if necessary. Here is a sample; alter the names:

```
Yoyodyne, Inc., hereby disclaims all copyright interest in the program
'Gnomovision' (which makes passes at compilers) written by James Hacker.
signature of Ty Coon, 1 April 1989
Ty Coon, President of Vice
```

This General Public License does not permit incorporating your program into proprietary programs. If your program is a subroutine library, you may consider it more useful to permit linking proprietary applications with the library. If this is what you want to do, use the GNU Library General Public License instead of this License.

FSF & GNU inquiries & questions to gnu@gnu.org.

Comments on these web pages to webmasters@www.gnu.org, send other questions to gnu@gnu.org.

Copyright notice above.

Free Software Foundation, Inc., 59 Temple Place - Suite 330, Boston, MA 02111, USA

Updated: 16 Feb 1998 tower

GNU LIBRARY GENERAL PUBLIC LICENSE

http://www.gnu.org/copyleft/lgpl.html

Version 2, June 1991

Copyright (©) 1991 Free Software Foundation, Inc. 59 Temple Place - Suite 330, Boston, MA 02111-1307, USA Everyone is permitted to copy and distribute verbatim copies of this license document, but changing it is not allowed.

Note

This is the first released version of the library GPL. It is numbered 2 because it goes with version 2 of the ordinary GPL.

Preamble

The licenses for most software are designed to take away your freedom to share and change it. By contrast, the GNU General Public Licenses are intended to guarantee your freedom to share and change free software — to make sure the software is free for all its users.

This license, the Library General Public License, applies to some specially designated Free Software Foundation software, and to any other libraries whose authors decide to use it. You can use it for your libraries, too.

When we speak of free software, we are referring to freedom, not price. Our General Public Licenses are designed to make sure that you have the freedom to distribute copies of free software (and charge for this service if you wish), that you receive source code or can get it if you want it, that you can change the software or use pieces of it in new free programs; and that you know you can do these things.

To protect your rights, we need to make restrictions that forbid anyone to deny you these rights or to ask you to surrender the rights. These restrictions translate to certain responsibilities for you if you distribute copies of the library, or if you modify it.

For example, if you distribute copies of the library, whether gratis or for a fee, you must give the recipients all the rights that we gave you. You must make sure that they, too, receive or can get the source code. If you link a program with the library, you must provide complete object files to the recipients so that they can relink them with the library, after making changes to the library and recompiling it. And you must show them these terms so they know their rights.

Our method of protecting your rights has two steps: (1) copyright the library, and (2) offer you this license which gives you legal permission to copy, distribute and/or modify the library.

Also, for each distributor's protection, we want to make certain that everyone understands that there is no warranty for this free library. If the library is modified by someone else and passed on, we want its recipients to know that what they have is not the original version, so that any problems introduced by others will not reflect on the original authors' reputations.

Finally, any free program is threatened constantly by software patents. We wish to avoid the danger that companies distributing free software will individually obtain patent licenses, thus in effect transforming the program into proprietary software. To prevent this, we have made it clear that any patent must be licensed for everyone's free use or not licensed at all.

Most GNU software, including some libraries, is covered by the ordinary GNU General Public License, which was designed for utility programs. This license, the GNU Library General Public License, applies to certain designated libraries. This license is quite different from the ordinary one; be sure to read it in full, and don't assume that anything in it is the same as in the ordinary license.

The reason we have a separate public license for some libraries is that they blur the distinction we usually make between modifying or adding to a program and simply using it. Linking a program with a library, without changing the library, is in some sense simply using the library, and is analogous to running a utility program or application program. However, in a textual and legal sense, the linked executable is a combined work, a derivative of the original library, and the ordinary General Public License treats it as such.

Because of this blurred distinction, using the ordinary General Public License for libraries did not effectively promote software sharing, because most developers did not use the libraries. We concluded that weaker conditions might promote sharing better.

However, unrestricted linking of non-free programs would deprive the users of those programs of all benefit from the free status of the libraries themselves. This Library General Public License is intended to permit developers of non-free programs to use free libraries, while preserving your freedom as a user of such programs to change the free libraries that are incorporated in them. (We have not seen how to achieve this as regards changes in header files, but we have achieved it as regards changes in the actual functions of the Library.) The hope is that this will lead to faster development of free libraries.

The precise terms and conditions for copying, distribution and modification follow. Pay close attention to the difference between a "work based on the library" and a "work that uses the library." The former contains code derived from the library, while the latter only works together with the library.

Note that it is possible for a library to be covered by the ordinary General Public License rather than by this special one.

TERMS AND CONDITIONS FOR COPYING, DISTRIBUTION AND MODIFICATION

0. This License Agreement applies to any software library which contains a notice placed by the copyright holder or other authorized party saying it may be distributed under the terms of this Library General Public License (also called "this License"). Each licensee is addressed as "you."

A "library" means a collection of software functions and/or data prepared so as to be conveniently linked with application programs (which use some of those functions and data) to form executables.

The "Library," below, refers to any such software library or work which has been distributed under these terms. A "work based on the Library" means either the Library or any derivative work under copyright law: that is to say, a work containing the Library or a portion of it, either verbatim or with modifications and/or translated straightforwardly into another language. (Hereinafter, translation is included without limitation in the term "modification.")

"Source code" for a work means the preferred form of the work for making modifications to it. For a library, complete source code means all the source code for all modules it contains, plus any associated interface definition files, plus the scripts used to control compilation and installation of the library.

Activities other than copying, distribution and modification are not covered by this License; they are outside its scope. The act of running a program using the Library is not restricted, and output from such a program is covered only if its contents constitute a work based on the Library (independent of the use of the Library in a tool for writing it). Whether that is true depends on what the Library does and what the program that uses the Library does.

1. You may copy and distribute verbatim copies of the Library's complete source code as you receive it, in any medium, provided that you conspicuously and appropriately publish on each copy an appropriate copyright notice and disclaimer of warranty; keep intact all the notices that refer to this License and to the absence of any warranty; and distribute a copy of this License along with the Library.

You may charge a fee for the physical act of transferring a copy, and you may at your option offer warranty protection in exchange for a fee.

2. You may modify your copy or copies of the Library or any portion of it, thus forming a work based on the Library, and copy and distribute such modifications or work under the terms of Section 1 above, provided that you also meet all of these conditions:

a) The modified work must itself be a software library.

b) You must cause the files modified to carry prominent notices stating that you changed the files and the date of any change.

c) You must cause the whole of the work to be licensed at no charge to all third parties under the terms of this License.

d) If a facility in the modified Library refers to a function or a table of data to be supplied by an application program that uses the facility, other than as an argument passed when the facility is invoked, then you must make a good faith effort to ensure that, in the event an application does not supply such function or table, the facility still operates, and performs whatever part of its purpose remains meaningful. (For example, a function in a library to compute square roots has a purpose that is entirely well-defined independent of the application. Therefore, Subsection 2d requires that any application-supplied function or table used by this function must be optional: if the application does not supply it, the square root function must still compute square roots.)

These requirements apply to the modified work as a whole. If identifiable sections of that work are not derived from the Library, and can be reasonably considered independent and separate works in themselves, then this License, and its terms, do not apply to those sections when you distribute them as separate works. But when you distribute the same sections as part of a whole which is a work based on the Library, the distribution of the whole must be on the terms of this License, whose permissions for other licensees extend to the entire whole, and thus to each and every part regardless of who wrote it.

Thus, it is not the intent of this section to claim rights or contest your rights to work written entirely by you; rather, the intent is to exercise the right to control the distribution of derivative or collective works based on the Library.

In addition, mere aggregation of another work not based on the Library with the Library (or with a work based on the Library) on a volume of a storage or distribution medium does not bring the other work under the scope of this License.

3. You may opt to apply the terms of the ordinary GNU General Public License instead of this License to a given copy of the Library. To do this, you must alter all the notices that refer to this License, so that they refer to the ordinary GNU General Public License, version 2, instead of to this License. (If a newer version than version 2 of the ordinary GNU General Public License has appeared, then you can specify that version instead if you wish.) Do not make any other change in these notices.

Once this change is made in a given copy, it is irreversible for that copy, so the ordinary GNU General Public License applies to all subsequent copies and derivative works made from that copy.

This option is useful when you wish to copy part of the code of the Library into a program that is not a library.

4. You may copy and distribute the Library (or a portion or derivative of it, under Section 2) in object code or executable form under the terms of Sections 1 and 2 above provided that you accompany it with the complete corresponding machine-readable source code, which must be distributed under the terms of Sections 1 and 2 above on a medium customarily used for software interchange.

If distribution of object code is made by offering access to copy from a designated place, then offering equivalent access to copy the source code from the same place satisfies the requirement to distribute the source code, even though third parties are not compelled to copy the source along with the object code.

5. A program that contains no derivative of any portion of the Library, but is designed to work with the Library by being compiled or linked with it, is called a "work that uses the Library." Such a work, in isolation, is not a derivative work of the Library, and therefore falls outside the scope of this License.

However, linking a "work that uses the Library" with the Library creates an executable that is a derivative of the Library (because it contains portions of the Library), rather than a "work that uses the library." The executable is therefore covered by this License. Section 6 states terms for distribution of such executables.

When a "work that uses the Library" uses material from a header file that is part of the Library, the object code for the work may be a derivative work of the Library even though the source code is not. Whether this is true is especially significant if the work can be linked without the Library, or if the work is itself a library. The threshold for this to be true is not precisely defined by law.

If such an object file uses only numerical parameters, data structure layouts and accessors, and small macros and small inline functions (ten lines or less in length), then the use of the object file is unrestricted, regardless of whether it is legally a derivative work. (Executables containing this object code plus portions of the Library will still fall under Section 6.)

Otherwise, if the work is a derivative of the Library, you may distribute the object code for the work under the terms of Section 6. Any executables containing that work also fall under Section 6, whether or not they are linked directly with the Library itself.

6. As an exception to the Sections above, you may also compile or link a "work that uses the Library" with the Library to produce a work containing portions of the Library, and distribute that work under terms of your choice, provided that the terms permit modification of the work for the customer's own use and reverse engineering for debugging such modifications.

You must give prominent notice with each copy of the work that the Library is used in it and that the Library and its use are covered by this License. You must supply a copy of this

License. If the work during execution displays copyright notices, you must include the copyright notice for the Library among them, as well as a reference directing the user to the copy of this License. Also, you must do one of these things:

a) Accompany the work with the complete corresponding machine-readable source code for the Library including whatever changes were used in the work (which must be distributed under Sections 1 and 2 above); and, if the work is an executable linked with the Library, with the complete machine-readable "work that uses the Library," as object code and/or source code, so that the user can modify the Library and then relink to produce a modified executable containing the modified Library. (It is understood that the user who changes the contents of definitions files in the Library will not necessarily be able to recompile the application to use the modified definitions.)

b) Accompany the work with a written offer, valid for at least three years, to give the same user the materials specified in Subsection 6a, above, for a charge no more than the cost of performing this distribution.

c) If distribution of the work is made by offering access to copy from a designated place, offer equivalent access to copy the above specified materials from the same place.

d) Verify that the user has already received a copy of these materials or that you have already sent this user a copy.

For an executable, the required form of the "work that uses the Library" must include any data and utility programs needed for reproducing the executable from it. However, as a special exception, the source code distributed need not include anything that is normally distributed (in either source or binary form) with the major components (compiler, kernel, and so on) of the operating system on which the executable runs, unless that component itself accompanies the executable.

It may happen that this requirement contradicts the license restrictions of other proprietary libraries that do not normally accompany the operating system. Such a contradiction means you cannot use both them and the Library together in an executable that you distribute.

7. You may place library facilities that are a work based on the Library side-by-side in a single library together with other library facilities not covered by this License, and distribute such a combined library, provided that the separate distribution of the work based on the Library and of the other library facilities is otherwise permitted, and provided that you do these two things:

   a) Accompany the combined library with a copy of the same work based on the Library, uncombined with any other library facilities. This must be distributed under the terms of the Sections above.

   b) Give prominent notice with the combined library of the fact that part of it is a work based on the Library, and explaining where to find the accompanying uncombined form of the same work.

8. You may not copy, modify, sublicense, link with, or distribute the Library except as expressly provided under this License. Any attempt otherwise to copy, modify, sublicense, link with, or distribute the Library is void, and will automatically terminate your rights under this License. However, parties who have received copies, or rights, from you under this License will not have their licenses terminated so long as such parties remain in full compliance.

9. You are not required to accept this License, since you have not signed it. However, nothing else grants you permission to modify or distribute the Library or its derivative works. These actions are prohibited by law if you do not accept this License. Therefore, by modifying or distributing the Library (or any work based on the Library), you indicate your acceptance of

this License to do so, and all its terms and conditions for copying, distributing or modifying the Library or works based on it.

10. Each time you redistribute the Library (or any work based on the Library), the recipient automatically receives a license from the original licensor to copy, distribute, link with or modify the Library subject to these terms and conditions. You may not impose any further restrictions on the recipients' exercise of the rights granted herein. You are not responsible for enforcing compliance by third parties to this License.

11. If, as a consequence of a court judgment or allegation of patent infringement or for any other reason (not limited to patent issues), conditions are imposed on you (whether by court order, agreement or otherwise) that contradict the conditions of this License, they do not excuse you from the conditions of this License. If you cannot distribute so as to satisfy simultaneously your obligations under this License and any other pertinent obligations, then as a consequence you may not distribute the Library at all. For example, if a patent license would not permit royalty-free redistribution of the Library by all those who receive copies directly or indirectly through you, then the only way you could satisfy both it and this License would be to refrain entirely from distribution of the Library.

If any portion of this section is held invalid or unenforceable under any particular circumstance, the balance of the section is intended to apply, and the section as a whole is intended to apply in other circumstances.

It is not the purpose of this section to induce you to infringe any patents or other property right claims or to contest validity of any such claims; this section has the sole purpose of protecting the integrity of the free software distribution system which is implemented by public license practices. Many people have made generous contributions to the wide range of software distributed through that system in reliance on consistent application of that system; it is up to the author/donor to decide if he or she is willing to distribute software through any other system and a licensee cannot impose that choice.

This section is intended to make thoroughly clear what is believed to be a consequence of the rest of this License.

12. If the distribution and/or use of the Library is restricted in certain countries either by patents or by copyrighted interfaces, the original copyright holder who places the Library under this License may add an explicit geographical distribution limitation excluding those countries, so that distribution is permitted only in or among countries not thus excluded. In such case, this License incorporates the limitation as if written in the body of this License.

13. The Free Software Foundation may publish revised and/or new versions of the Library General Public License from time to time. Such new versions will be similar in spirit to the present version, but may differ in detail to address new problems or concerns.

Each version is given a distinguishing version number. If the Library specifies a version number of this License which applies to it and "any later version," you have the option of following the terms and conditions either of that version or of any later version published by the Free Software Foundation. If the Library does not specify a license version number, you may choose any version ever published by the Free Software Foundation.

14. If you wish to incorporate parts of the Library into other free programs whose distribution conditions are incompatible with these, write to the author to ask for permission. For software which is copyrighted by the Free Software Foundation, write to the Free Software Foundation; we sometimes make exceptions for this. Our decision will be guided by the two goals of preserving the free status of all derivatives of our free software and of promoting the sharing and reuse of software generally.

NO WARRANTY

15. BECAUSE THE LIBRARY IS LICENSED FREE OF CHARGE, THERE IS NO WARRANTY FOR THE LIBRARY, TO THE EXTENT PERMITTED BY APPLICABLE LAW. EXCEPT WHEN OTHERWISE STATED IN WRITING THE COPYRIGHT HOLDERS AND/OR OTHER PARTIES PROVIDE THE LIBRARY "AS IS" WITHOUT WARRANTY OF ANY KIND, EITHER EXPRESSED OR IMPLIED, INCLUDING, BUT NOT LIMITED TO, THE IMPLIED WARRANTIES OF MERCHANTABILITY AND FITNESS FOR A PARTICULAR PURPOSE. THE ENTIRE RISK AS TO THE QUALITY AND PERFORMANCE OF THE LIBRARY IS WITH YOU. SHOULD THE LIBRARY PROVE DEFECTIVE, YOU ASSUME THE COST OF ALL NECESSARY SERVICING, REPAIR OR CORRECTION.

16. IN NO EVENT UNLESS REQUIRED BY APPLICABLE LAW OR AGREED TO IN WRITING WILL ANY COPYRIGHT HOLDER, OR ANY OTHER PARTY WHO MAY MODIFY AND/OR REDISTRIBUTE THE LIBRARY AS PERMITTED ABOVE, BE LIABLE TO YOU FOR DAMAGES, INCLUDING ANY GENERAL, SPECIAL, INCIDENTAL OR CONSEQUENTIAL DAMAGES ARISING OUT OF THE USE OR INABILITY TO USE THE LIBRARY (INCLUDING BUT NOT LIMITED TO LOSS OF DATA OR DATA BEING RENDERED INACCURATE OR LOSSES SUSTAINED BY YOU OR THIRD PARTIES OR A FAILURE OF THE LIBRARY TO OPERATE WITH ANY OTHER SOFTWARE), EVEN IF SUCH HOLDER OR OTHER PARTY HAS BEEN ADVISED OF THE POSSIBILITY OF SUCH DAMAGES.

END OF TERMS AND CONDITIONS

How to Apply These Terms to Your New Libraries

If you develop a new library, and you want it to be of the greatest possible use to the public, we recommend making it free software that everyone can redistribute and change. You can do so by permitting redistribution under these terms (or, alternatively, under the terms of the ordinary General Public License).

To apply these terms, attach the following notices to the library. It is safest to attach them to the start of each source file to most effectively convey the exclusion of warranty; and each file should have at least the "copyright" line and a pointer to where the full notice is found.

```
one line to give the library's name and an idea of what it does. Copyright (C)
year  name of author
This library is free software; you can redistribute it and/or modify it under
the terms of the GNU Library General Public License as published by the Free
Software Foundation; either version 2 of the License, or (at your option) any
later version.
This library is distributed in the hope that it will be useful, but WITHOUT ANY
WARRANTY; without even the implied warranty of MERCHANTABILITY or FITNESS FOR A
PARTICULAR PURPOSE. See the GNU Library General Public License for more details.
You should have received a copy of the GNU Library General Public License along
with this library; if not, write to the Free Software Foundation, Inc., 59
Temple Place - Suite 330, Boston, MA  02111-1307, USA.
```

Also add information on how to contact you by electronic and paper mail.

You should also get your employer (if you work as a programmer) or your school, if any, to sign a "copyright disclaimer" for the library, if necessary. Here is a sample; alter the names:

```
Yoyodyne, Inc., hereby disclaims all copyright interest in the library 'Frob' (a
library for tweaking knobs) written by James Random Hacker.
signature of Ty Coon, 1 April 1990
Ty Coon, President of Vice
```

That's all there is to it!

FSF & GNU inquiries & questions to gnu@gnu.org.

Comments on these web pages to webmasters@www.gnu.org, send other questions to gnu@gnu.org.

Copyright notice above. Free Software Foundation, Inc., 59 Temple Place - Suite 330, Boston, MA 02111, USA

Updated: 8 May 1999 jonas

GNU LESSER GENERAL PUBLIC LICENSE

Version 2.1, February 1999

`http://www.gnu.org/copyleft/lesser.txt`

Copyright (©) 1991, 1999 Free Software Foundation, Inc. 59 Temple Place, Suite 330, Boston, MA02111-1307USA Everyone is permitted to copy and distribute verbatim copies of this license document, but changing it is not allowed.

 Note

This is the first released version of the Lesser GPL. It also counts as the successor of the GNU Library Public License, version 2, hence the version number 2.1.

Preamble

The licenses for most software are designed to take away your freedom to share and change it. By contrast, the GNU General Public Licenses are intended to guarantee your freedom to share and change free software — to make sure the software is free for all its users.

This license, the Lesser General Public License, applies to some specially designated software packages — typically libraries — of the Free Software Foundation and other authors who decide to use it. You can use it too, but we suggest you first think carefully about whether this license or the ordinary General Public License is the better strategy to use in any particular case, based on the explanations below.

When we speak of free software, we are referring to freedom of use, not price. Our General Public Licenses are designed to make sure that you have the freedom to distribute copies of free software (and charge for this service if you wish); that you receive source code or can get it if you want it; that you can change the software and use pieces of it in new free programs; and that you are informed that you can do these things.

To protect your rights, we need to make restrictions that forbid distributors to deny you these rights or to ask you to surrender these rights. These restrictions translate to certain responsibilities for you if you distribute copies of the library or if you modify it.

For example, if you distribute copies of the library, whether gratis or for a fee, you must give the recipients all the rights that we gave you. You must make sure that they, too, receive or can get the source code. If you link other code with the library, you must provide complete object files to the recipients, so that they can relink them with the library after making changes to the library and recompiling it. And you must show them these terms so they know their rights.

We protect your rights with a two-step method: (1) we copyright the library, and (2) we offer you this license, which gives you legal permission to copy, distribute and/or modify the library.

To protect each distributor, we want to make it very clear that there is no warranty for the free library. Also, if the library is modified by someone else and passed on, the recipients should know that what they have is not the original version, so that the original author's reputation will not be affected by problems that might be introduced by others.

Finally, software patents pose a constant threat to the existence of any free program. We wish to make sure that a company cannot effectively restrict the users of a free program by obtaining a restrictive license from a patent holder. Therefore, we insist that any patent license obtained for a version of the library must be consistent with the full freedom of use specified in this license.

Most GNU software, including some libraries, is covered by the ordinary GNU General Public License. This license, the GNU

Lesser General Public License, applies to certain designated libraries, and is quite different from the ordinary General Public License. We use this license for certain libraries in order to permit linking those libraries into non-free programs.

When a program is linked with a library, whether statically or using a shared library, the combination of the two is legally speaking a combined work, a derivative of the original library. The ordinary General Public License therefore permits such linking only if the entire combination fits its criteria of freedom. The Lesser General Public License permits more lax criteria for linking other code with the library.

We call this license the "Lesser" General Public License because it does Less to protect the user's freedom than the ordinary General Public License. It also provides other free software developers Less of an advantage over competing non-free programs. These disadvantages are the reason we use the ordinary General Public License for many libraries. However, the Lesser license provides advantages in certain special circumstances.

For example, on rare occasions, there may be a special need to encourage the widest possible use of a certain library, so that it becomes a de-facto standard. To achieve this, non-free programs must be allowed to use the library. A more frequent case is that a free library does the same job as widely used non-free libraries. In this case, there is little to gain by limiting the free library to free software only, so we use the Lesser General Public License.

In other cases, permission to use a particular library in non-free programs enables a greater number of people to use a large body of free software. For example, permission to use the GNU C Library in non-free programs enables many more people to use the whole GNU operating system, as well as its variant, the GNU/Linux operating system.

Although the Lesser General Public License is Less protective of the users' freedom, it does ensure that the user of a program that is linked with the Library has the freedom and the wherewithal to run that program using a modified version of the Library.

The precise terms and conditions for copying, distribution and modification follow. Pay close attention to the difference between a "work based on the library" and a "work that uses the library." The former contains code derived from the library, whereas the latter must be combined with the library in order to run.

GNU LESSER GENERAL PUBLIC LICENSE TERMS AND CONDITIONS FOR COPYING, DISTRIBUTION AND MODIFICATION

0. This License Agreement applies to any software library or other program which contains a notice placed by the copyright holder or other authorized party saying it may be distributed under the terms of this Lesser General Public License (also called "this License"). Each licensee is addressed as "you."

A "library" means a collection of software functions and/or data prepared so as to be conveniently linked with application programs (which use some of those functions and data) to form executables.

The "Library," below, refers to any such software library or work which has been distributed under these terms. A "work based on the Library" means either the Library or any derivative work under copyright law: that is to say, a work containing the Library or a portion of it, either verbatim or with modifications and/or translated straightforwardly into another language.(Hereinafter, translation is included without limitation in the term "modification.")

"Source code" for a work means the preferred form of the work for making modifications to it. For a library, complete source code means all the source code for all modules it contains, plus any associated interface definition files, plus the scripts used to control compilation and installation of the library.

Activities other than copying, distribution and modification are not covered by this License; they are outside its scope. The act of running a program using the Library is not restricted, and output from such a program is covered only if its contents constitute a work based on the Library (independent of the use of the Library in a tool for writing it).Whether that is true depends on what the Library does and what the program that uses the Library does.

1. You may copy and distribute verbatim copies of the Library's complete source code as you receive it, in any medium, provided that you conspicuously and appropriately publish on each copy an appropriate copyright notice and disclaimer of warranty; keep intact all the notices that refer to this License and to the absence of any warranty; and distribute a copy of this License along with the Library.

   You may charge a fee for the physical act of transferring a copy, and you may at your option offer warranty protection in exchange for a fee.

2. You may modify your copy or copies of the Library or any portion of it, thus forming a work based on the Library, and copy and distribute such modifications or work under the terms of Section 1 above, provided that you also meet all of these conditions:

   a) The modified work must itself be a software library.

   b) You must cause the files modified to carry prominent notices stating that you changed the files and the date of any change.

   c) You must cause the whole of the work to be licensed at no charge to all third parties under the terms of this License.

   d) If a facility in the modified Library refers to a function or a table of data to be supplied by an application program that uses the facility, other than as an argument passed when the facility is invoked, then you must make a good faith effort to ensure that, in the event an application does not supply such function or table, the facility still operates, and performs whatever part of its purpose remains meaningful.

(For example, a function in a library to compute square roots has a purpose that is entirely well-defined independent of the application. Therefore, Subsection 2d requires that any application-supplied function or table used by this function must be optional: if the application does not supply it, the square root function must still compute square roots.)

These requirements apply to the modified work as a whole. If identifiable sections of that work are not derived from the Library, and can be reasonably considered independent and separate works in themselves, then this License, and its terms, do not apply to those sections when you distribute them as separate works. But when you distribute the same sections as part of a whole which is a work based on the Library, the distribution of the whole must be on the terms of this License, whose permissions for other licensees extend to the entire whole, and thus to each and every part regardless of who wrote it.

Thus, it is not the intent of this section to claim rights or contest your rights to work written entirely by you; rather, the intent is to exercise the right to control the distribution of derivative or collective works based on the Library.

In addition, mere aggregation of another work not based on the Library with the Library (or with a work based on the Library) on a volume of a storage or distribution medium does not bring the other work under the scope of this License.

3. You may opt to apply the terms of the ordinary GNU General Public License instead of this License to a given copy of the Library. To do this, you must alter all the notices that refer to this License, so that they refer to the ordinary GNU General Public License, version 2, instead of to this License. (If a newer version than version 2 of the ordinary GNU General Public License has appeared, then you can specify that version instead if you wish.)Do not make any other change in these notices.

Once this change is made in a given copy, it is irreversible for that copy, so the ordinary GNU General Public License applies to all subsequent copies and derivative works made from that copy.

This option is useful when you wish to copy part of the code of the Library into a program that is not a library.

4. You may copy and distribute the Library (or a portion or derivative of it, under Section 2) in object code or executable form under the terms of Sections 1 and 2 above provided that you accompany it with the complete corresponding machine-readable source code, which must be distributed under the terms of Sections 1 and 2 above on a medium customarily used for software interchange.

   If distribution of object code is made by offering access to copy from a designated place, then offering equivalent access to copy the source code from the same place satisfies the requirement to distribute the source code, even though third parties are not compelled to copy the source along with the object code.

5. A program that contains no derivative of any portion of the Library, but is designed to work with the Library by being compiled or linked with it, is called a "work that uses the Library." Such a work, in isolation, is not a derivative work of the Library, and therefore falls outside the scope of this License.

   However, linking a "work that uses the Library" with the Library creates an executable that is a derivative of the Library (because it contains portions of the Library), rather than a "work that uses the library." The executable is therefore covered by this License. Section 6 states terms for distribution of such executables.

   When a "work that uses the Library" uses material from a header file that is part of the Library, the object code for the work may be a derivative work of the Library even though the source code is not. Whether this is true is especially significant if the work can be linked without the Library, or if the work is itself a library. The threshold for this to be true is not precisely defined by law.

If such an object file uses only numerical parameters, data structure layouts and accessors, and small macros and small inline functions (ten lines or less in length), then the use of the object file is unrestricted, regardless of whether it is legally a derivative work.(Executables containing this object code plus portions of the Library will still fall under Section 6.)

Otherwise, if the work is a derivative of the Library, you may distribute the object code for the work under the terms of Section 6. Any executables containing that work also fall under Section 6, whether or not they are linked directly with the Library itself.

6. As an exception to the Sections above, you may also combine or link a "work that uses the Library" with the Library to produce a work containing portions of the Library, and distribute that work under terms of your choice, provided that the terms permit modification of the work for the customer's own use and reverse engineering for debugging such modifications.

   You must give prominent notice with each copy of the work that the Library is used in it and that the Library and its use are covered by this License. You must supply a copy of this License. If the work during execution displays copyright notices, you must include the copyright notice for the Library among them, as well as a reference directing the user to the copy of this License. Also, you must do one of these things:

   a) Accompany the work with the complete corresponding machine-readable source code for the Library including whatever changes were used in the work (which must be distributed under Sections 1 and 2 above); and, if the work is an executable linked with the Library, with the complete machine-readable "work that uses the Library", as object code and/or source code, so that the user can modify the Library and then relink to produce a modified executable containing the modified Library.(It is understood that the user who changes the contents of definitions files in the Library will not necessarily be able to recompile the application to use the modified definitions.)

b) Use a suitable shared library mechanism for linking with the Library. A suitable mechanism is one that (1) uses at run time a copy of the library already present on the user's computer system, rather than copying library functions into the executable, and (2) will operate properly with a modified version of the library, if the user installs one, as long as the modified version is interface-compatible with the version that the work was made with.

c) Accompany the work with a written offer, valid for at least three years, to give the same user the materials specified in Subsection 6a, above, for a charge no more than the cost of performing this distribution.

d) If distribution of the work is made by offering access to copy from a designated place, offer equivalent access to copy the above specified materials from the same place.

e) Verify that the user has already received a copy of these materials or that you have already sent this user a copy.

For an executable, the required form of the "work that uses the Library" must include any data and utility programs needed for reproducing the executable from it. However, as a special exception, the materials to be distributed need not include anything that is normally distributed (in either source or binary form) with the major components (compiler, kernel, and so on) of the operating system on which the executable runs, unless that component itself accompanies the executable.

It may happen that this requirement contradicts the license restrictions of other proprietary libraries that do not normally accompany the operating system. Such a contradiction means you cannot use both them and the Library together in an executable that you distribute.

7. You may place library facilities that are a work based on the Library side-by-side in a single library together with other library facilities not covered by this License, and distribute such a combined library, provided that the separate distribution of the work based on the Library and of the other library facilities is otherwise permitted, and provided that you do these two things:

   a) Accompany the combined library with a copy of the same work based on the Library, uncombined with any other library facilities. This must be distributed under the terms of the Sections above.

   b) Give prominent notice with the combined library of the fact that part of it is a work based on the Library, and explaining where to find the accompanying uncombined form of the same work.

8. You may not copy, modify, sublicense, link with, or distribute the Library except as expressly provided under this License. Any attempt otherwise to copy, modify, sublicense, link with, or distribute the Library is void, and will automatically terminate your rights under this License. However, parties who have received copies, or rights, from you under this License will not have their licenses terminated so long as such parties remain in full compliance.

9. You are not required to accept this License, since you have not signed it. However, nothing else grants you permission to modify or distribute the Library or its derivative works. These actions are prohibited by law if you do not accept this License. Therefore, by modifying or distributing the Library (or any work based on the Library), you indicate your acceptance of this License to do so, and all its terms and conditions for copying, distributing or modifying the Library or works based on it.

10. Each time you redistribute the Library (or any work based on the Library), the recipient automatically receives a license from the original licensor to copy, distribute, link with or modify the Library subject to these terms and conditions. You may not impose any further restrictions on the recipients' exercise of the rights granted herein. You are not responsible for enforcing compliance by third parties with this License.

11. If, as a consequence of a court judgment or allegation of patent infringement or for any other reason (not limited to patent issues), conditions are imposed on you (whether by court order, agreement or otherwise) that contradict the conditions of this License, they do not excuse you from the conditions of this License. If you cannot distribute so as to satisfy simultaneously your obligations under this License and any other pertinent obligations, then as a consequence you may not distribute the Library at all. For example, if a patent license would not permit royalty-free redistribution of the Library by all those who receive copies directly or indirectly through you, then the only way you could satisfy both it and this License would be to refrain entirely from distribution of the Library.

If any portion of this section is held invalid or unenforceable under any particular circumstance, the balance of the section is intended to apply, and the section as a whole is intended to apply in other circumstances.

It is not the purpose of this section to induce you to infringe any patents or other property right claims or to contest validity of any such claims; this section has the sole purpose of protecting the integrity of the free software distribution system which is implemented by public license practices. Many people have made generous contributions to the wide range of software distributed through that system in reliance on consistent application of that system; it is up to the author/donor to decide if he or she is willing to distribute software through any other system and a licensee cannot impose that choice.

This section is intended to make thoroughly clear what is believed to be a consequence of the rest of this License.

12. If the distribution and/or use of the Library is restricted in certain countries either by patents or by copyrighted interfaces, the original copyright holder who places the Library under this License may add an explicit geographical distribution limitation excluding those countries, so that distribution is permitted only in or among countries not thus excluded. In such case, this License incorporates the limitation as if written in the body of this License.

13. The Free Software Foundation may publish revised and/or new versions of the Lesser General Public License from time to time. Such new versions will be similar in spirit to the present version, but may differ in detail to address new problems or concerns.

Each version is given a distinguishing version number. If the Library specifies a version number of this License which applies to it and "any later version," you have the option of following the terms and conditions either of that version or of any later version published by the Free Software Foundation. If the Library does not specify a license version number, you may choose any version ever published by the Free Software Foundation.

14. If you wish to incorporate parts of the Library into other free programs whose distribution conditions are incompatible with these, write to the author to ask for permission. For software which is copyrighted by the Free Software Foundation, write to the Free Software Foundation; we sometimes make exceptions for this. Our decision will be guided by the two goals of preserving the free status of all derivatives of our free software and of promoting the sharing and reuse of software generally.

NO WARRANTY

15. BECAUSE THE LIBRARY IS LICENSED FREE OF CHARGE, THERE IS NO WARRANTY FOR THE LIBRARY, TO THE EXTENT PERMITTED BY APPLICABLE LAW. EXCEPT WHEN OTHERWISE STATED IN WRITING THE COPYRIGHT HOLDERS AND/OR OTHER PARTIES PROVIDE THE LIBRARY "AS IS" WITHOUT WARRANTY OF ANY KIND, EITHER EXPRESSED OR IMPLIED, INCLUDING, BUT NOT LIMITED TO, THE IMPLIED WARRANTIES OF MERCHANTABILITY AND FITNESS FOR A PARTICULAR PURPOSE.THE ENTIRE RISK AS TO THE QUALITY AND PERFORMANCE OF THE LIBRARY IS WITH YOU.SHOULD THE LIBRARY PROVE DEFECTIVE, YOU ASSUME THE COST OF ALL NECESSARY SERVICING, REPAIR OR CORRECTION.

16. IN NO EVENT UNLESS REQUIRED BY APPLICABLE LAW OR AGREED TO IN WRITING WILL ANY COPYRIGHT HOLDER, OR ANY OTHER PARTY WHO MAY MODIFY AND/OR REDISTRIBUTE THE LIBRARY AS PERMITTED ABOVE, BE LIABLE TO YOU FOR DAMAGES, INCLUDING ANY GENERAL, SPECIAL, INCIDENTAL OR CONSEQUENTIAL DAMAGES ARISING OUT OF THE USE OR INABILITY TO USE THE LIBRARY (INCLUDING BUT NOT LIMITED TO LOSS OF DATA OR DATA BEING RENDERED INACCURATE OR LOSSES SUSTAINED BY YOU OR THIRD PARTIES OR A FAILURE OF THE LIBRARY TO OPERATE WITH ANY OTHER SOFTWARE), EVEN IF SUCH HOLDER OR OTHER PARTY HAS BEEN ADVISED OF THE POSSIBILITY OF SUCH DAMAGES.

END OF TERMS AND CONDITIONS

How to Apply These Terms to Your New Libraries

If you develop a new library, and you want it to be of the greatest possible use to the public, we recommend making it free software that everyone can redistribute and change. You can do so by permitting redistribution under these terms (or, alternatively, under the terms of the ordinary General Public License).

To apply these terms, attach the following notices to the library. It is safest to attach them to the start of each source file to most effectively convey the exclusion of warranty; and each file should have at least the "copyright" line and a pointer to where the full notice is found.

one line to give the library's name and a brief idea of what it does. Copyright

(C) year name of author

This library is free software; you can redistribute it and/or modify it under

the terms of the GNU Lesser General Public License as published by the Free

Software Foundation; either version 2 of the License, or (at your option) any

later version.

This library is distributed in the hope that it will be useful, but WITHOUT ANY

WARRANTY; without even the implied warranty of MERCHANTABILITY or FITNESS FOR A

PARTICULAR PURPOSE. See the GNU Lesser General Public License for more details.

You should have received a copy of the GNU Lesser General Public License along

with this library; if not, write to the Free Software Foundation, Inc., 59

Temple Place, Suite 330, Boston, MA02111-1307USA

Also add information on how to contact you by electronic and paper mail.

You should also get your employer (if you work as a programmer) or your school, if any, to sign a "copyright disclaimer" for the library, if necessary. Here is a sample; alter the names:

Yoyodyne, Inc., hereby disclaims all copyright interest in the library `Frob' (a

library for tweaking knobs) written by James Random Hacker.

signature of Ty Coon, 1 April 1990 Ty Coon, President of Vice

That's all there is to it!

FSF & GNU inquiries & questions to gnu@gnu.org.

Comments on these web pages to webmasters@www.gnu.org, send other questions to gnu@gnu.org.

Copyright notice above.

Free Software Foundation, Inc., 59 Temple Place - Suite 330, Boston, MA 02111, USA

Updated: 5 Jun 1999 jonas

The Open Source Definition

http://opensource.org/osd.html

(Version 1.7)

Open source doesn't just mean access to the source code. The distribution terms of open-source software must comply with the following criteria:

1. Free Redistribution

The license may not restrict any party from selling or giving away the software as a component of an aggregate software distribution containing programs from several different sources. The license may not require a royalty or other fee for such sale.

2. Source Code

The program must include source code, and must allow distribution in source code as well as compiled form. Where some form of a product is not distributed with source code, there must be a well-publicized means of obtaining the source code for no more than a reasonable reproduction cost -- preferably, downloading via the Internet without charge. The source code must be the preferred form in which a programmer would modify the program. Deliberately obfuscated source code is not allowed. Intermediate forms such as the output of a preprocessor or translator are not allowed.

3. Derived Works

The license must allow modifications and derived works, and must allow them to be distributed under the same terms as the license of the original software.

4. Integrity of The Author's Source Code.

The license may restrict source-code from being distributed in modified form only if the license allows the distribution of "patch files" with the source code for the purpose of modifying the program at build time. The license must explicitly permit distribution of software built from modified source code. The license may require derived works to carry a different name or version number from the original software.

5. No Discrimination Against Persons or Groups.

The license must not discriminate against any person or group of persons.

6. No Discrimination Against Fields of Endeavor.

The license must not restrict anyone from making use of the program in a specific field of endeavor. For example, it may not restrict the program from being used in a business, or from being used for genetic research.

7. Distribution of License.

The rights attached to the program must apply to all to whom the program is redistributed without the need for execution of an additional license by those parties.

8. License Must Not Be Specific to a Product.

The rights attached to the program must not depend on the program's being part of a particular software distribution. If the program is extracted from that distribution and used or distributed within the terms of the program's license, all parties to whom the program is redistributed should have the same rights as those that are granted in conjunction with the original software distribution.

9. License Must Not Contaminate Other Software.

The license must not place restrictions on other software that is distributed along with the licensed software. For example, the license must not insist that all other programs distributed on the same medium must be open-source software.

Conformance

(This section is not part of the Open Source Definition.)

We think the Open Source Definition captures what the great majority of the software community originally meant, and still mean, by the term "Open Source". However, the term has become widely used and its meaning has lost some precision. The **OSI Certified** mark is OSI's way of certifying that the license under which the software is distributed conforms to the OSD; the generic term "Open Source" cannot provide that assurance, but we still encourage use of the term "Open Source" to mean conformance to the OSD. For information about the **OSI Certified** mark, and for a list of licenses that OSI has approved as conforming to the OSD, see [*list given below*].

Change history:

1.0 – identical to DFSG, except for addition of MPL and QPL to clause 10.

1.1 – added LGPL to clause 10.

1.2 – added public-domain to clause 10.

1.3 – retitled clause 10 and split off the license list, adding material on procedures.

1.4 – Now explicit about source code requirement for PD software.

1.5 – allow ``reasonable reproduction cost" to meet GPL terms.

1.6 – Edited section 10; this material has moved.

1.7 – Section 10 replaced with new "Conformance" section.

Bruce Perens wrote the first draft of this document as 'The Debian Free Software Guidelines,' and refined it using the comments of the Debian developers in a month-long e-mail conference in June, 1997. He removed the Debian-specific references from the document to create the `Open Source Definition'.

Send questions or suggestions about this page to webmaster@ opensource.org

The Approved Licenses

http://www.opensource.org/licenses/

For your convenience, we have collected here copies of the licenses certified by OSI. Commonly-used abbreviations in parentheses follow some full names.

The first four are the `classic' licenses most commonly used for open-source software before the Mozilla release in early 1998. The Mozilla Public license has since become widely used.

The GNU General Public License (GPL);

The GNU Library or `Lesser' Public License (LGPL);

The BSD license;

The MIT license (sometimes called called the `X Consortium license');

The Artistic license;

The Mozilla Public License (MPL);

The Qt Public License (QPL).

The IBM Public License.

The MITRE Collaborative Virtual Workspace License (CVW License).

The Ricoh Source Code Public License.

The Python license.

The zlib/libpng license.

Other conforming licenses include the IJG JPEG library license and the OPL (OpenLDAP Public License).

The "Artistic License"

`http://language.perl.com/misc/Artistic.html`

Preamble

The intent of this document is to state the conditions under which a Package may be copied, such that the Copyright Holder maintains some semblance of artistic control over the development of the package, while giving the users of the package the right to use and distribute the Package in a more-or-less customary fashion, plus the right to make reasonable modifications.

Definitions

"Package" refers to the collection of files distributed by the Copyright Holder, and derivatives of that collection of files created through textual modification.

"Standard Version" refers to such a Package if it has not been modified, or has been modified in accordance with the wishes of the Copyright Holder as specified below.

"Copyright Holder" is whoever is named in the copyright or copyrights for the package.

"You" is you, if you're thinking about copying or distributing this Package.

"Reasonable copying fee" is whatever you can justify on the basis of media cost, duplication charges, time of people involved, and so on. (You will not be required to justify it to the Copyright Holder, but only to the computing community at large as a market that must bear the fee.)

"Freely Available" means that no fee is charged for the item itself, though there may be fees involved in handling the item. It also means that recipients of the item may redistribute it under the same conditions they received it.

1. You may make and give away verbatim copies of the source form of the Standard Version of this Package without restriction, provided that you duplicate all of the original copyright notices and associated disclaimers.

2. You may apply bug fixes, portability fixes and other modifications derived from the Public Domain or from the Copyright Holder. A Package modified in such a way shall still be considered the Standard Version.

3. You may otherwise modify your copy of this Package in any way, provided that you insert a prominent notice in each changed file stating how and when you changed that file, and provided that you do at least ONE of the following:

   a. place your modifications in the Public Domain or otherwise make them Freely Available, such as by posting said modifications to Usenet or an equivalent medium, or placing the modifications on a major archive site such as uunet.uu.net, or by allowing the Copyright Holder to include your modifications in the Standard Version of the Package.

   b. use the modified Package only within your corporation or organization.

   c. rename any non-standard executables so the names do not conflict with standard executables, which must also be provided, and provide a separate manual page for each non-standard executable that clearly documents how it differs from the Standard Version.

   d. make other distribution arrangements with the Copyright Holder.

4. You may distribute the programs of this Package in object code or executable form, provided that you do at least ONE of the following:

   a. distribute a Standard Version of the executables and library files, together with instructions (in the manual page or equivalent) on where to get the Standard Version.

b. accompany the distribution with the machine-readable source of the Package with your modifications.

c. give non-standard executables non-standard names, and clearly document the differences in manual pages (or equivalent), together with instructions on where to get the Standard Version.

d. make other distribution arrangements with the Copyright Holder.

5. You may charge a reasonable copying fee for any distribution of this Package. You may charge any fee you choose for support of this Package. You may not charge a fee for this Package itself. However, you may distribute this Package in aggregate with other (possibly commercial) programs as part of a larger (possibly commercial) software distribution provided that you do not advertise this Package as a product of your own. You may embed this Package's interpreter within an executable of yours (by linking); this shall be construed as a mere form of aggregation, provided that the complete Standard Version of the interpreter is so embedded.

6. The scripts and library files supplied as input to or produced as output from the programs of this Package do not automatically fall under the copyright of this Package, but belong to whomever generated them, and may be sold commercially, and may be aggregated with this Package. If such scripts or library files are aggregated with this Package via the so-called "undump" or "unexec" methods of producing a binary executable image, then distribution of such an image shall neither be construed as a distribution of this Package nor shall it fall under the restrictions of Paragraphs 3 and 4, provided that you do not represent such an executable image as a Standard Version of this Package.

7. C subroutines (or comparably compiled subroutines in other languages) supplied by you and linked into this Package in order to emulate subroutines and variables of the language

defined by this Package shall not be considered part of this Package, but are the equivalent of input as in Paragraph 6, provided these subroutines do not change the language in any way that would cause it to fail the regression tests for the language.

8. Aggregation of this Package with a commercial distribution is always permitted provided that the use of this Package is embedded; that is, when no overt attempt is made to make this Package's interfaces visible to the end user of the commercial distribution. Such use shall not be construed as a distribution of this Package.

9. The name of the Copyright Holder may not be used to endorse or promote products derived from this software without specific prior written permission.

10. THIS PACKAGE IS PROVIDED "AS IS" AND WITHOUT ANY EXPRESS OR IMPLIED WARRANTIES, INCLUDING, WITHOUT LIMITATION, THE IMPLIED WARRANTIES OF MERCHANTIBILITY AND FITNESS FOR A PARTICULAR PURPOSE.

The End

QT FREE EDITION LICENSE

http://www.troll.no/free-license.html

Copyright (©) 1992-1998 Troll Tech AS. All rights reserved.

This is the license for the latest version of Qt Free Edition; it covers private use, use of third-party application programs based on Qt, and development of free software for the free software community.

COPYRIGHT AND RESTRICTIONS

The Qt toolkit is a product of Troll Tech AS. The Qt Free Edition is limited to use with the X Window System.

You may copy this version of the Qt Free Edition provided that the entire archive is distributed unchanged and as a whole, including this notice.

You may use this version of the Qt Free Edition to compile, link and run application programs legally developed by third parties.

You may use the Qt Free Edition to create application programs provided that:

You accept this license.

Your software does not require modifications to Qt Free Edition.

You satisfy ONE of the following three requirements:

EITHER

Users of your software can freely obtain source code for the software, freely modify the source code (possibly with restrictions on copyright notices, attributions and legal responsibility), and freely redistribute original or modified versions of the software.

OR

Your software is distributed under the GNU GENERAL PUBLIC LICENSE, version 2 or later, as defined by the Free Software Foundation.

OR

Your software is distributed under the GNU LIBRARY GENERAL PUBLIC LICENSE, version 2 or later, as defined by the Free Software Foundation.

If you are paid to develop something with Qt Free Edition or it is a part of your job the following conditions also apply:

Your software must not require libraries, programs, data or documentation that are not available outside your organization in order to compile or use.

If and when your organization starts using the software, you must notify Troll Tech AS of the following:

Your organization's name and purpose.

The software's name and purpose.

The software's license.

That your organization considers the software to be free software.

You may also use the Qt Free Edition to create reusable components (such as libraries) provided that you accept the terms above, and in addition that:

Your components' license includes the following text:

[Your package] requires the Qt library, which is copyright Troll Tech AS. Freely distributable programs may generally use Qt Free Edition free of charge, see [README.QT] for details.

README.QT is distributed along with your components.

Qt Free Edition is not distributed as an integral part of your components.

LIMITATIONS OF LIABILITY

Troll Tech AS makes no obligation under this license to support or upgrade Qt Free Edition, or assist in the use of Qt Free Edition.

In no event shall Troll Tech AS be liable for any lost revenue or profits or other direct, indirect, special, incidental or consequential damages, even if Troll Tech has been advised of the possibility of such damages.

QT FREE EDITION IS PROVIDED AS IS WITH NO WARRANTY OF ANY KIND, INCLUDING THE WARRANTY OF DESIGN, MERCHANTABILITY AND FITNESS FOR A PARTICULAR PURPOSE.

THE Q PUBLIC LICENSE version 1.0

Copyright (©) 1999 Troll Tech AS, Norway.

Everyone is permitted to copy and distribute this license document.

The intent of this license is to establish freedom to share and change the software regulated by this license under the open source model.

This license applies to any software containing a notice placed by the copyright holder saying that it may be distributed under the terms of the Q Public License version 1.0. Such software is herein referred to as the Software. This license covers modification and distribution of the Software, use of third-party application programs based on the Software, and development of free software which uses the Software.

Granted Rights

1. You are granted the non-exclusive rights set forth in this license provided you agree to and comply with any and all conditions in this license. Whole or partial distribution of the Software, or software items that link with the Software, in any form signifies acceptance of this license.

2. You may copy and distribute the Software in unmodified form provided that the entire package, including — but not restricted to — copyright, trademark notices and disclaimers, as released by the initial developer of the Software, is distributed.

3. You may make modifications to the Software and distribute your modifications, in a form that is separate from the Software, such as patches. The following restrictions apply to modifications:

   a. Modifications must not alter or remove any copyright notices in the Software.

   b. When modifications to the Software are released under this license, a non-exclusive royalty-free right is granted to the initial developer of the Software to distribute your modification in future versions of the Software provided such versions remain available under these terms in addition to any other license(s) of the initial developer.

4. You may distribute machine-executable forms of the Software or machine-executable forms of modified versions of the Software, provided that you meet these restrictions:

  a. You must include this license document in the distribution.

  b. You must ensure that all recipients of the machine-executable forms are also able to receive the complete machine-readable source code to the distributed Software, including all modifications, without any charge beyond the costs of data transfer, and place prominent notices in the distribution explaining this.

  c. You must ensure that all modifications included in the machine-executable forms are available under the terms of this license.

5. You may use the original or modified versions of the Software to compile, link and run application programs legally developed by you or by others.

6. You may develop application programs, reusable components and other software items that link with the original or modified versions of the Software. These items, when distributed, are subject to the following requirements:

  a. You must ensure that all recipients of machine-executable forms of these items are also able to receive and use the complete machine-readable source code to the items without any charge beyond the costs of data transfer.

  b. You must explicitly license all recipients of your items to use and re-distribute original and modified versions of the items in both machine-executable and source code forms. The recipients must be able to do so without any charges whatsoever, and they must be able to re-distribute to anyone they choose.

c. If the items are not available to the general public, and the initial developer of the Software requests a copy of the items, then you must supply one.

Limitations of Liability

In no event shall the initial developers or copyright holders be liable for any damages whatsoever, including — but not restricted to — lost revenue or profits or other direct, indirect, special, incidental or consequential damages, even if they have been advised of the possibility of such damages, except to the extent invariable law, if any, provides otherwise.

No Warranty

The Software and this license document are provided AS IS with NO WARRANTY OF ANY KIND, INCLUDING THE WARRANTY OF DESIGN, MERCHANTABILITY AND FITNESS FOR A PARTICULAR PURPOSE.

Choice of Law

This license is governed by the Laws of Norway. Disputes shall be settled by Oslo City Court.

Apache License

http://www.apache.org/docs/LICENSE
Copyright (©) 1995-1999 The Apache Group. All rights reserved.

Redistribution and use in source and binary forms, with or without modification, are permitted provided that the following conditions are met:

1. Redistributions of source code must retain the above copyright notice, this list of conditions and the following disclaimer.

2. Redistributions in binary form must reproduce the above copyright notice, this list of conditions and the following disclaimer in the documentation and/or other materials provided with the distribution.

3. All advertising materials mentioning features or use of this software must display the following acknowledgment: "This product includes software developed by the Apache Group for use in the Apache HTTP server project (http://www. apache.org/)."

4. The names "Apache Server" and "Apache Group" must not be used to endorse or promote products derived from this software without prior written permission. For written permission, please contact apache@apache.org.

5. Products derived from this software may not be called "Apache" nor may "Apache" appear in their names without prior written permission of the Apache Group.

6. Redistributions of any form whatsoever must retain the following acknowledgment: "This product includes software developed by the Apache Group for use in the Apache HTTP server project (http://www.apache.org/)."

THIS SOFTWARE IS PROVIDED BY THE APACHE GROUP "AS IS" AND ANY EXPRESSED OR IMPLIED WARRANTIES, INCLUDING, BUT NOT LIMITED TO, THE IMPLIED WARRANTIES OF MERCHANTABILITY AND FITNESS FOR A PARTICULAR PURPOSE ARE DISCLAIMED. IN NO EVENT SHALL THE APACHE GROUP OR ITS CONTRIBUTORS BE LIABLE FOR ANY DIRECT, INDIRECT, INCIDENTAL, SPECIAL, EXEMPLARY, OR CONSEQUENTIAL DAMAGES (INCLUDING, BUT NOT LIMITED TO, PROCUREMENT OF SUBSTITUTE GOODS OR SERVICES; LOSS OF USE, DATA, OR PROFITS; OR BUSINESS INTERRUPTION) HOWEVER

CAUSED AND ON ANY THEORY OF LIABILITY, WHETHER IN CONTRACT, STRICT LIABILITY, OR TORT (INCLUDING NEGLIGENCE OR OTHERWISE) ARISING IN ANY WAY OUT OF THE USE OF THIS SOFTWARE, EVEN IF ADVISED OF THE POSSIBILITY OF SUCH DAMAGE.

This software consists of voluntary contributions made by many individuals on behalf of the Apache Group and was originally based on public domain software written at the National Center for Supercomputing Applications, University of Illinois, Urbana-Champaign. For more information on the Apache Group and the Apache HTTP server project, please see <http://www.apache.org/>.

The 4.4 BSD Copyright

http://www.freebsd.org/copyright/license.html

All of the documentation and software included in the 4.4BSD and 4.4BSD-Lite Releases is copyrighted by The Regents of the University of California.

Copyright 1979, 1980, 1983, 1986, 1988, 1989, 1991, 1992, 1993, 1994 The Regents of the University of California. All rights reserved.

Redistribution and use in source and binary forms, with or without modification, are permitted provided that the following conditions are met:

1. Redistributions of source code must retain the above copyright notice, this list of conditions and the following disclaimer.

2. Redistributions in binary form must reproduce the above copyright notice, this list of conditions and the following disclaimer in the documentation and/or other materials provided with the distribution.

3. All advertising materials mentioning features or use of this software must display the following acknowledgement:

This product includes software developed by the University of California, Berkeley and its contributors.

4. Neither the name of the University nor the names of its contributors may be used to endorse or promote products derived from this software without specific prior written permission.

THIS SOFTWARE IS PROVIDED BY THE REGENTS AND CONTRIBUTORS ``AS IS" AND ANY EXPRESS OR IMPLIED WARRANTIES, INCLUDING, BUT NOT LIMITED TO, THE IMPLIED WARRANTIES OF MER-CHANTABILITY AND FITNESS FOR A PARTICULAR PURPOSE ARE DISCLAIMED. IN NO EVENT SHALL THE REGENTS OR CONTRIBUTORS BE LIABLE FOR ANY DIRECT, INDIRECT, INCIDENTAL, SPECIAL, EXEMPLARY, OR CONSEQUENTIAL DAMAGES (INCLUDING, BUT NOT LIMITED TO, PROCUREMENT OF SUBSTITUTE GOODS OR SERVICES; LOSS OF USE, DATA, OR PROFITS; OR BUSINESS INTERRUPTION) HOWEVER CAUSED AND ON ANY THEORY OF LIABIL-ITY, WHETHER IN CONTRACT, STRICT LIABILITY, OR TORT (INCLUDING NEGLIGENCE OR OTHERWISE) ARISING IN ANY WAY OUT OF THE USE OF THIS SOFTWARE, EVEN IF ADVISED OF THE POSSIBILITY OF SUCH DAMAGE.

The Institute of Electrical and Electronics Engineers and the American National Standards Committee X3, on Information Processing Systems have given us permission to reprint portions of their documentation.

In the following statement, the phrase "this text" refers to por-tions of the system documentation.

Portions of this text are reprinted and reproduced in electronic form in the second BSD Networking Software Release, from IEEE

Std 1003.1-1988, IEEE Standard Portable Operating System Interface for Computer Environments (POSIX), copyright C 1988 by the Institute of Electrical and Electronics Engineers, Inc. In the event of any discrepancy between these versions and the original IEEE Standard, the original IEEE Standard is the referee document.

In the following statement, the phrase "This material" refers to portions of the system documentation.

This material is reproduced with permission from American National Standards Committee X3, on Information Processing Systems. Computer and Business Equipment Manufacturers Association (CBEMA), 311 First St., NW, Suite 500, Washington, DC 20001-2178. The developmental work of Programming Language C was completed by the X3J11 Technical Committee.

The views and conclusions contained in the software and documentation are those of the authors and should not be interpreted as representing official policies, either expressed or implied, of the Regents of the University of California.

freebsd-questions@FreeBSD.ORG

X Window System License - X11R6.4

http://www.x.org/xlicense.html

THE SOFTWARE IS PROVIDED "AS IS," WITHOUT WARRANTY OF ANY KIND, EXPRESS OR IMPLIED, INCLUDING BUT NOT LIMITED TO THE WARRANTIES OF MERCHANTABIL- ITY, FITNESS FOR A PARTICU- LAR PURPOSE AND NONINFRINGEMENT. IN NO EVENT SHALL THE OPEN GROUP BE LIABLE FOR ANY CLAIM, DAMAGES OR OTHER LIABILITY, WHETHER IN AN ACTION OF CONTRACT, TORT OR OTHERWISE, ARISING FROM, OUT OF OR IN CONNECTION WITH THE SOFTWARE OR THE USE OR OTHER DEALINGS IN THE SOFTWARE.

Except as contained in this notice, the name of The Open Group shall not be used in advertising or otherwise to promote the sale, use or other dealings in this Software without prior written authorization from The Open Group.

X Window System is a trademark of The Open Group

(©)1997-1999, The Open Group. All rights reserved. Open Software Foundation, OSF, the OSF logo, OSF/1, OS F/Motif, Motif, X/Open, and UNIX are registered trademarks, and The Open Group, the "X" device, X Consortium and X Window System are trademarks, of The Open Group. All other trademarks mentioned are the property of their respective owners.

MOZILLA PUBLIC LICENSE

Version 1.1
`http://www.mozilla.org/NPL/NPL-1_1Final.html`

1. Definitions.

1.0.1. "Commercial Use" means distribution or otherwise making the Covered Code available to a third party.

1.1. "Contributor" means each entity that creates or contributes to the creation of Modifications.

1.2. **"Contributor Version"** means the combination of the Original Code, prior Modifications used by a Contributor, and the Modifications made by that particular Contributor.

1.3. **"Covered Code"** means the Original Code or Modifications or the combination of the Original Code and Modifications, in each case including portions thereof.

1.4. **"Electronic Distribution Mechanism"** means a mechanism generally accepted in the software development community for the electronic transfer of data.

1.5. **"Executable"** means Covered Code in any form other than Source Code.

1.6. **"Initial Developer"** means the individual or entity identified as the Initial Developer in the Source Code notice required by **Exhibit A.**

1.7. **"Larger Work"** means a work which combines Covered Code or portions thereof with code not governed by the terms of this License.

1.8. **"License"** means this document.

1.8.1. **"Licensable"** means having the right to grant, to the maximum extent possible, whether at the time of the initial grant or subsequently acquired, any and all of the rights conveyed herein.

1.9. **"Modifications"** means any addition to or deletion from the substance or structure of either the Original Code or any previous Modifications. When Covered Code is released as a series of files, a Modification is:

A. Any addition to or deletion from the contents of a file containing Original Code or previous Modifications.

B. Any new file that contains any part of the Original Code or previous Modifications.

1.10. **"Original Code"** means Source Code of computer software code which is described in the Source Code notice required by **Exhibit A** as Original Code, and which, at the time of its release under this License is not already Covered Code governed by this License.

1.10.1. **"Patent Claims"** means any patent claim(s), now owned or hereafter acquired, including without limitation, method, process, and apparatus claims, in any patent Licensable by grantor.

1.11. **"Source Code"** means the preferred form of the Covered Code for making modifications to it, including all modules it contains, plus any associated interface definition files, scripts used to control compilation and installation of an Executable, or source code differential comparisons against either the Original Code or another well known, available Covered Code of the Contributor's choice. The Source Code can be in a compressed or archival form, provided the appropriate decompression or de-archiving software is widely available for no charge.

1.12. **"You"** **(or "Your")** means an individual or a legal entity exercising rights under, and complying with all of the terms of, this License or a future version of this License issued under Section 6.1. For legal entities, "You" includes any entity which controls, is controlled by, or is under common control with You. For purposes of this definition, "control" means (a) the power, direct or indirect, to cause the direction or management of such entity, whether by contract or otherwise, or (b) ownership of more than fifty percent (50%) of the outstanding shares or beneficial ownership of such entity.

2. Source Code License.

2.1. The Initial Developer Grant.

The Initial Developer hereby grants You a world-wide, royalty-free, non-exclusive license, subject to third party intellectual property claims:(a)under intellectual property rights (other than patent or trademark) Licensable by Initial Developer to use, reproduce, modify, display, perform, sublicense and distribute the Original Code (or portions thereof) with or without Modifications, and/or as part of a Larger Work; and

- under Patents Claims infringed by the making, using or selling of Original Code, to make, have made, use, practice, sell, and offer for sale, and/or otherwise dispose of the Original Code (or portions thereof).(c) the licenses granted in this Section 2.1(a) and (b) are effective on the date Initial Developer first distributes Original Code under the terms of this License.

- Notwithstanding Section 2.1(b) above, no patent license is granted: 1) for code that You delete from the Original Code; 2) separate from the Original Code; or 3) for infringements caused by: i) the modification of the Original Code or ii) the combination of the Original Code with other software or devices.

2.2. Contributor Grant.

Subject to third party intellectual property claims, each Contributor hereby grants You a world-wide, royalty-free, non-exclusive license

(a) under intellectual property rights (other than patent or trademark) Licensable by Contributor, to use, reproduce, modify, display, perform, sublicense and distribute the Modifications created by such Contributor (or portions thereof)either on an unmodified basis, with other Modifications, as Covered Code and/or as part of a Larger Work; and

(b) under Patent Claims infringed by the making, using, or selling of Modifications made by that Contributor either alone and/or in combination with its Contributor Version (or portions of such combination), to make, use, sell, offer for sale, have made, and/or otherwise dispose of: 1) Modifications made by that Contributor (or portions thereof); and 2) the combination of Modifications made by that Contributor with its Contributor Version (or portions of such combination).

(c) the licenses granted in Sections 2.2(a) and 2.2(b) are effective on the date Contributor first makes Commercial Use of the Covered Code.

(d) Notwithstanding Section 2.2(b) above, no patent license is granted: 1) for any code that Contributor has deleted from the Contributor Version; 2)separate from the Contributor Version;3)for infringements caused by: i) third party modifications of Contributor Version or ii)the combination of Modifications made by that Contributor with other software(except as part of the Contributor Version) or other devices; or 4) under Patent Claims infringed by Covered Code in the absence of Modifications made by that Contributor.

3. Distribution Obligations.

3.1. Application of License.

The Modifications which You create or to which You contribute are governed by the terms of this License, including without limitation Section 2.2. The Source Code version of Covered Code may be distributed only under the terms of this License or a future version of this License released under Section 6.1, and You must include a copy of this License with every copy of the Source Code You distribute. You may not offer or impose any terms on any Source Code version that alters or restricts the applicable version of this License or the recipients' rights hereunder. However, You may include an additional document offering the additional rights described in Section 3.5.

3.2. Availability of Source Code.

Any Modification which You create or to which You contribute must be made available in Source Code form under the terms of this License either on the same media as an

Executable version or via an accepted Electronic Distribution Mechanism to anyone to whom you made an Executable version available; and if made available via Electronic Distribution Mechanism, must remain available for at least twelve (12) months after the date it initially became available, or at least six (6) months after a subsequent version of that particular Modification has been made available to such recipients. You are responsible for ensuring that the Source Code version remains available even if the Electronic Distribution Mechanism is maintained by a third party.

3.3. Description of Modifications.

You must cause all Covered Code to which You contribute to contain a file documenting the changes You made to create that Covered Code and the date of any change. You must include a prominent statement that the Modification is derived, directly or indirectly, from Original Code provided by the Initial Developer and including the name of the Initial Developer in (a) the Source Code, and (b) in any notice in an Executable version or related documentation in which You describe the origin or ownership of the Covered Code.

3.4. Intellectual Property Matters

(a) Third Party Claims.

If Contributor has knowledge that a license under a third party's intellectual property rights is required to exercise the rights granted by such Contributor under Sections 2.1 or 2.2, Contributor must include a text file with the Source Code distribution titled "LEGAL" which describes the claim and the party making the claim in sufficient detail that a recipient will know whom to contact. If Contributor obtains such knowledge after the Modification is made available as described in Section 3.2, Contributor shall promptly modify the LEGAL file in all copies Contributor makes available thereafter and shall take other steps (such as notifying appropriate mailing lists or newsgroups) reasonably calculated to inform those who received the Covered Code that new knowledge has been obtained.

(b)   Contributor APIs.

If Contributor's Modifications include an application programming interface and Contributor has knowledge of patent licenses which are reasonably necessary to implement that API, Contributor must also include this information in the LEGAL file.(c)Representations. Contributor represents that, except as disclosed pursuant to Section 3.4(a)above, Contributor believes that Contributor's Modifications are Contributor's original creation(s) and/or Contributor has sufficient rights to grant the rights conveyed by this License.

3.5. Required Notices.

You must duplicate the notice in **Exhibit A** in each file of the Source Code. If it is not possible to put such notice in a particular Source Code file due to its structure, then You must include such notice in a location (such as a relevant directory) where a user would be likely to look for such a notice. If You created one or more Modification(s) You may add your name as a Contributor to the notice described in **Exhibit A**. You must also duplicate this License in any documentation for the Source Code where You describe recipients' rights or ownership rights relating to Covered Code. You may choose to offer, and to charge a fee for, warranty, support, indemnity or liability obligations to one or more recipients of Covered Code. However, You may do so only on Your own behalf, and not on behalf of the Initial Developer or any Contributor. You must make it absolutely clear than any such warranty, support, indemnity or liability obligation is offered by You alone, and You hereby agree to indemnify the Initial Developer and every Contributor for any liability incurred by the Initial Developer or such Contributor as a result of warranty, support, indemnity or liability terms You offer.

3.6. Distribution of Executable Versions.

You may distribute Covered Code in Executable form only if the requirements of Section 3.1-3.5 have been met for that Covered Code, and if You include a notice stating that the Source Code version of the Covered Code is available under the terms of this License, including a description of how and where You have fulfilled the obligations of Section 3.2. The notice must be conspicuously included in any notice in an Executable version, related documentation or collateral in which You describe recipients' rights relating to the Covered Code. You may distribute the Executable version of Covered Code or ownership rights under a license of Your choice, which may contain terms different from this License, provided that You are in compliance with the terms of this License and that the license for the Executable version does not attempt to limit or alter the recipient's rights in the Source Code version from the rights set forth in this License. If You distribute the Executable version under a different license You must make it absolutely clear that any terms which differ from this License are offered by You alone, not by the Initial Developer or any Contributor. You hereby agree to indemnify the Initial Developer and every Contributor for any liability incurred by the Initial Developer or such Contributor as a result of any such terms You offer.

3.7. Larger Works.

You may create a Larger Work by combining Covered Code with other code not governed by the terms of this License and distribute the Larger Work as a single product. In such a case, You must make sure the requirements of this License are fulfilled for the Covered Code.

4. Inability to Comply Due to Statute or Regulation.

If it is impossible for You to comply with any of the terms of this License with respect to some or all of the Covered Code due to statute, judicial order, or regulation then You must: (a) comply with the terms of this License to the maximum extent possible; and (b)describe the limitations and the code they affect. Such description must be included in the LEGAL file described in Section 3.4 and must be included with all distributions of the Source Code. Except to the extent prohibited by statute or regulation, such description must be sufficiently detailed for a recipient of ordinary skill to be able to understand it.

5. Application of this License.

This License applies to code to which the Initial Developer has attached the notice in Exhibit A and to related Covered Code.

6. Versions of the License.

6.1. New Versions.

Netscape Communications Corporation ("Netscape") may publish revised and/or new versions of the License from time to time. Each version will be given a distinguishing version number.

6.2. Effect of New Versions.

Once Covered Code has been published under a particular version of the License, You may always continue to use it under the terms of that version. You may also choose to use such Covered Code under the terms of any subsequent version of the License published by Netscape. No one other than Netscape has the right to modify the terms applicable to Covered Code created under this License.

6.3. Derivative Works.

If You create or use a modified version of this License (which you may only do in order to apply it to code which is not already Covered Code governed by this License), You must (a) rename Your license so that the phrases "Mozilla," "MOZILLAPL," "MOZPL," "Netscape," "MPL," "NPL" or any confusingly similar phrase do not appear in your license (except to note that your license differs from this License) and (b)otherwise make it clear that Your version of the license contains terms which differ from the Mozilla Public License and Netscape Public License. (Filling in the name of the Initial Developer, Original Code or Contributor in the notice described in Exhibit A shall not of themselves be deemed to be modifications of this License.)

7. DISCLAIMER OF WARRANTY.

COVERED CODE IS PROVIDED UNDER THIS LICENSE ON AN "AS IS" BASIS, WITHOUT WARRANTY OF ANY KIND, EITHER EXPRESSED OR IMPLIED, INCLUDING, WITHOUT LIMITATION, WARRANTIES THAT THE COVERED CODE IS FREE OF DEFECTS, MER-CHANTABLE, FIT FOR A PARTICULAR PURPOSE OR NON-INFRINGING. THE ENTIRE RISK AS TO THE QUALITY AND PERFORMANCE OF THE COVERED CODE IS WITHYOU. SHOULD ANY COVERED CODE PROVE DEFECTIVE IN ANY RESPECT, YOU (NOT THE INITIAL DEVELOPER OR ANY OTHER CONTRIBUTOR) ASSUME THE COST OF ANY NECESSARY SERVICING, REPAIR OR CORRECTION. THIS DISCLAIMER OF WARRANTY CONSTITUTES AN ESSENTIAL PART OF THIS LICENSE. NO USE OF ANY COVERED CODE IS AUTHORIZED HERE UNDER EXCEPT UNDER THIS DISCLAIMER.

8. TERMINATION.

8.1. This License and the rights granted hereunder will terminate automatically if You fail to comply with terms herein and fail to cure such breach within 30 days of becoming aware of the breach. All sublicenses to the Covered Code which are properly granted shall survive any termination of this License. Provisions which, by their nature, must remain in effect beyond the termination of this License shall survive.

8.2. If You initiate litigation by asserting a patent infringement claim (excluding declatory judgment actions) against Initial Developer or a Contributor (the Initial Developer or Contributor against whom You file such action is referred to as "Participant")alleging that:

(a) such Participant's Contributor Version directly or indirectly infringes any patent, then any and all rights granted by such Participant to You under Sections 2.1 and/or 2.2 of this License shall, upon 60 days notice from Participant terminate prospectively, unless if within 60 days after receipt of notice You either: (i)agree in writing to pay Participant a mutually agreeable reasonable royalty for Your past and future use of Modifications made by such Participant, or (ii) withdraw Your litigation claim with respect to the Contributor Version against such Participant. If within 60 days of notice, a reasonable royalty and payment arrangement are not mutually agreed upon in writing by the parties or the litigation claim is not withdrawn, the rights granted by Participant to You under Sections 2.1 and/or 2.2 automatically terminate at the expiration of the 60 day notice period specified above.

(b) any software, hardware, or device, other than such Participant's Contributor Version, directly or indirectly infringes any patent, then any rights granted to You by such Participant under Sections 2.1(b) and 2.2(b) are revoked effective as of the date You first made, used, sold, distributed, or had made, Modifications made by that Participant.

8.3. If You assert a patent infringement claim against Participant alleging that such Participant's Contributor Version directly or indirectly infringes any patent where such claim is resolved (such as by license or settlement) prior to the initiation of patent infringement litigation, then the reasonable value of the licenses granted by such Participant under Sections 2.1 or 2.2 shall be taken into account in determining the amount or value of any payment or license.

8.4. In the event of termination under Sections 8.1 or 8.2 above, all end user license agreements (excluding distributors and resellers) which have been validly granted by You or any distributor hereunder prior to termination shall survive termination.

9. LIMITATION OF LIABILITY.

UNDER NO CIRCUMSTANCES AND UNDER NO LEGAL THEORY, WHETHER TORT (INCLUDING NEGLIGENCE), CONTRACT, OR OTHERWISE, SHALL YOU, THE INITIAL DEVELOPER, ANY OTHER CONTRIBUTOR, OR ANY DISTRIBUTOR OF COVERED CODE, OR ANY SUPPLIER OF ANY OF SUCH PARTIES, BE LIABLE TO ANY PERSON FOR ANY INDIRECT, SPECIAL, INCIDENTAL, OR CONSEQUENTIAL DAMAGES OF ANY CHARACTER INCLUDING, WITHOUT LIMITATION, DAMAGES FOR LOSS OF GOODWILL, WORK STOPPAGE, COMPUTER FAILURE OR MALFUNCTION, OR

ANY AND ALL OTHER COMMERCIAL DAMAGES OR LOSSES, EVEN IF SUCH PARTY SHALL HAVE BEEN INFORMED OF THE POSSIBILITY OF SUCH DAMAGES. THIS LIMITATION OF LIABILITY SHALL NOT APPLY TO LIABILITY FOR DEATH OR PERSONAL INJURY RESULTING FROM SUCH PARTY'S NEGLIGENCE TO THE EXTENT APPLICABLE LAW PROHIBITS SUCH LIMITATION. SOME JURISDICTIONS DO NOT ALLOW THE EXCLUSION OR LIMITATION OF INCIDENTAL OR CONSEQUENTIAL DAMAGES, SO THIS EXCLUSION AND LIMITATION MAY NOT APPLY TO YOU.

10. U.S. GOVERNMENT END USERS.

The Covered Code is a "commercial item," as that term is defined in 48 C.F.R. 2.101(Oct. 1995), consisting of "commercial computer software" and "commercial computer software documentation," as such terms are used in 48 C.F.R. 12.212 (Sept. 1995).Consistent with 48 C.F.R. 12.212 and 48 C.F.R. 227.7202-1 through 227.7202-4(June 1995), all U.S. Government End Users acquire Covered Code with only those rights set forth herein.

11. MISCELLANEOUS.

This License represents the complete agreement concerning subject matter hereof. If any provision of this License is held to be unenforceable, such provision shall be reformed only to the extent necessary to make it enforceable. This License shall be governed by California law provisions (except to the extent applicable law, if any, provides otherwise), excluding its conflict-of-law provisions. With respect to disputes in which at least one party is a citizen of, or an entity chartered or registered to do business in the United States of America, any litigation relating to this License shall be subject to the jurisdiction of the Federal Courts of the Northern District of California, with venue lying in Santa Clara County, California, with the losing party responsible for costs, including without limitation, court costs and reasonable attorneys' fees and expenses. The application of the United Nations Convention on Contracts for the International Sale of Goods is expressly excluded. Any law or regulation which provides that the language of a contract shall be construed against the drafter shall not apply to this License.

12. RESPONSIBILITY FOR CLAIMS.

As between Initial Developer and the Contributors, each party is responsible for claims and damages arising, directly or indirectly, out of its utilization of rights under this License and You agree to work with Initial Developer and Contributors to distribute such responsibility on an equitable basis. Nothing herein is intended or shall be deemed to constitute any admission of liability.

13. MULTIPLE-LICENSED CODE.

Initial Developer may designate portions of the Covered Code as "Multiple-Licensed." "Multiple-Licensed" means that the Initial Developer permits you to utilize portions of the Covered Code under Your choice of the NPL or the alternative licenses, if any, specified by the Initial Developer in the file described in Exhibit A.

EXHIBIT A – Mozilla Public License.

"The contents of this file are subject to the Mozilla Public License Version 1.1 (the "License"); you may not use this file except in compliance with the License. You may obtain a copy of the License at http://www.mozilla.org/MPL/

Software distributed under the License is distributed on an "AS IS" basis, WITHOUT WARRANTY OF ANY KIND, either express or implied. See the License for the specific language governing rights and limitations under the License.

The Original Code is _____.

The Initial Developer of the Original Code is _____.

Portions created by_____ are Copyright (©) _____. All Rights Reserved.

Contributor(s): _____.

Alternatively, the contents of this file may be used under the terms of the _____ license(the "[___] License"), in which case the provisions of [_____] License are applicable instead of those above. If you wish to allow use of your version of this file only under the terms of the [___] License and not to allow others to use your version of this file under the MPL, indicate your decision by deleting the provisions above and replace them with the notice and other provisions required by the [___] License. If you do not delete the provisions above, a recipient may use your version of this file under either the MPL or the [___] License."

[NOTE: The text of this Exhibit A may differ slightly from the text of the notices in the Source Code files of the Original Code. You should use the text of this Exhibit A rather than the text found in the Original Code Source Code for Your Modifications.]

AMENDMENTS

The Netscape Public License Version 1.1 ("NPL") consists of the Mozilla Public License Version 1.1 with the following Amendments, including Exhibit A-Netscape Public License. Files identified with "Exhibit A-Netscape Public License" are governed by the Netscape Public License Version 1.1.

Additional Terms applicable to the Netscape Public License.

I. Effect.

These additional terms described in this Netscape Public License -- Amendments shall apply to the Mozilla Communicator client code and to all Covered Code under this License.

II. "Netscape's Branded Code" means Covered Code that Netscape distributes and/or permits others to distribute under one or more trademark(s)which are controlled by Netscape but which are not licensed for use under this License.

III. Netscape and logo.

This License does not grant any rights to use the trademarks "Netscape", the "Netscape N and horizon" logo or the "Netscape lighthouse" logo, "Netcenter," "Gecko," "Java" or "JavaScript," "Smart Browsing" even if such marks are included in the Original Code or Modifications.

IV. Inability to Comply Due to Contractual Obligation.

Prior to licensing the Original Code under this License, Netscape has licensed third party code for use in Netscape's Branded Code. To the extent that Netscape is limited contractually from making such third party code available under this License, Netscape may choose to reintegrate such code into Covered Code without being required to distribute such code in Source Code form, even if such code would otherwise be considered "Modifications" under this License.

V. Use of Modifications and Covered Code by Initial Developer.

V.1. In General.

The obligations of Section 3 apply to Netscape, except to the extent specified in this Amendment, Section V.2 and V.3.

V.2. Other Products.

Netscape may include Covered Code in products other than the Netscape's Branded Code which are released by Netscape during the two(2) years following the release date of the Original Code, without such additional products becoming subject to the terms of this License, and may license such additional products on different terms from those contained in this License.

V.3. Alternative Licensing.

Netscape may license the Source Code of Netscape's Branded Code, including Modifications incorporated therein, without such Netscape Branded Code becoming subject to the terms of this License, and may license such Netscape Branded Code on different terms from those contained in this License.

VI. Litigation.

Notwithstanding the limitations of Section 11 above, the provisions regarding litigation in Section 11(a), (b) and (c) of the License shall apply to all disputes relating to this License.

EXHIBIT A - Netscape Public License.

"The contents of this file are subject to the Netscape Public License Version 1.1 (the "License"); you may not use this file except in compliance with the License. You may obtain a copy of the License at http://www.mozilla.org/NPL/

Software distributed under the License is distributed on an "AS IS" basis, WITHOUT WARRANTY OF ANY KIND, either express or implied. See the License for the specific language governing rights and limitations under the License.

The Original Code is Mozilla Communicator client code, released March 31,1998.

The Initial Developer of the Original Code is Netscape Communications Corporation. Portions created by Netscape are Copyright (©) 1998-1999Netscape Communications Corporation. All Rights Reserved.

Contributor(s): _____. Alternatively, the contents of this file may be used under the terms of the _____license (the "[___] License"), in which case the provisions of [_____] License are applicable instead of those above. If you wish to allow use of your version of this file only under the terms of the [___] License and not to allow others to use your version of this file under the NPL, indicate your decision by deleting the provisions above and replace them with the notice and other provisions required by the [___] License. If you do not delete the provisions above, a recipient may use your version of this file under either the NPL or the [___] License."

Copyright (©) 1998-1999 The Mozilla Organization.

IBM PUBLIC LICENSE VERSION 1.0 - JIKES COMPILER

`http://www.research.ibm.com/jikes/license/license3.htm`

THE ACCOMPANYING PROGRAM IS PROVIDED UNDER THE TERMS OF THIS IBM PUBLIC LICENSE ("AGREEMENT"). ANY USE, REPRODUCTION OR DISTRIBUTION OF THE PROGRAM CONSTITUTES RECIPIENT'S ACCEPTANCE OF THIS AGREEMENT.

1. DEFINITIONS

"Contribution" means:

a. in the case of International Business Machines Corporation ("IBM"), the Original Program, and

b. in the case of each Contributor,

  i. changes to the Program, and

  ii. additions to the Program;

where such changes and/or additions to the Program originate from and are distributed by that particular Contributor. A Contribution 'originates' from a Contributor if it was added to the Program by such Contributor itself or anyone acting on such Contributor's behalf. Contributions do not include additions to the Program which:

(i) are separate modules of software distributed in conjunction with the Program under their own license agreement, and

(ii) are not derivative works of the Program.

"Contributor" means IBM and any other entity that distributes the Program.

"Licensed Patents " mean patent claims licensable by a Contributor which are necessarily infringed by the use or sale of its Contribution alone or when combined with the Program.

"Original Program" means the original version of the software accompanying this Agreement as released by IBM, including source code, object code and documentation, if any.

"Program" means the Original Program and Contributions.

"Recipient" means anyone who receives the Program under this Agreement, including all Contributors.

2. GRANT OF RIGHTS

a. Subject to the terms of this Agreement, each Contributor hereby grants Recipient a non-exclusive, worldwide, royalty-free copyright license to reproduce, prepare derivative works of, publicly display, publicly perform, distribute and sublicense the Contribution of such Contributor, if any, and such derivative works, in source code and object code form.

b. Subject to the terms of this Agreement, each Contributor hereby grants Recipient a non-exclusive, worldwide, royalty-free patent license under Licensed Patents to make, use, sell, offer to sell, import and otherwise transfer the Contribution of such Contributor, if any, in source code and object code form. This patent license shall apply to the combination of the Contribution and the Program if, at the time the Contribution is added by the Contributor, such addition of the Contribution causes such combination to be covered by the Licensed Patents. The patent license shall not apply to any other combinations which include the Contribution. No hardware per se is licensed hereunder.

c. Recipient understands that although each Contributor grants the licenses to its Contributions set forth herein, no assurances are provided by any Contributor that the Program does not infringe the patent or other intellectual property rights of any other entity. Each Contributor disclaims any liability to Recipient for claims brought by any other entity based on infringement of intellectual property rights or otherwise. As a condition to exercising the rights and licenses granted hereunder, each Recipient hereby assumes sole responsibility to secure any other intellectual property rights needed, if any. For example, if a third party patent license is required to allow Recipient to distribute the Program, it is Recipient's responsibility to acquire that license before distributing the Program.

d. Each Contributor represents that to its knowledge it has sufficient copyright rights in its Contribution, if any, to grant the copyright license set forth in this Agreement.

3. REQUIREMENTS

A Contributor may choose to distribute the Program in object code form under its own license agreement, provided that:

a. it complies with the terms and conditions of this Agreement; and

b. its license agreement:

i. effectively disclaims on behalf of all Contributors all warranties and conditions, express and implied, including warranties or conditions of title and non-infringement, and implied warranties or conditions of merchantability and fitness for a particular purpose;

ii. effectively excludes on behalf of all Contributors all liability for damages, including direct, indirect, special, incidental and consequential damages, such as lost profits;

iii. states that any provisions which differ from this Agreement are offered by that Contributor alone and not by any other party; and

iv. states that source code for the Program is available from such Contributor, and informs licensees how to obtain it in a reasonable manner on or through a medium customarily used for software exchange.

When the Program is made available in source code form:

a. it must be made available under this Agreement; and

b. a copy of this Agreement must be included with each copy of the Program.

Each Contributor must include the following in a conspicuous location in the Program:

Copyright (©) 1996, 1999 International Business Machines Corporation and others. All Rights Reserved.

In addition, each Contributor must identify itself as the originator of its Contribution, if any, in a manner that reasonably allows subsequent Recipients to identify the originator of the Contribution.

4. COMMERCIAL DISTRIBUTION

Commercial distributors of software may accept certain responsibilities with respect to end users, business partners and the like. While this license is intended to facilitate the commercial use of the Program, the Contributor who includes the Program in a commercial product offering should do so in a manner which does not create potential liability for other Contributors. Therefore, if a Contributor includes the Program in a commercial product offering, such Contributor ("Commercial Contributor") hereby agrees to defend and indemnify every other Contributor ("Indemnified Contributor") against any losses, damages and costs (collectively "Losses") arising from claims, lawsuits and other legal actions brought by a third party against the Indemnified Contributor to the extent caused by the acts or omissions of such Commercial Contributor in connection with its distribution of the Program in a commercial product offering. The obligations in this section do not apply to any claims or Losses relating to any actual or alleged intellectual property infringement. In order to qualify, an Indemnified Contributor must:

a) promptly notify the Commercial Contributor in writing of such claim, and

b) allow the Commercial Contributor to control, and cooperate with the Commercial Contributor in, the defense and any related settlement negotiations. The Indemnified Contributor may participate in any such claim at its own expense.

For example, a Contributor might include the Program in a commercial product offering, Product X. That Contributor is then a Commercial Contributor. If that Commercial Contributor then makes performance claims, or offers warranties related to Product X, those performance claims and warranties are such Commercial Contributor's responsibility alone.

Under this section, the Commercial Contributor would have to defend claims against the other Contributors related to those performance claims and warranties, and if a court requires any other Contributor to pay any damages as a result, the Commercial Contributor must pay those damages.

5. NO WARRANTY

EXCEPT AS EXPRESSLY SET FORTH IN THIS AGREEMENT, THE PROGRAM IS PROVIDED ON AN "AS IS" BASIS, WITHOUT WARRANTIES OR CONDITIONS OF ANY KIND, EITHER EXPRESS OR IMPLIED INCLUDING, WITHOUT LIMITATION, ANY WARRANTIES OR CONDITIONS OF TITLE, NON-INFRINGEMENT, MERCHANTABILITY OR FITNESS FOR A PARTICULAR PURPOSE. Each Recipient is solely responsible for determining the appropriateness of using and distributing the Program and assumes all risks associated with its exercise of rights under this Agreement, including but not limited to the risks and costs of program errors, compliance with applicable laws, damage to or loss of data, programs or equipment, and unavailability or interruption of operations.

6. DISCLAIMER OF LIABILITY

EXCEPT AS EXPRESSLY SET FORTH IN THIS AGREE-MENT, NEITHER RECIPIENT NOR ANY CONTRIBU-TORS SHALL HAVE ANY LIABILITY FOR ANY DIRECT, INDIRECT, INCIDENTAL, SPECIAL, EXEMPLARY, OR CONSEQUENTIAL DAMAGES (INCLUDING WITHOUT LIMITATION LOST PROFITS), HOWEVER CAUSED AND ON ANY THEORY OF LIABILITY, WHETHER IN CON-TRACT, STRICT LIABILITY, OR TORT (INCLUDING NEGLIGENCE OR OTHERWISE) ARISING IN ANY WAY OUT OF THE USE OR DISTRIBUTION OF THE PRO-GRAM OR THE EXERCISE OF ANY RIGHTS GRANTED HEREUNDER, EVEN IF ADVISED OF THE POSSIBILITY OF SUCH DAMAGES.

7. GENERAL

If any provision of this Agreement is invalid or unenforceable under applicable law, it shall not affect the validity or enforceability of the remainder of the terms of this Agreement, and without further action by the parties hereto, such provision shall be reformed to the minimum extent necessary to make such provision valid and enforceable.

If Recipient institutes patent litigation against a Contributor with respect to a patent applicable to software (including a cross-claim or counterclaim in a lawsuit), then any patent licenses granted by that Contributor to such Recipient under this Agreement shall terminate as of the date such litigation is filed. In addition, if

Recipient institutes patent litigation against any entity (including a cross-claim or counterclaim in a lawsuit) alleging that the Program itself (excluding combinations of the Program with other software or hardware) infringes such Recipient's patent(s), then such Recipient's rights granted under Section 2(b) shall terminate as of the date such litigation is filed.

All Recipient's rights under this Agreement shall terminate if it fails to comply with any of the material terms or conditions of this Agreement and does not cure such failure in a reasonable period of time after becoming aware of such noncompliance.

If all Recipient's rights under this Agreement terminate, Recipient agrees to cease use and distribution of the Program as soon as reasonably practicable. However, Recipient's obligations under this Agreement and any licenses granted by Recipient relating to the Program shall continue and survive.

IBM may publish new versions (including revisions) of this Agreement from time to time. Each new version of the Agreement will be given a distinguishing version number. The Program (including Contributions) may always be distributed subject to the version of the Agreement under which it was received. In addition, after a new version of the Agreement is published, Contributor may elect to distribute the Program (including its Contributions) under the new version. No one other than IBM has the right to modify this Agreement. Except as expressly stated in Sections 2(a) and 2(b) above,

Recipient receives no rights or licenses to the intellectual property of any Contributor under this Agreement, whether expressly, by implication, estoppel or otherwise. All rights in the Program not expressly granted under this Agreement are reserved.

This Agreement is governed by the laws of the State of New York and the intellectual property laws of the United States of America. No party to this Agreement will bring a legal action under this Agreement more than one year after the cause of action arose. Each party waives its rights to a jury trial in any resulting litigation.

BitKeeper

BitKeeper License draft 1.21, 12/16/99

`http://bitkeeper.com/license.html`

1. DEFINITIONS

BKL: This license in its entirety, also known as the BitKeeper License.

You: The licensee of the BitKeeper Software.

BitMover: The licensor of the BitKeeper Software.

GPL: The Free Software Foundation's General Public License, version 2.

BitKeeper Software:

+ In the case of a binary distribution, the complete set of executable programs and any accompanying files, such as documentation, known as the BitKeeper Software.

+ In the case of an installation for use, the complete set of executable programs and any accompanying files, such as documentation, known as the BitKeeper Software.

+ In the case of a source distribution, the complete set of source files, known as the BitKeeper Software.

+ In any case, the set of files distributed must include all files and programs distributed by BitMover, Inc. as part of the BitKeeper Software.

Open Logging: The transmission of meta information, such as change commentaries about the data managed by the BitKeeper Software, to a functioning Open Logging server in the openlogging.org domain (or an alternative domain as posted on www.bitkeeper.com/logging).

Conforming Software: BitKeeper Software that:

(i) passes all of the current regression tests for that version of the Bit Keeper Software; the tests must be unmodified and are not licensed under the BKL;

(ii) performs Open Logging identically to a current or recent (less than one year old) version of the BitKeeper Software as distributed by BitMover, Inc.; and

(iii) is distributed under the terms of the BKL.

BitKeeper Project: A set of files managed by the same BitKeeper ChangeSet file. There may be multiple instances of the project; each instance is called a repository.

Single user BitKeeper project: A BitKeeper project wherein all changes to all files are made by the same person.

2. LICENSE GRANTS

(a) Licensees may freely install, use, copy, and distribute unmodified BitKeeper Software.

(b) Licensees may create, install, use, and distribute, derivative works which are (or, in the case of a source distribution, will produce) Conforming Software.

(c) The subset of the system known as the MDBM library is also available under the terms of the GPL.

(d) The subset of the system known as the LEAKS library is also available under the terms of the GPL.

(f) The subset of the system known as the INSTALLER is also available under the terms of the GPL.

3. LICENSEE OBLIGATIONS

(a) Maintaining Open Logging Feature: You hereby warrant that you will not take any action to disable or otherwise interfere with the Open Logging feature of the BitKeeper Software. You hereby warrant that you will take any necessary action to enable the transmission of the log messages, provided that it is possible for electronic mail to be sent from your site.

(b) Modifications: You may provide, at your option, modifications to BitMover. By doing so, You grant BitMover permission to distribute the modification under any license.

This provision survives any termination of your license. In return, BitMover promises that future versions of the BitKeeper Software that contain your modification will be available under the BKL.

(c) Inclusion with another application having source and/or configuration management features: If you include the BitKeeper Software for use with a system having source and/or configuration management features, that system must inform the user, at each execution of BitKeeper code, "This software is using part of the BitKeeper configuration management system."

4. NON-CONFORMING USE

4.1. Single user projects

For single user BitKeeper projects, Open Logging is optional.

4.2. Closed Use

Closed use is the use of the BitKeeper Software without Open Logging. Closed use of the BitKeeper Software requires that you (or your organization) purchase closed use licenses for all users of the BitKeeper Software within your organization. Closed use licensees receive support, tested upgrades, and may choose to disable Open Logging. The BKL does not convey authority to make closed use of the BitKeeper Software.

4.3. Logging Waivers

Sites which do not wish to have their changes logged on an Open Logging server, such as educational or research institutes, should apply for, and may be granted, a written waiver from BitMover, Inc. After applying for a written waiver, such an institution may use the BitKeeper Software without Open Logging, for up to 90 days, or until a response is received from BitMover, Inc., whichever comes first. Should BitMover not grant your waiver request, you have the option of converting to Open Logging, immediately terminating your use of the BitKeeper Software or continuing your use after purchasing closed use license[s].

4.4. Damages

Use, copying, or distribution of non-conforming software without purchasing a closed use license, receiving a logging waiver, or using BitKeeper Software only for single user projects is a violation of copyrights held by BitMover on the BitKeeper Software. Damages for copyright infringement are the greater of actual damages or statutory damages, which are currently up to $100,000 per infringement.

5. CONVERSION TO THE GPL

The BitKeeper Software will be made available under the terms of the GPL in the event that all Open Logging servers cease to function for a continuous period of 180 days starting on or after June 1st 2000.

6. DISCLAIMER OF WARRANTY

COVERED CODE IS PROVIDED UNDER THIS LICENSE ON AN "AS IS" BASIS, WITHOUT WARRANTY OR INDEMNIFICATION OF ANY KIND, EITHER EXPRESSED OR IMPLIED, INCLUDING, WITHOUT LIMITATION, WARRANTIES OR INDEMNITIES CONCERNING INTELLECTUAL PROPERTIES (E.G. PATENTS OR COPYRIGHTS), WARRANTIES THAT THE COVERED CODE IS FREE OF DEFECTS, MERCHANTABLE, FIT FOR A PARTICULAR PURPOSE OR NON-INFRINGING.

SHOULD ANY PORTION OF BITKEEPER SOFTWARE PROVE DEFECTIVE IN ANY RESPECT, YOU ASSUME THE COST OF ANY RESULTING DAMAGES, NECESSARY SERVICING, REPAIR OR

CORRECTION. THIS DISCLAIMER OF WAR-
RANTY CONSTITUTES AN ESSENTIAL PART OF
THIS LICENSE. NO USE OF BITKEEPER SOFT-
WARE IS AUTHORIZED HERE UNDER EXCEPT
SUBJECT TO THIS DISCLAIMER.

7. TERMINATION

+ This License and the rights granted hereunder will terminate automatically if you fail to comply with terms herein.
Provisions which, by their nature, should remain in effect
beyond the termination of this License shall survive
including, without limitation, Section 3(b).

+ If the Open Logging requirement is found to be unenforceable, then this license automatically terminates unless You
continue to comply with the Open Logging requirement.

+ Should You or your organization choose to institute
patent, copyright, and/or intellectual property litigation
against BitMover, Inc. with respect to the BitKeeper
Software, then this License and the rights granted hereunder will terminate automatically as of the date such litigation is filed.

8. LIMITATION OF LIABILITY

TO THE FULL EXTENT ALLOWED BY APPLICA-
BLE LAW, BITMOVER'S LIABILITY TO YOU FOR
CLAIMS RELATING TO THIS LICENSE, WHETHER
FOR BREACH OR IN TORT, SHALL BE LIMITED
TO ONE HUNDRED PERCENT (100%) OF THE
AMOUNT HAVING THEN ACTUALLY BEEN PAID
BY YOU TO BITMOVER FOR ALL COPIES
LICENSED HERE UNDER OF THE PARTICULAR
ITEMS GIVING RISE TO SUCH CLAIM, IF ANY.

IN NO EVENT WILL BITMOVER BE LIABLE
FOR ANY INDIRECT, PUNITIVE, SPECIAL, INCI-
DENTAL OR CONSEQUENTIAL DAMAGES IN

CONNECTION WITH OR ARISING OUT OF THIS LICENSE (INCLUDING, WITHOUT LIMITATION, LOSS OF PROFITS, USE, DATA, OR OTHER ECONOMIC ADVANTAGE), HOWEVER IT ARISES AND ON ANY THEORY OF LIABILITY, WHETHER IN AN ACTION FOR CONTRACT, STRICT LIABILITY OR TORT (INCLUDING NEGLIGENCE) OR OTHERWISE, WHETHER OR NOT SUCH PARTY HAS BEEN ADVISED OF THE POSSIBILITY OF SUCH DAMAGE AND NOTWITHSTANDING THE FAILURE OF ESSENTIAL PURPOSE OF ANY REMEDY.

9. MISCELLANEOUS

9.1. Merger

This License represents the complete agreement between You and BitMover regarding the BitKeeper Software covered by this License.

9.2. Assignment

BitMover may assign this License, and its rights and obligations hereunder, at its sole discretion.

9.3. Severability

If any provision of this License is held to be unenforceable, such provision shall be reformed only to the extent necessary to make it enforceable.

9.4. Governing Law/Jurisdiction

This License shall be governed by the laws of the US and the State of California, as applied to contracts entered into and to be performed in California between California residents.

BKL   Copyright (©) 1999 BitMover, Inc.   BKL

Appendix B

Web Resources

Open Source software lives on the Internet; that there are so many constantly changing sources is a great help to Community members and a hindrance for outsiders. The links given here are by no means all the links listed in the book; for specific topics the Index may be a better guide because it will take you to the pages discussing the topic, where you will probably find some pertinent Internet sites.

Open Source and Linux Links

Even under the topics listed in this appendix, the sites listed are hardly complete, but they are often good places to begin; many of them have good link listings of their own. Some of the sites in this list are not mentioned elsewhere in this book.

General information sites

You can get some general information about Linux from the following sites:

About Linux (`http://AboutLinux.com`)

CNet Help.com Linux (`http://searchlinux.com`)

Feedmag Links to Articles (`http://www.feedmag.com/oss/ossjournalism.html`)

Google Linux Search (`http://www.google.com/linux`)

justlinux (http://www.justlinux.com/)

Linux Events (http://linsight.com)

Linux Focus (http://linuxfocus.org/English)

Linux on Laptops (http://www.cs.utexas.edu/users/kharker/linux-laptop)

Linux Laughs! (http://laughs.linuxlots.com)

Linux Links (http://www.linuxlinks.com)

Linux Newbie (http://linuxnewbie.org/)

Linux Online! (http://www.linux.org)

Linux Ports (http://perso.wanadoo.es/xose/linux/linux_ports.html)

Linux Savvy (http://www.linuxsavvy.com/resources/)

LinuxStart (http://linuxstart.com/)

Linux Web Watcher (http://webwatcher.org/)

Open Directory (a Yahoo!-like portal built with Community editors and labor) (http://directory.mozilla.org)

Open Source IT (http://www.opensourceit.com/)

O'Reilly Linux Center (http://linux.oreilly.com)

OS Opinion (http://www.osopinion.com)

PegaSoft Portal Site (http://www.vaxxine.com/pegasoft/portal)

Software in the Public Interest (http://www.spi-inc.org/)

The Ultimate Directory of Linux Software (http://www.tudols.com)

Linux-Magazin (German) (http://www.linux-magazin.de)

Linux StartSeite (German) (http://homepages.go.com/~linux_linux/Linux.htm)

Newsworthy sites

You find out about the lastest news on Linux from the following sites:

32BitsOnline (`http://32bitsonline.com/`)

DeployLinux.Net (news for the enterprise) (`http://www.deploylinux.net`)

Geek News (`http://www.geeknews.org`)

ICE-News (`http://linuxinside.org`)

INFORMATION WEEK Linux Toolbox (`http://www.informationweek.com/center/linux`)

Linux Announce (`http://tile.net/news/composlinuxannounce.html`)

Linux Planet (has distro reviews) (`http://www.linuxplanet.com`)

Linux Power (`http://linuxpower.org`)

The Linux Show (`http://www.thelinuxshow.com`)

LinuxStockNews.com (`http://www.linuxstocknews.com`)

Linux Today (`http://www.linuxtoday.com`)

Linux UK News (`http://www.linuxuk.co.uk`)

Linux Weekly News (`http://lwn.net`)

LinuxWorld (`http://linuxworld.com/`)

Open Resources News (`http://www.openresources.com/news/`)

Slashdot (News for Geeks) (`http://slashdot.org/`)

Technocrat.Net (`http://technocrat.net/`)

Temple of the Screaming Penguin (sorts news by source) (`http://www.screaming-penguin.com`)

Transmetazone (tracks Transmeta Corporation) (`http://www.transmetazone.com`)

ZD Enterprise Linux News (http://www.zdnet.com/enterprise/linux)

German Linux News (http://linuxbbs.org)

Linux NetMag (German, with some English) (http://www.linuxnetmag.de)

Linux Ticker (http://linuxticker.com): German sites

Developers sites

Sites that me be of interest to Linux developers follow:

CodeCatalog.com (Open Source code search engine) (http://www.codecatalog.com/)

CPU Review (http://www.cpureview.com/)

FreeCode (applications and so forth with source code) (http://www.freecode.com/index.html)

freshmeat.net (http://freshmeat.net/)

IBM developerWorks Linux Zone (http://www.ibm.com/developer/linux)

Kernel Traffic (Linux kernel discussions) (http://kt.linuxcare.com/)

Linux Developer Network (http://linuxdev.net/index.shtml)

Linux Development Projects (http://www.linuxdoc.org/devel.html)

Linux from Scratch (http://www.linuxfromscratch.org/)

Linux Mafia (Slackware resources) (http://www.linuxmafia.org/)

Mozillazine (news of Mozilla) (http://www.mozillazine.org/)

OrphanSource (for orphaned code, programs, and projects) (http://orphansource.org/)

Penguin Computing Antarctica Project (project hosting) (http://www.penguincomputing.com/antarctic.html)

Pyrite (http://pyrite.linuxbox.com/): Palm Pilot connectivity/data toolkit

Review of Operating Systems (links to projects) (http://www.tunes.org/Review/OSes.html)

Scripting News (cross platform) (http://www.scripting.com/)

SEUL Simple End-User Linux Project (advocacy, education, and hosting of related projects) (http://www.seul.org)

Slashcode Project (source code that runs Slashdot site) (http://slashcode.com)

SourceForge (Open Source project hosting site and developers' portal) (http://sourceforge.net/)

SmartBeak (SMARTBEAK developer resources) (http://www.smartbeak.com)

Trillian Project (Linux on the Intel Itanium processor) (http://www.linuxia64.org)

Distribution sites

Here are some distribution sites:

Kernel Notes (http://kernelnotes.org/dist-index.html)

LinuxISO.org (ISOs of Linux distros) (http://www.linux-iso.org/)

Woven Goods (http://www.fokus.gmd.de/linux/linux-distrib.html)

RedHatIsNotLinux.Org (against a de facto Red Hat standard) (http://www.redhatisnotlinux.org/)

Business sites

Here are some business-oriened sites:

Freely Redistributable Software in Business (http://www.cyber.com.au/misc/frsbiz/)

Linux Business Applications (http://www.m-tech.ab.ca/linux-biz/index.html)

Linux Business Expo (http://www.linuxbizexpo.com)

Linux Capital Group (http://linuxvc.com)

Linux Commercial HOWTO (http://www.linuxdoc.org/HOWTO/Commercial-HOWTO.html)

Linux Consultants HOW-TO (worldwide listing of Linux consultants) (http://linux-rep.fnal.gov/howtos/Consultants-HOWTO.html)

Linux in Business (cases) (http://www.LinuxBusiness.com)

Linux Investments (http://www.linuxinvestments.com)

Linux News for the Corporate World (http://www.geocities.com/SiliconValley/Haven/6087/news.html)

LinuxGram Business News (http://www.g2news.com/linuxgram.html)

Business Users of Linux-Mandrake (http://www.linux-mandrake.com/bizcase/)

LinuxPorts for the Corporation (http://www.linuxports.com)

Linux Support and Resource Center for Consultants (http://www.bynari.com/BCG/index.html)

OSInvestor.com (http://www.osinvestor.com/)

Sm@rt Reseller InfoPak on Linux (http://www.zdnet.com/sr/filters/linux/?chkpt=entelse-linux): from reseller point of view

WhatifLinux.com (for systems administrators considering Open Source) (http://www.whatiflinux.com)

Shopping sites

Here are some sites at which you can shop:

Cheap Bytes (http://www.cheapbytes.com)

Copyleft.Net (http://copyleft.net/)

eLinux.com (http://www.elinux.com)

Linux Mall (http://linuxmall.com/)

ThinkGeek (http://www.thinkgeek.com)

History sites

The following sites offer information on the history of Linux:

CNet (http://home.cnet.com/category/0-3662-7-286385.html?dd.cn.txt.0603.01)

The Mozilla Museum (http://home.snafu.de/tilman/mozilla/index.html)

some *Salon* Magazine Stories on Free Software (http://www.salonmagazine.com/21st/feature/1998/12/11list.html)

Software Panorama (Open Source Software Educational Society) (http://www.softpanorama.org/)

The Sourceware Operating System Proposal (1993 paper on future of UNIX) (http://www.bitmover.com/lm/papers/srcos.html)

UNIX Heritage Society (http://minnie.cs.adfa.oz.au/TUHS)

Graphics and art sites

The following sites offer information or tools for working with graphics and art:

Free GUI Toolkits (http://www.geocities.com/SiliconValley/Vista/7184/guitool.html)

HelixCode (GNOME development and support) (http://www.helixcode.com/)

LIMP: Linux Image Montage Poster Project (http://linux.remotepoint.com)

Linux Artist (http://linuxartist.org)

Linux Graphics Advocacy (http://linas.org/linux/graphics-ad.html)

Linux Penguins on the Web (http://www.tunes.org/~do/penguindex.html)

Logos for 2.2 Linux (http://www-mddsp.enel.ucalgary.ca/People/adilger/logo)

LWN Penguin picture gallery (http://lwn.net/Gallery)

MAVERIK (Open Source VR engine) (http://aig.cs.man.ac.uk/systems/Maverik/)

MindsEye (Open Source 3D rendering project) (http://mindseye.luna.net/info.html)

Xi Graphics (commercial display servers for Linux and UNIX) (http://www.xig.com)

Application sites

The following sites have downloadable applications:

AppWatch.com (http://appwatch.com/Linux/): news about Open Source applications

BeOpen (news about Open Source applicationsPortal) (http://www.beopen.org/ BeOpen)

DOSEMU (DOS emulation) (http://www.dosemu.org)

IceWalkers (database of applications) (http://www.icewalk.com/)

Linux Applications (http://www.linuxapps.com)

Linux Applications and Utilities Page (http://home.xnet.com/~blatura/linapps.shtml)

Scientific Applications on Linux (http://SAL.KachinaTech.COM/index.shtml)

VMware (concurrent NT and Linux) (http://www.vmware.com/products/appscenarios.html)

Support sites

The following sites offer support:

Question Exchange (http://www.questionexchange.com): help auction

L.U.S.T. (Linux User Support Team) (http://www.ch4549.org/lust)

Statistics sites

The following sites provide statistical data:

A Quantitative Profile of a Community of Open Source Linux Developers (http://metalab.unc.edu/osrt/develpro.html)

The Internet Operating System Counter (tracks use of Linux, BSD, and others; tracks many domains, but not .com) (http://www.leb.net/hzo/ioscount/index.html)

The Linux Counter (register here to be counted as a user) (http://counter.li.org/)

Netcraft Web Server Survey (http://www.netcraft.com/survey)

Red Hat Wealth Monitor (http://prosthetic-monkey.com/RHWM)

Brokering users or developers for Open Source projects

Here are some sites for brokering users or developers for Open Source projects:

sourceXchange (http://www.sourcexchange.com/)

Cosource.com (http://www.cosource.com/)

Asynchrony (http://www.asynchrony.com/)

Free Software Bazaar (http://visar.csustan.edu/bazaar/bazaar.html)

Group sites

The following sites are organized by various various Linux groups:

Bay Area Linux Group (http://hugin.imat.com/bale)

Linux International (http://www.LI.org/)

Linux User Groups Map (worldwide) (http://vancouver-webpages.com/geo/lugmap.html)

Open Source Initiative (http://www.opensource.org/)

Public Software Institute (http://www.public-software.com/)

Silicon Valley Linux Users Group Home Page (http://www.svlug.org)

Linux User Groups Worldwide (http://lugww.counter.li.org)

Tux.Org (umbrella site for user groups and developers) (http://www.tux.org/)

Economics and licensing sites

The following sites provide economics and licensing information:

Andrew Leonard (in *Salon*) (http://www.salon.com/tech/fsp/index.html)

Brave GNU World (http://www.gnu.org/brave-gnu-world/brave-gnu-world.en.html)

Clay Shirky (on the Internet, Open Source, and so on) (http://www.shirky.com/opensource)

Cyberspaces.org (material on cyberlaw) (http://cyberspaces.org/)

Electronic Property (http://www.virtualschool.edu/mon/ElectronicProperty/index.html)

Free Software Business Discussion Archives (http://www.apocalypse.org/pub/fsb/)

Free Software Licensing (http://www.cs.mu.oz.au/~trd/www-free/software_licenses.html)

French Law on Open Source (http://www.osslaw.org/)

Open Source Initiative License Discussion Archive (http://www.crynwr.com/cgi-bin/ezmlm-cgi/3)

Open Source Software Licensing Page (http://www.stromian.com/Open_Source_Licensing.htm)

Microsoft sites

The following sites provide information about Microsoft:

Boycott Microsoft (http://www0.vcnet.com/bms)

LINUX FUD Factor FAQ (also discusses standards tactics) (http://www.geocities.com/SiliconValley/Hills/9267/fud2.html)

Linux Myths Explained (Microsoft's Linux Myths Web Page refuted)(http://www.hinterlands.f9.co.uk/linuxmyths.html)

Linux Today Counter-FUD Site (to answer the Linux Myths page at Microsoft) (http://noFUD.linuxtoday.com)

From MSWord to MSWorld (strategy) (http://www.netaction.org/msoft/world)

The Next 10 Minutes (Nicholas Petreley series on NT) (http://www.ncworldmag.com/ncw-03-1998/ncw-03-nextten.html)

The UNIX-vs-NT Organization (http://www.unix-vs-nt.org)

NT vs Linux Site (http://www.jimmo.com/Linux-NT_Debate)

NT vs. UNIX (http://www.unix-vs-nt.org/kirch)

Embedded sites

The following sites that offer information on embedding:

Embedded Linux (portal) (http://www.embedlinux.net/)

Linux Embedded (http://linux-embedded.com)

Linux Devices (http://www.linuxdevices.com)

Clinux (The Linux Microcontroller Project) (http://ryeham.ee.ryerson.ca/uClinux)

Real-Time Linux Portal (http://realtimelinux.org/)

High-end computing sites

The following sites offer high-end computing information:

Beowulf Project (http://www.beowulf.org/)

Beowulf Portal (http://www.beowulf-underground.org/)

Extreme Linux (http://www.extremelinux.org/)

High-Availability Linux Project (http://www.henge.com/~alanr/ha)

Linux Enterprise Computing (http://linas.org/linux)

Top 500 Supercomputer Sites (http://www.top500.org/)

Training and certification and standards sites

The following sites offer information on training and certification and standards:

Basic Linux Training (http://basiclinux.hypermart.net/basic/index.html)

Free Standards Group (http://www.freestandards.org/)

Java Community Process (http://www.java.sun.com/aboutJava/communityprocess/)

Learn Linux (http://www.learnlinux.com)

Linux Internationalization Initiative (http://li18nux.net/)

Linux Professional Institute (http://www.lpi.org)

Linux Standard Base (http://www.linuxbase.org)

Linux Training (http://training.linsight.com/): list of sites

Sair LinuxGNU Certification
(http://www.linuxcertification.org)

Publishing sites

The following sites offer information on publishing:

Essential Open Book Project (http://www.linuxworld.com/idgbooks-openbook/home.html): IDG Books Worldwide

The Linux Documentation Project: Homepage (http://sunsite.unc.edu/mdw/linux.html)

Linux Press (`http://www.linuxpress.com`)

Open Content (`http://opencontent.org/`)

Open Docs (`http://www.opendocs.org/FAQ.html`)

Open Source Writers Group (`http://www.oswg.org:8080/oswg`)

Prime Time Freeware (OSS code and documentation) (`http://www.ptf.com`)

Glossary

Active Server Pages (ASP)
The generation of Web pages, not by coding them individually with HTML, but by writing material from one or more databases to the page in answer to a query from a client.

Application Programming Interface (API)
A set of commands that a developer can use to take advantage of the functions of a piece of software from another piece of software. If the commands and their parameters are published, then any developer can use the functionality in the software.

Application Service Provider (ASP)
Hosts applications on an Internet-enabled server that lets client machines use the hosted applications remotely.

Beowulf
Open Source software used with Linux to join separate small computers (Intel 486 or better) to provide computing power on the order of a supercomputer. Many government research agencies have built Beowulf supercomputers.

Berkeley Software Distribution (BSD)
The original UNIX clone; its variants today include FreeBSD, BSD OS, and NetBSD. Its license allows you to change the source code and keep it private, even if you distribute the resulting software.

Client
A desktop computer, linked to a larger central computer called a server; also the name for software that runs on the client machine.

Cluster
A group of processors joined together to take advantage of their combined computing power.

Command Line Interface (CLI)
Often called the Console, as contrasted with a Graphical User Interface, or GUI.

Commercial
Often used loosely to mean proprietary. Any software that is sold could be called commercial, even if there is a Free or Open Source version of it given away. Restrictions on the modifying and distribution of the software determine whether it is proprietary or not.

Community
General term for everyone involved in moving Linux or Open Source software forward.

Complete product
The concept that a technology product cannot exist in a marketplace without a number of ancillary features, devices, and services; Linux has had to show the world that it can provide support, training, device drivers, systems integrators and channels, as well as standards and easy installation.

Copyleft
Process for sharing copyrighted material, whether software or publications, by copyrighting them to establish control, and then using that control to grant a license and source code to users, provided the licensee, when passing on the work and its derivatives, grants an identical license to all recipients, along with the software source code. The license allows the licensee to copy, distribute, and modify the software.

COTS
For Commercial Off-The-Shelf parts, and the practice of using these in building open systems, particularly cluster supercomputers.

Covered code
Open Source code supplied with special provisions in its accompanying license that do not necessarily apply to the code that others bundle with the covered code. The term originates in the Netscape Public License (MozPL). The license specifies (among other provisions) that modifications to the covered code must also be distributed under the NPL, while additions to the package that merely call the APIs in the covered code may be shipped binary-only and under another license if the developer desires.

Cracker

See the distinction drawn under Hacker.

Distribution, Distro

"Distribution" usually refers to the channels of delivery for software sales; it is also used to refer to a particular edition of Linux or other Open Source software put out by a particular publisher, as in "the SuSE distribution of Linux." The term "distro" is used to refer to this second sense.

Early adopters

In the second stage of the Technology Adoption Life Cycle, these visionaries watch the innovators for new technologies to adopt them for a strategic advantage over (nonadopting) competitors. They have influence and often have sizable budgets to do the pilot work in adopting the new technology. They are a small percentage of the total market for a technology.

Early majority

In the third stage of the Technology Adoption Life Cycle these pragmatists watch their fellow pragmatists, and want to use the same technologies they are using. They are concerned with stability and standards across their industries, and are a harder sell than the early adopters, who generally sell themselves. The early majority are the early half of the eventual majority adopters of a technology.

Filters

The conversion software that translates one data format into another; any non-Microsoft productivity application will need filters so that its users can interact with the Microsoft users and their data. Filters are needed because the majority of users have made the Microsoft formats into a de facto standard.

Forking

The splitting of a software project into two or more branches, which continue in parallel, but incorporating different code and probably addressing different problems for a different set of users.

Free Software

Copylefted software; that is, software issued under the GNU General Public License. Some Open Source software is Free Software.

Free Software Foundation (FSF)
Founded by Richard Stallman, and holder of the copyrights for the GNU software development tools, promotes the idea of distributing all software as Free Software under the GNU General Public License.

gcc
GNU C Compiler, a widespread tool from the Free Software Foundation.

GIMP, The
The Linux answer to Adobe PhotoShop.

glibc
One of the GNU C libraries, for graphics.

GNU Network Object Model Environment (GNOME)
Begun with the dual purpose of providing functionality like that of the Microsoft objects (now called COM) as Free Software, and of providing a desktop untrammeled by the licensing requirements underlying KDE.

GPL
Short name for the GNU General Public License (see Copyleft).

GTK and GTK+
The GNOME Toolkit (for the C language) and the GNOME Toolkit for object-oriented C++ and written as Free Software without the encumbering licensing of the Qt Toolkit.

Hacker
A clever programmer who has the power to make software and hardware achieve beyond what people thought they could do. A acker who goes beyond the bounds of innocent excitement to the extent of harming others becomes a cracker. There is some disagreement about where to draw the line.

High availability
A quality of dependability in computer systems that must be available continuously with no downtime. They are built on some combination of reliable hardware and software with multiple backup systems and the automatic ability to substitute good components for bad.

IBM PL
IBM Public License.

Independent Software Vendor (ISV)
An originator and/or publisher of software.

Innovators
Originators of the technology in its first stage of the Technology Adoption Life Cycle. Innovators love technology for its own sake, and rarely have power or budgets.

Intellectual Property (IP)
Property protected either by copyright or by patent.

Internet Service Provider (ISP)
A company that sells connections to the Internet.

K Desktop Environment, The (KDE)
Originated in Germany as an Open Source alternative to the CDE, or Common Desktop Environment, it is, however, built on the proprietary Qt Toolkit (see Licensing Dependencies). GNOME arose as a Free Software alternative to KDE.

Late majority
In the Technology Adoption Life Cycle these are the most conservative, and account for about half the market for a technology.

Lesser General Public License (LGPL)
Covers the linking of software not licensed under the GPL with software that is under the GPL. Originally called the Library General Public License.

Licensing dependencies
Series of influences exerted by underlying software's licensing on other software that uses the underlying software. Because KDE uses the Qt Toolkit software, it must observe the Q Public License, which specifies that software using Qt must be distributed with its source code, except in those cases for which a developer purchases a commercial Qt license.

Linux Software Map, The (LSM)
A database of the applications available for Linux, built by organizing the filled-out forms that accompany each submission of software to the server. These forms are commonly called LSMs.

Mozilla
Code-name for the Netscape browser intended to kill the Mosaic browser. The name, along with the software code, came to the Mozilla Open Source project funded by Netscape to encourage Open Source community work on a new version of Mozilla.

Open Source Definition
Series of requirements proposed by the Open Source Initiative; software should meet these requirements in order to be called "Open Source."

Open Source software
Used loosely, it refers to software whose source code can be viewed. Used more strictly, it is software that conforms to the Open Source Definition.

Productivity applications or products
Software used on the job, such as word processors or spreadsheets that increase a user's productivity.

Proprietary software
All software is proprietary, unless its creator specifically disavows rights under copyright and places it in the public domain, but the term generally means (copyrighted) software that is not distributed as Free or Open Source software. Some software may regard itself as Open Source, but will be judged by the Open Source community as actually proprietary, depending on the actual licensing terms. Most commercial software is proprietary.

RHAD
Red Hat Advanced Development Laboratories.

Sun Community Source License, The (SCSL)
One of a number of attempts by Sun Microsystems to accommodate the Open Source way of doing things while still protecting its intellectual property rights and foreclosing any possible Forking of the code.

Technology Adoption Life Cycle
A model that explains the behavior of the software market. Technology passes through four stages of adoption by different market segments: innovators, early adopters, early majority, and late majority.

World domination

The goal of the Linux movement. In its modest form it may mean simply a choice of operating systems for the average user; in its extreme form it encompasses the destruction of Microsoft, generally because Linux believers hold that a 15 percent market share for Linux will inevitably lead to an 85 percent share.

X License

The simple license for X Window software that allows a developer to take the source code, modify it, and distribute it as binary-only code. The BSD License also allows this practice.

X Window

Open Source software to manage the Graphical User Interface (GUI) in UNIX and similar operating systems. It is separate from the operating system.

Index

Continued

Continued

IDG BOOKS WORLDWIDE, INC. OPEN CONTENT LICENSE

v0.1, August 10, 1999

Please read this Open Content License ("License") for our Open Content Work published by IDG Books Worldwide, Inc. ("IDGB"). You acknowledge that you accept the terms of our License.

1. **License; Requirements for Modified and Unmodified Versions.**

   a. **Grant.** IDGB grants to you a non-exclusive license to reproduce and distribute, in whole or in part, in print or electronic media, the Open Content Work, including for commercial redistribution. If you reproduce or distribute the Open Content Work, you must adhere to the terms of this License and this License or an incorporation of it by reference as set forth in Section 2 below must be displayed in any reproduction. IDGB reserves all rights not expressly granted herein.

   b. **Attribution.** Any publication in standard (paper) book form requires citation to the original author and IDGB. The original author's and IDGB's names shall appear prominently on the covers and spine of the Open Content Work.

2. **Incorporation by Reference.** Proper form for an incorporation by reference is as follows:

   This is an Open Content Work published by IDG Books Worldwide, Inc. You may reproduce and distribute this material provided that you adhere to the terms and conditions set forth in the IDG Books Worldwide, Inc. Open Content License (the latest version is presently available at `http://www.linuxworld.com/idgbooks-openbook/lw-oclicense.html`).

   This reference must be immediately followed with the author(s) and/or IDGB's options in Section 7 below displayed.

3. **Copyright.** Copyright to the Open Content Work is owned by IDGB or the author.

4. **License Application and Disclaimer.** The following terms apply to the Open Content Work, unless otherwise expressly stated in this License:

   a. **Application.** Mere aggregation or compilation of the Open Content Work or a portion of the Open Content Work with other works or programs on the same media shall not cause this License to apply to those other works or programs. The aggregate work or compilation shall contain a notice specifying the inclusion of the material from the Open Content Work and a copyright notice in the name of its copyright owner.

   b. **NO WARRANTY.** THIS OPEN CONTENT WORK IS BEING LICENSED "AS IS" WITHOUT WARRANTIES OF ANY KIND, EXPRESS OR IMPLIED, INCLUDING WITHOUT LIMITATION ANY WARRANTY OF NON-INFRINGEMENT OR IMPLIED WARRANTIES OF MERCHANTABILITY AND FITNESS FOR A PARTICULAR PURPOSE, WITH RESPECT TO (I) THE MATERIAL IN THE OPEN CONTENT WORK, (II) THE SOFTWARE AND THE SOURCE CODE CONTAINED THEREIN, AND/OR (III) THE TECHNIQUES DESCRIBED IN THE OPEN CONTENT WORK.

5. **Requirements for Modified Works.** If you modify this Open Content Work, including in translations, anthologies, compilations, and partial documents, you must:

   a. **Designation.** Designate within the modified work that the modification is a translation, anthology, compilation, portion of, or other modification of the Open Content Work.

   b. **Identity.** Identify yourself as the person making the modifications and date the modification.

c. Acknowledgment of Original Author and IDGB. Acknowledge the Open Content Work's original author and IDGB in accordance with standard academic citation practices, including a reference to the original ISBN under which the work was published.

d. Location of Original Work. Identify the original Open Content Work's location.

e. License. Display this License or incorporate it by reference as set forth in Section 2 above.

f. No Endorsement. Not use the original author(s)' name(s) or IDGB's name to indicate an endorsement by them of your modifications, without their prior written permission.

6. **Good Practice Recommendations.** In addition to the terms and conditions of this License, the author and IDGB request, and strongly recommend, that redistributors of the Open Content Work adhere to the following:

    a. E-mail Notification. If you intend to distribute modifications of the Open Content Work in print media or on CD ROM, you should provide e-mail notification to the host not later than thirty (30) days prior to your redistribution, in order to give IDGB or the author(s) sufficient time to provide you with updated material to the Open Content Work. Your e-mail notification should include descriptions of your modifications.

    b. Identification of Modifications. You should clearly indicate, by marking up the document to reference the modifications, the substantive modifications and deletions you make to the Open Content Work.

    c. Free Copy of Modifications. While not mandatory, you should offer a free copy of the modifications, whether in print or on CD-ROM, to the original author(s) and to IDGB.

7. **License Options.** The following provision(s) are considered part of the License and must be included when you reproduce the License (or its incorporation by reference) in modifications of the Open Content Work.

   a. **Paper/Book Versions.** E-mail notification to the host is required not less than thirty (30) days prior to distribution of the Open Content Work or a derivative thereof in any standard (paper) book form.

8. **General.** This License constitutes the entire understanding between the parties as to the subject matter hereof. This License shall be governed by California law and the U.S. Copyright Act of 1976, as amended, and case law thereunder. In the event one or more provisions contained in this License are held by any court or tribunal to be illegal or otherwise unenforceable, the remaining provisions of this License shall remain in full force and effect.

CONTRIBUTORS AGREEMENT

If you desire to contribute to the Open Content Work and the intellectual development of its subject matter by providing written comments, additions, supplements, fixes, patches, or other contributions (collectively, "Contributions"), you acknowledge and agree that:

   a. Your Contribution may be used by IDGB or the author(s) on a non-exclusive basis, in whole or in part, to reproduce, modify, fix, patch, display, redistribute, and otherwise use in print or electronic media, in the Open Content Work, revised editions, and otherwise throughout the world. You also understand that IDGB and the author(s) cannot guarantee that either of them will use your Contribution in any manner.

b. Based on the quality, extent, and use of your Contribution, you will receive a general or special acknowledgment, and may receive a contributor's honorarium, from IDGB. In this regard, you hereby give IDGB permission to acknowledge your Contribution by posting and otherwise reproducing your name and e-mail address.

c. To your best knowledge, you represent and warrant that (i) your Contribution does not violate any copyright, trademark, or any other registered or common law intellectual property or proprietary right of any person or entity, (ii) all statements in your Contribution are true and accurate and do not violate the property or privacy rights of any third party, (iii) your Contribution does not contain information or instructions that could reasonably cause injury to person or property, and (iv) you have full authority to agree to the terms herein and to make these representations.

my2cents.idgbooks.com